RUNNING A SMALL LIBRARY

A How-To-Do-It Manual

Edited by
JOHN A. MOORMAN

HOW-TO-DO-IT MANUALS
FOR LIBRARIANS

NUMBER 149

NEAL-SCHUMAN PUBLISHERS, INC.
New York   London

Published by Neal-Schuman Publishers, Inc.
100 William St., Suite 2004
New York, NY 10038

Printed and bound in the United States of America.

The paper used in this publication meets the minimum requirements of American National Standard for Information Sciences—Permanence of Paper for Printed Library Materials, ANSI Z39.48–1992.

Library of Congress Cataloging-in-Publication Data

   Running a small library : a how-to-do-it manual / edited by John A. Moorman.
     p. cm. — (How-to-do-it manuals for librarians ; no. 149)
   Includes bibliographical references and index.
   ISBN 1-55570-549-9 (alk. paper)
 1. Small libraries—Administration—Handbooks, manuals, etc. I. Moorman, John A. II. Series: How-to-do-it manuals for libraries ; no. 149.
Z675.S57R86 2006
025.1—dc22   2006012457

For my wife,

Ileen G. Moorman.

Her love, support, and

encouragement

of my work and my life

made this project possible.

CONTENTS

LIST OF FIGURES

PREFACE

Every library, regardless of size, has an ambitious mission and the potential to provide excellent opportunities and benefits to its community. Operating a small library poses a large question: How can an organization charged with doing so much with a few (or even one) staff members and very limited resources be managed successfully? *Running a Small Library: A How-To-Do-It Manual* recognizes both the trials and rewards of working in such institutions. It provides practical guidance for the day-to-day and the out-of-the-ordinary services, activities, and issues facing all types of small libraries.

As the book's editor and an author of some chapters, I have tried to design this handbook to tackle big-picture concepts as well as specific issues. The individual chapter authors are a unique mix of librarians, administrators, consultants, and users. All possess considerable experience in their chosen topics in the small library setting. I hope our explanations, instruction, and advice will meet your needs and help you better serve your community whatever your role—manager, professional, paraprofessional, trustee, or volunteer—or level of experience. The common thread linking us is a desire to support the continued success of people, who, like you, make up the backbone of our information society.

Running a Small Library: A How-To-Do-It Manual covers six major areas: management, administration, public services, collection development, computers and automation, and sources for more information.

Part I, "Introducing the Small Library," contains five chapters, each devoted to the unique characteristics of library settings in college, community college, special, school, and public libraries. Experts explore these different service sectors, presenting the history, current state, and future challenges for their respective institutions. They also examine how the institution can assess and respond to the unique needs of its users.

Part II, "Administration in the Small Library," brings together nine chapters that cover the major facets of library management such as budgets, policies, staffing, facilities, and development.

- Chapter 6, "Budgeting," assists readers in creating a financial plan that works. From types of budgets—line-item or zero-based—to key financial considerations, this chapter provides valuable and often overlooked guidance.
- Establishing firm standards helps organizations run smoothly and Chapter 7, "Policies and Procedures," makes

the creation of institutional regulations easier. It outlines necessary topics that must be covered and provides guidance for authoring effective statements.

- Personnel are important in any library and probably more so in the small library. Chapter 8, "Staffing," factors human elements into the management equation, describing how to create job descriptions, interview candidates, train staff, balance schedules, and supervise and evaluate workers.
- Chapter 9, "Buildings," covers how to plan, finance, construct, furnish, remodel, and maintain facilities.
- Library services are too important to be left to chance, so Chapter 10, "Planning," shows why and how you should prepare for long- and short-term goals.
- Chapter 11, "Governing Boards and Governmental Relations," demonstrates both how these bodies work for you and how you work with them—from establishment to assessment.
- Chapter 12, "Friends Groups and Foundations," explains the differences between these two support bodies; walks readers through their formation; and provides guidance for setting bylaws, fundraising, and keeping both groups active.
- Libraries are ideal organizations for partnerships and Chapter 13, "Community Partnership," presents solid advice for those organizations looking to partner. In addition to model relationships, you will find management techniques and suggestions for maximizing the benefits to your institution.
- Even a small library is a growing library. Chapter 14, "Development," describes various aspects of fundraising, including annual funds, special project or special purpose funding, and endowments.

Part III, "Public Services in the Small Library," is divided into two broad chapters: Chapter 15, "Adult Services," and Chapter 16, "Youth Services." These act as guides through reference, programming, customer service, and reader's advisory. The youth chapter includes special direction for improving literacy and understanding children's literature.

Part IV, "Collection Development in the Small Library," addresses the issues and topics related to your materials and collections.

- Chapter 17, "Selection," helps to establish selection and collection policies; identify key resources for aiding in the evaluation of titles; and offers direction in handling challenges to materials.

- Once desired titles have been identified, Chapter 18, "Ordering," explains how to get them to the library. This chapter discusses options for ordering; steps in the process; and tools for managing your acquisitions.
- Chapter 19, "Cataloging," outlines the two systems of classification and subject headings; discusses authority control; and presents options for making your books available to users.
- Chapter 20, "Circulation," helps to determine a circulation policy, recover overdue materials, and return materials to your shelves.
- When materials no longer meet the needs of users, you can turn to Chapter 21, "Weeding," to ensure that your library is taking the correct action in discarding worn or obsolete materials.

Computers are an important part of any library's services. Part V, "Computers and Automation in the Small Library," contains two chapters that address the unique issues surrounding technology in smaller institutions. Chapter 22, "Personal Computers and In-house Networks," will help you evaluate and purchase new equipment, protect current resources, and plan for future technologies. It also provides suggestions for setting usage policies, selecting management software, and creating networks. Because many traditional library functions are now automated, Chapter 23, "Integrated Library Systems," will help to understand how the ILS can streamline services and improve access for users. The chapter reviews the modules of an ILS—cataloging, circulation, and online public access catalogs (OPACS)—and helps libraries determine their systems' needs.

"Running a Small Library Sourcebook" rounds out the final part of this manual. This section provides a list of state library agencies, book and periodical vendors, library furniture and supply vendors, automation vendors, professional organizations, and a bibliography of useful materials. This information will prove valuable as you seek additional resources or knowledge on particular topics.

This manual is designed to help you better serve your community—whether in the academic, public, special, or school setting—by providing a better understanding of the essential functions of a small library. I hope that professionals, paraprofessionals, volunteers, and library supporters will find this volume a useful introduction and guide to the small library.

ACKNOWLEDGMENTS

I thank Charles Harmon, director of publishing at Neal-Schuman, for his confidence in my ability to accomplish this project. Without his support and encouragement this book would not have been possible.

Michael Kelley, of Neal-Schuman, has been a wonderful editor and I have enjoyed working with and learning from him.

I also thank the contributing authors whose willingness to share their experiences and knowledge has substantially enriched the content of this book.

Part I

Introducing the Small Library

1 COLLEGE LIBRARIES

Karin Borei

DEFINITION

The National Center for Education Statistics defines an academic library as follows:

"The library for an accredited degree-granting institution of higher education or a non-accredited institution with a program of four years or more." Academic libraries are identified by the post-secondary institution of which they are a part.

An academic library provides the following:

1. An organized collection of printed or other materials or a combination thereof;
2. A staff trained to provide and interpret such materials as required to meet the informational, cultural, recreational, or educational needs of clientele;
3. An established schedule in which services of the staff are available to clientele; and
4. The physical facilities necessary to support such a collection, staff, and schedule. (NCES 2006a).

JSTOR, the highly respected electronic archive of scholarly journal literature, provides a definition of the "small academic library," which is a combination of Carnegie academic institution classifications modified by student FTE (full-time equivalent) numbers. That is, the definition is an intersection of the academic purposes of the parent institution and the size of the student body of that institution.

> Small Institutions: Those Doctoral II and Masters I institutions with enrollments below 2,500 are "Small," while those below 1,000 are "Very Small." [and] All Masters II and Bachelors I colleges with FTE enrollments

of 1,000 or more are regarded as "Small," while those below 1,000 are "Very Small." (JSTOR, 2005)

In practical terms, this means that a "small academic library" primarily serves an undergraduate institution with a student body of up to about 2,500 students. Often, though not always, such a library is a "college library: A type of academic library maintained by an independent four-year college, or by one of several colleges within a larger university, for the use of students and faculty. (Reitz, 2004). Within that definition, library staff and collection sizes will vary.

OVERVIEW

This chapter covers:

- Services
- Budgeting
- Statistics
- Staff
- Challenges for the future

INTRODUCTION

The first academic library in what was to become the United States started out with 400 volumes willed by John Harvard to the two-year-old college in Cambridge, Massachusetts, which was to bear his name. Many academic libraries in the United States have at one time been "small," even if some have since grown very large. Many others, however, have chosen to remain more modest in size; and in doing so, have often developed very different cultures and management approaches from their larger cousins.

The exact number of small academic libraries now in the United States cannot easily be calculated exactly, though a reasonable estimate is 1,000–1,200. The three standard published sources of information about academic libraries provide the following enumerations (which are not likely to change much from year to year).

- 3,617 "University & College" libraries are listed in the 2004 American Library Directory, although this number is not broken down by size of parent institution (ALA 2004, xii).

- The 2004 Bowker Annual Library and Book Trade Almanac, in describing its statistical tables, states that "Colleges are the 1,472 responding [to the National Center for Education Statistics' biannual ... *Academic Library Survey*] institutions with master's and baccalaureate programs" (Bowker 2004, 450).
- The annual Association of College and Research Libraries (ACRL) statistical survey, *Academic Library Trends and Statistics*, numbers its "population" of United States academic libraries as 2,568; and of those, 1,325 were "Carnegie Classification: Master's Colleges and Institutions [and] Baccalaureate Colleges." Again, however, this number is not broken down by size of parent institution (ACRL 2005).

How-to writings on managing small academic libraries are not a new idea nor, in many ways, have the broad issues addressed by such writing changed much over time. For instance, much of *College Librarianship*, which was written in 1981, is just as applicable today, only with more technology as part of the mix. In the introduction to this work, the editors provide a description of the small academic library, which applies just as well these twenty-five years later:

> The college library, physically and financially unable to gather and store all of the information that students could use, must concentrate on furthering the educational process by teaching research skills and making students aware of the universe of informational resources available. This is not to say that the college library should not attempt to gather stores of information, but rather that it must selectively gather the informational materials that best facilitate the educational process. Since the college library can never acquire everything, it should then aspire to the acquisition of the most useful things. (Miller 1981, 2)

The joys of the small academic library center on the immediacy of contact with both the entire library staff and with the library's users, and on the efficiency of action that smallness makes possible.

LIBRARY SERVICES

Every library should have a mission statement that reflects the library's service philosophy. The process of devising and periodically reviewing such a statement helps the library staff to be clear about what it should and should not be doing, as well as about how it should be doing what it does. The mission statement makes clear as well to the rest of the campus where the library fits into the bigger picture.

The Mission of Staley Library is:

- To enhance students' ability to understand, pursue, and satisfy their own research needs, by stimulating their critical thinking and problem solving capabilities, both for their academic careers and for lifelong learning.
- To advance the University's academic programs and scholarly processes through instruction and collaboration.
- To provide the physical and virtual resources and learning spaces that support the academic research needs of students, faculty and staff.

This mission is relatively typical for a small academic library. It is posted on the library's Web site.

The services of the smaller academic library tend, as do those of their parent institutions, to focus on instruction, whether (for the library) in classes or at the reference desk. The library instruction will have as its ultimate objective that of teaching students how to do their own research, to find and evaluate resources that best meet their needs, and how to use those resources to create the best research results. "Research" in this context will be primarily at the undergraduate level.

The library collection of the small academic library will reflect that same reality (primary focus on an institution-specific undergraduate curriculum rather than on a larger research agenda); although with the many electronic resources and services so broadly available today, no library's immediately available resources are as restricted as they used to be. The library should in any case have and maintain a collection development policy, for one reason because developing and referring to such a policy clarifies for the librarians what the collection focus should be, and for another because such a policy can be referred to in case of questions from someone outside the library.

In technical services, small academic libraries tend not to have the kind of processing backlogs that large libraries often accumulate, meaning that what is obtained today is often available for use tomorrow. In part this is of course because less material is being obtained in the first place. However, it is reasonable to suggest that the more important reason is that in the smaller library, fewer steps are involved in any processing (acquisitions, receiving, cataloging, labeling), fewer staff handle the materials, not to mention the smaller physical distances required to move materials around.

As to technology, although the small academic library will have access to, and need for, services from the campus information technology (computer) staff, the library also requires some computer proficiency in its own staff, for immediate troubleshooting, for Web page development and maintenance, and for work with whatever computer system(s) the library uses.

The ideal situation for the small academic library is to be part of some kind of consortium, both for its library systems implementation, upgrading, enhancement and maintenance, and for group pricing for its databases. A consortium also provides a ready community of colleagues for the director and other librarians as well as for the rest of the library staff for collaborations and assistance.

THE LIBRARY BUDGET

Small academic libraries are given budgets as one unit of the larger academic institution, and are thus dependent on the budgetary priorities of that larger institution. The libraries are budgeted as an "expense" to the larger institutions, generally without any expectation of corresponding revenue generation. This can sometimes make it difficult to justify the need for specific library budgets, beyond some generic "the library is the heart of the institution."

Other units within the parent institution usually can refer to criteria more easily understood by the larger institution when justifying a budget request. Academic departments, for instance, can have their budgets be dependent on the number of students that major in their discipline, or the number of credit hours that their faculty teach, or the total number of students that enroll in their courses. While such contingencies can be frustrating for those departments come budget time, at least those are clearly defined criteria. For the library, few such clear corresponding criteria are available. This makes it even more imperative to develop good justifications for every library budget request.

There are several things to keep in mind when justifying a budget request:

- It is always appropriate for the library to be asked for justification of its budget. Being asked for justification is not a question of lack of either trust or appreciation. Rather it is an opportunity to educate a larger audience about what the library's services consist of, and what those services cost.
- The budget justification must be written in language that someone who is not a librarian can understand, without being insulting and without overexplaining.
- Though it can feel frustrating to keep justifying the same thing repeatedly, especially as it is likely that not everything that is requested will be granted, the need for repetition, and gracious repetition at that, should be expected. Repetition, even over multiple years, as often as not does eventually lead to enough success to make repetition worthwhile.
- The process of formulating the justification will often clarify for the budget creator as well as the parent institution's budget office exactly why the library needs the requested funds.

Often the library will, in addition to its regular annual budget, have some "restricted" funds, that is, endowments gifts that generate income that can be spent in areas specified by the donors. There are two main advantages to such funds: (1) they are extras beyond the regular budget, and (2) they do not disappear at the end of the fiscal year, the way any unspent funds in the annual budget usually will (though there can be institutional variations in what funds may be carried over from one budget year to the next).

Obtaining grants is a way to stretch the library's budget beyond what the parent institution can or will support, though it should never be in place of institutional support for the library's core services. Onetime gifts are of course also always welcome, if with the same caveat.

STATISTICS

Every library will maintain statistics on various parts of its operations. Most of these statistics will come from the various computer systems that the library uses. Statistics will encompass staff size, collection size (such as volumes, subscriptions, and databases), service quantities (circulation, interlibrary loans, instruction sessions, reference questions), and budget allocations and uses.

Statistics are needed for a number of reasons:

- Most years they will be required for at least one, and sometimes more than one, national statistical survey. The two major statistical surveys for small academic libraries are the annual ACRL Statistics Questionnaire and the bi-annual NCES (National Center for Education Statistics) Academic Libraries Survey. Both are conducted electronically through the Internet. The library director will be notified by the surveying agencies with instructions and deadlines.
- Chances are good that the library will also be asked to contribute numbers to a regional or consortial group. With luck, that group will use the same statistical definitions as the above national ones, but it is not something that can be counted on.
- A regular but infrequent (typically every ten years) use of library statistics is for the accreditation self-study that is mandated for entire academic institutions by regional academic accreditation bodies. A compilation from the annual ACRL and NCES surveys will usually serve this situation well.

Although accrediting bodies will differ from region to region in their processes, a primary source for questions to shape the library's accreditation self-study is ACRL's Standards for Libraries in Higher Education. "The standards and key principles are designed as a tool to help libraries establish individual goals within the context of their institutional goals" (ACRL 2004b). That is, these standards are a general planning tool for academic libraries of all sizes.

- It is also likely that the library will be asked by one or another department on campus, academic and/or administrative, to provide particular numbers. For instance, schools of music and education within the parent institution need specialized library statistics for their discipline-mandated accreditation reports (which may be more frequent than the institution-wide accreditation study). Some of these requests can be anticipated because they are recurring, while others come out of the blue. It is in

the library's best interest to always respond to these requests with good grace, regardless of deadlines. "We are too busy" is not an acceptable excuse, even if it is true.
- Various statistics will also be needed for requests or reports or grants generated by the library.
- Comparing one's own statistics to those of the parent institution's defined peer (same-as) and aspiration institutions can be very useful in generating arguments for increased budgetary and other forms of support from the parent institution.
- Statistics should also be used to evaluate and adjust library services and library work flows.

LIBRARY STAFF

THE DIRECTOR

Consider the leadership structure of your own [academic] institution and the different kinds of responsibilities the director of the college library is expected, in the normal course of things, to assume. Who other than the library director must deal with the sum of: a professional staff; a non-professional staff; student assistants; the entire faculty; the entire student body; a large and complicated budget; a complex procurement and storage operation, including the need to keep abreast of new items of various kinds; long-range planning, but also the day-to-day functioning of a many-faceted system comprehending innumerable small details; upkeep problems for one or more buildings; and concern for public relations with people beyond the campus? . . . a president's or a dean's job may be more difficult, more demanding, in some ways; but no one [else]'s attention is pulled in so many directions simultaneously . . . " (Maurer 1981, 97–98)

Today, the library director must also be knowledgeable about and up-to-date with ever-expanding computer technology and with electronic resources and services, and must work with local, statewide, and regional consortia that manage some aspects of the individual library's services. The library director is also part of the administrative team of the larger institution (college or university), and as such has responsibilities to that larger institution that may at times conflict with her/his responsibility to the library.

The reporting structure for the director of the small academic library follows two basic models. The first model considers the library an academic endeavor; and as such, the director of the library (sometimes called college librarian or university librarian) reports to the vice president for academic affairs or the provost. The second model looks on the library in a more limited way, as another technology function; and as such, the library director reports to whomever heads campus computer technology. Although the first model is intuitively preferable, the director usually has no say in this matter.

Regardless of reporting structure, the library director's supervisor may have limited understanding of what the library is or does ("Everything isn't available on the Internet for free?"). Ideally, the supervisor will trust the library director to manage the library without interference, expecting only a few basic courtesies:

- Make her/him and the parent institution look good, and the corollary, to not make her/him or the parent institution look bad.
- Manage the library budget so as to obtain the most with the least, and preferably not ask for more.
- Provide occasional reports, in whatever format the supervisor prefers (oral or written, superficial or detailed, seldom or often—the director needs to learn the reporting style preferred by the supervisor, and to adjust her/his own style as needed).

As to other campus constituencies—faculty, students, administration, staff—their needs, too, will be reasonably straightforward:

- That students' and others' intellectual resource needs will be met without reference to budgetary or other constraints.
- That the library director will be a respectful colleague.
- Bonus: that the library director will be an intelligent and interesting person with a sense of humor.

The group that will have the greatest expectations of the director of the small academic library is the library staff. In contrast to the director of a larger library, in the smaller library the director will not be shielded in any way from that staff; and expectations will be high. (More on this later in this chapter.)

NON-DIRECTOR

The first rule for being a successful manager is having a good staff, the rest being then secondary. That said, it is obvious that this is an oversimplification; and it is equally obvious that there are myriad other things involved in managing a small academic library that can make the director's life more or less challenging, more or less interesting, more or less rewarding (in whatever ways these terms may be defined). Nevertheless, it remains true that a competent, dependable, committed, and reasonably satisfied staff is key to the success of the director of a small academic library, and especially so when the accent is on "small."

When a new director arrives at the new-to-the-director library, a staff will already be in place of course. The best assumption to make in the beginning is that what is already in place is wonderful, and that the staff is only waiting for a good director to lead them. It is unlikely that this will prove to be an entirely correct assumption; and in a few unfortunate cases, even all the best efforts to shape the staff to meet the director's vision will come to naught. However, the odds are ultimately in favor of a positive outcome when that is the implied expectation.

Small academic libraries differ in their staffing not only in size, but also in having a flatter structure and in having broader responsibilities within each position. Flexibility in responsibilities is more likely, and also makes more sense, in the smaller library.

HIRING A GOOD STAFF

Hiring an academic librarian involves much the same extensive search process as the hiring of a faculty member for an academic department of the college or university. ACRL's (Association of College & Research Libraries) *A Guideline for the Screening and Appointment of Academic Librarians Using a Search Committee* provides a blueprint for most of the steps in a successful search to fill a librarian vacancy even at a small academic library, including doing national advertising and using a search committee, conducting telephone interviews and thorough reference checks, and having finalists come to campus for full-day interviews with a broad range of people, including meeting the full library staff. In this way there is broad input into and acceptance of the final choice (ACRL 2004a).

Even for the librarian who wants to end up working in a larger library, a small library is a good professional starting point. In a large library, it is hard for either librarians or support staff to get a sense of the larger picture, the broader context, or the variety of tasks that go into the totality of a library's services. In contrast, the staff of a small library is far more likely to become aware of and learn about every aspect of academic librarianship.

An excellent pool of librarian candidates for the small academic library is the brand-new or relatively recent library school graduate. True, these graduates may not stay for very long, which means more frequent searches to fill vacancies. On the positive side, however, new librarians will often be hungry for the more varied and often more responsible experiences than a more departmentalized larger library can offer, they will have fresher knowledge and often a more open mind about possibilities, and, perhaps, unfortunately for them but luckily for the hiring library, they will more likely be willing and able to work for the often lesser pay that a smaller library can offer.

When considering candidates for librarian positions at a small academic library, the following questions may aid in seeking out positive characteristics, in addition to core competencies:

- Is the candidate genuinely interested in performing a broad range of tasks? A candidate who wants to specialize might not be happy in the smaller library.
- Is the candidate able to work independently while at the same time keeping in mind the collaborative necessities of a small staff?
- Will the candidate "fit in" with the existing staff? This does not mean hiring clones of existing staff; but a genuine loner would not be successful within a small staff.

For support staff vacancies, an abbreviated version of the librarian search process will work well. Support staff will probably be performing a narrower range of tasks than the librarians; but many of same considerations that apply to librarians apply to support staff also.

Most commonly for small academic libraries, the parent institution will have a human resources (personnel) office that will be knowledgeable about benefits and other employment particulars, most especially in the area of conforming to what sometimes seems a bewildering array of laws dealing with hiring, promotion, and other employment practices. That office will also have specific record keeping requirements for all searches, and the library must be sure to comply with such external requirements.

KEEPING A GOOD STAFF

What, then, will a library staff want from its director? Their desires reflect the hands-on reality of managing any small organization, the expectation of collaboration that is part of the academic environment, and a desire for intelligent and respectful leadership. Thus, the library staff will want the library director to:

- obtain the largest possible budget, including the best possible pay and benefits;
- monitor and manage that budget to greatest benefit;
- act as a buffer against the larger institution and world;
- hire the best possible staff;
- mediate conflict among staff to mutually satisfactory conclusions;
- tactfully rectify individual staff underperformance or misbehavior;
- involve staff in planning and decision making in a meaningful way;
- communicate with and keep staff informed;
- give clear directions of desired results, and then leave the staff to accomplish these results in ways they judge to be the most effective;
- understand, appreciate, and respect what each staff member does at work;
- know enough specifics about every aspect of library operations to make decisions that make sense to those who know more about each specific aspect;
- model any desired behavior, and be fair and even-handed;
- give appropriate public credit when deserved, and criticism only in private;
- devise rewards that are appropriate to each individual's reward structure (flexibility, time off, and pizza are tops on this list);
- mentor when desired;
- sometimes but not always join staff for breaks;
- be tolerant and have a sense of humor.

Librarians should be expected to collaborate in library-wide planning and decision making and also to have some specific administrative responsibilities of their own, while support staff members more usually want primarily to know about anything that affects them and to be given clear directions as to what they are to accomplish.

Some librarians may also want faculty status, the same as or similar to the status of academic faculty members. The attraction is understandable: participation in campus-wide faculty governance on a peer basis, potentially higher salaries, access to paid sabbaticals, tenure options, and, presumably, increased respect at least from other faculty. However and on the other hand, librarians in small academic libraries invariably have twelve-month contracts with forty-hour scheduled workweeks, in contrast to the academic faculty's nine-month contracts with flexible workweeks; and in addition, if librarians go through the campus faculty promotion and tenure process, they will to their disadvantage be judged by criteria that are mostly not applicable to their own professional standards and responsibilities. This is an issue that most directors of small academic libraries will at some time encounter.

CHALLENGES FOR THE FUTURE

It is of course risky to presume to be able to foretell the future. However, without doubt everything in the following incomplete list of trends will inevitably affect academic libraries of all sizes, including the small academic library, in the next few years. Most of these trends reflect realities for the larger institutions of which the libraries are a part.

- Sustained proliferation of "non-traditional" academic programs such as distance education (where "distance" can mean anything from across town to across the world), degree completion programs, and continuing education is a certainty. Some academic institutions and their libraries have been working with such programs for many years already, but now the trend is towards ubiquity. This will affect almost every aspect of library operations.
- The face of the traditional student body is also changing, growing more multicultural and sometimes multilingual. International students are also being recruited to campuses in growing numbers, both to broaden overall campus perspectives and to help pay the bills (international students often pay a larger percent of individual tuition charges than do the sometimes heavily discounted, that is, subsidized domestic students).
- The already rapidly growing use of computer-based delivery of library services is further hastened by the spread of nontraditional academic programs, by online delivery of traditional academic courses and programs, and by a generalized demand by all students for electronic services. This will cover not only broad database licenses and electronic 24/7 reference via e-mail or chat, but also will af-

fect how library research instruction is delivered and, by extension, how all library staff is scheduled.

- New library technology such as federated searching (software that allows a single Google-like search of multiple library resources) and link resolvers (leading to instances of article full text anywhere in a library's resources) raise questions of how best to present and teach such resources to the campus community. It is, by the way, difficult to imagine how the small academic library with its small staff could introduce such resources without belonging to a larger group such as a consortium that can provide technical implementation expertise.

- The use of electronic books has so far not spread as rapidly as originally predicted. This however may change as better access technologies for these materials are developed.

- Increasing pressures for formalized assessment of library services is a reality already. LibQUAL is a relatively new tool to accomplish such assessment in a more uniform way than the self-designed surveys libraries having been using for years. "LibQUAL is a survey developed by the Association of Research Libraries (ARL) to provide libraries with a standardized, effective method to measure the quality of library services based on the perceptions of faculty, students and staff" (LibQUAL 2005). LibQUAL may be too ambitious an approach for the small academic library; but through this tool or something else, some forms of assessment will soon be imperative for academic libraries of all sizes.

- Related to assessment is an increasing demand from regulatory groups for reliance on commonly accepted service standards. Academic libraries are fortunate in this area to be able to refer to the already existing broad range of standards developed by ACRL.

- Financial pressures on parent institutions will likely continue to grow in the next several years, which will of course translate into similar financial pressures on libraries.

CONCLUSION

The bottom line: managing a small academic library is an always interesting, sometimes frustrating but ultimately satisfying mix of the strategic and the hands-on; and it provides a very immediate feeling that one is making a significant contribution to the education of college undergraduates.

REFERENCES

ACRL. 2004a. "A guideline for the screening and appointment of academic librarians using a search committee." www.ala.org/ala/acrl/acrlstandards/screenapguide.htm (accessed April 20, 2005).

ACRL. 2004b. "Standards for libraries in higher education." www.ala.org/ala/acrl/acrlstandards/standardslibraries.htm (accessed January 8, 2006).

ACRL. 2005. *Academic library trends and statistics for Carnegie classification master's colleges and institutions [and] baccalaureate colleges.* Chicago: Association of College and Research Libraries.

ACRL. 2006. "What is the Association of College & Research Libraries?" www.ala.org/ala/acrl/aboutacrl/whatisacrl/whatacrl.htm (accessed January 8, 2006).

ALA. 2004. *American library directory, 2004–2005.* Medford, NJ: Information Today.

Bowker. 2004. *Bowker annual library and book trade almanac, 2004.* Medford, NJ: Information Today.

Carnegie Foundation. 2005. "The Carnegie classification of institutions of higher education." www.carnegiefoundation.org/classifications/index.asp (accessed January 6, 2006).

JSTOR. 2005. "JSTOR classifications for U.S. academic or other research institutions." www.jstor.org/about/us.html#classification (accessed April 20, 2005).

LibQUAL. 2005. "Welcome to LibQUAL+TM!" www.libqual.org/ (accessed April 20, 2005).

Maurer, Charles B. 1981. "Close encounters of diverse kinds: A management panorama for the director of the smaller college library." In *College librarianship*, edited by William Miller and D. Stephen Rockwood. Metuchen, NJ and London: Scarecrow Press.

Miller, William , and D. Stephen Rockwood, eds. 1981. *College librarianship*. Metuchen, NJ and London: Scarecrow Press.

NCES. 2005. "Welcome to compare academic libraries." www.nces.ed.gov/surveys/libraries/compare/Index.asp?LibraryType=Academic (accessed December 20, 2005).

NCES. 2006a. "What is an academic library?" www.nces.ed.gov/surveys/libraries/AcaWhatIs.asp (accessed January 6, 2006).

NCES. 2006b. "Welcome." www.nces.ed.gov/index.asp (accessed January 9, 2006).

Reitz, Joan M. 2004. "ODLIS—Online dictionary for library and information science." www.lu.com/odlis/ (accessed December 12, 2005).

FURTHER READING

Every academic librarian should read the weekly *The Chronicle of Higher Education* on a regular basis in order to keep current with the broader environment in which academic libraries function. Limited online access is available at http://chronicle.com/, with full access available with a subscription to the paper version.

The academic librarian should also remain conversant with the full range of ACRL (Association of College & Research Libraries) publications (that is, not necessarily have read it all, but know what is available and then use as needed), including ACRL's range of standards for most aspects of academic library management. ACRL publications are listed at www.ala.org/ala/acrl/acrlpubs/publications.htm (accessed April 20, 2005). ACRL standards are compiled at www.ala.org/ala/acrl/acrlstandards/standards guidelines.htm (accessed April 20, 2005).

Another important category of information for the academic librarian is the many and varied e-mail lists for the profession. Librarians are generally very generous in sharing information about their experiences and practices: just ask. One source of information about such lists is *Library-Oriented Lists & Electronic Serials*, a compilation of links that is maintained through the Washington Research Library Consortium. www.aladin.wrlc.org/gsdl/cgi-bin/library?p=about&c=liblists (accessed May 27, 2005).

Libweb (http://lists.webjunction.org/libweb/Academic_main.html) provides a list of links to academic libraries in the United States by region and state.

E.D. TAB: *Academic Libraries: 2000.* "This report is based on information from the 2000 Academic Libraries Survey. The tables in this publication summarize library services, library staff, library collections, and library expenditures for libraries in degree-granting postsecondary institutions in the 50 states and the District of Columbia." Published in November 2003 by the National Center for Education Statistics. "ED TABs are a collection of tables, presented with minimal analyses. The purpose of an E.D. TAB is to make tabular data available quickly." Downloadable as a pdf file at http://nces.ed.gov/pubs2004/2004317.pdf (accessed December 14, 2005).

2 COMMUNITY COLLEGE LIBRARIES

Mary Mayer-Hennelly

DEFINITION

Community college libraries provide facilities, services, collections, and learning resources that support their mission of collegiate education and training for adults of all ages and backgrounds. The goals of teaching, learning, and research guide the operations and use of budgets. To be successful, library services must be available to all students and faculty, on-site or by remote access. They must be an integral part of teaching and learning at their institutions. The physical locations of libraries, their collections, equipment, and learning resources should be directly related to the college's curriculum and the institution's identity as an organization fostering learning.

OVERVIEW

This chapter covers:

- A general introduction to community colleges
- Individualized service
- Serving added student constituencies
- Joint library ventures

INTRODUCTION

Libraries serving community colleges have much in common with other academic libraries. Most have mature professional and support staff and acknowledge a need to add diversity to the professional ranks. The perceived lack of glamour in librarianship, the noticeable growth in online, off-site use of library resources versus traditional visits, staff resistance to continuous technological change, uneven funding, and the need to claim institutional recognition are common challenges.

In all higher education settings, academic librarians have been instrumental in providing research assistance to faculty. The knowledge and skills required in the academic setting and librarians' ability to establish and nurture strong positive relationships with faculty are integral to a successful library. These include, but are not limited to, effective bibliographic and information literacy instruction, collection development, understanding of the college's curricula and awareness of search strategies.

Community colleges boast libraries that are academic in nature, responsive in ways familiar to the public library and deliver personalized information responses on a special library level. For example, Tidewater Community College in Virginia states that its " . . . vision is centered around a core mission to providing the highest quality education, both for students seeking a baccalaureate degree in a four-year institution and for those seeking an education in occupational and technical fields to prepare for entry or advancement in the workforce" (Tidewater Community College, 2000). Clearly, much is included in community colleges' territory.

Their precursors, junior colleges and technical colleges, had strictly defined focuses. Developed in the 1960s, community colleges have a wider mission, that of entry into comprehensive higher education and workforce development. Programs and courses of instruction culminate with certificates, often in vocational fields such as automotive repair or horticulture, or an associate's degree. Transferable credit courses and articulation agreements enable students to move forward to four-year institutions. Modest tuition, always less than that of four-year colleges, enables wide access.

In addition to faculty and students, community college libraries are utilized by community patrons, members of the public library, by choice. Their needs and interests vary just as they do at the public library. Most community colleges provide full services to community patrons. The location of a campus and level of local public library resources affect the community patron presence. Urban community college libraries often have the same issues with community patrons that their public library counterparts experience.

Several distinct challenges exist now for community college libraries, often known as Learning Resource Centers (LRCs)*. These include the exceptional role of one-on-one individualized instruction with students, the libraries' unique need to respond with services and collections for constituencies considered non-traditional, even within the community college academic framework, and joint facility overtures from local communities.

INDIVIDUALIZED SERVICE

The statistical profile of a community college student does not parallel that of an entry-level university student. Fewer students arrive directly from high school. Most have been in the workforce or the military. Thirty-two percent of community college students are 30 years of age or older; 46 percent are 25 years or older (American Association of Community Colleges). About two-thirds of all community college students attend classes part time while working or managing family responsibilities; thus, completion of an associate's degree often takes longer than two years. The length of time for earning a credential in certificate programs varies (Educational Statistics Quarterly). Significant numbers of those stepping into higher education via the community college are economically challenged and the first in their families to earn any kind of degree.

The open admissions policy of community colleges is a major factor in planning library services. As library users, entering students may possess few information literacy skills. Some may have skills gained from recent secondary education or learned in the workplace.

Recognized as user friendly, campus libraries naturally attract new community college students. Because they arrive with varied skills sets, often the instruction, support, and encouragement received at the library are key to a student's success. Assembling a research paper, for example, may seem an insurmountable assignment for an individual who has not been in a formal classroom for ten years. How does one use a database? Where are specific

* Learning Resource Centers is a common label for an organization that may include all or some of the following: a traditional library, AV, media services, and electronic services such as computer labs.

instructions on how to cite a resource located on the Internet? It is the personalized library instruction that supports a student's progress; many need that one-on-one guidance.

Community college librarians, as academic librarians, are responsible for freshman orientation classes and specialized subject instruction. But, it is the individualized attention and guidance for students that help "level the playing field." It is from librarians that students learn how to obtain materials at consortial institutions and what virtual resources are. At library service desks, students receive instruction on how to access their campus e-mail and the institution's student information system (SIS). Through the library, a student realizes that resources for a project may be available in a media format such as DVD as well as in print or online resources. The rewards of enabling students to move to a higher level of information literacy are enormous.

SERVING ADDED STUDENT CONSTITUENCIES

By 2000, nearly all states had some variation of dual enrollment community college programs. The term dual enrollment is defined as high school students who are allowed to meet high school graduation requirements by simultaneously earning college credit. Dual enrollment's purpose is to improve the transition of students into higher education, provide high school students with first-hand exposure to college-level work, encourage grade 12 students to engage in demanding coursework, and offer high school seniors a wider array of curricular choices (Virginia Community College System).

Another offering is the middle college program, also known as early college. Collaboration between high schools (grades 9–12) and community colleges is considered by some a way to connect younger students to a higher education goal earlier in their secondary experience and targets at-risk students. Depending upon the program, it can bring high school students to the community college campus for coursework.

Community college libraries are closely involved with dual enrollment and middle college programs by providing basic orientation, library skills, and instruction targeted to topics such as search engines. The student participants are younger than even the traditional college age and their skills are uneven. Apart from their less mature profile, serving dual enrollment and middle college students may require other considerations such as adaptation or clarification of the institution's online use policy if the public school system involved has Internet access restrictions.

These programs have tremendous growth potential and the library leadership in community colleges needs to address the issues of dual enrollment and middle college students in their strategic planning.

JOINT LIBRARY VENTURES

Library partnerships of all kinds have increased, many necessitated by shrinking funds at all levels and initiated by economic incentives. One type of partnership that has received greatly increased consideration is shared, cooperative libraries in which two distinct entities combine resources in a single library facility. Because community college libraries have an academic core yet also share certain public library characteristics, including accessible services to the general community of citizens, they have a clear potential to become partners in many collaborative projects with city or county governments.

A literature search of library buildings designed and erected in the last three decades of the twentieth century reveals occasional shared library projects. Examples include a public school sharing library space with a public library branch within the school's walls, and a recreation center and public library branch under one roof, separated by a lobby area. A number of those projects had the common factor of serving a modest population over a wide service area. Having several public services combined in one facility is attractive as a single destination for busy citizens.

Proposals for collaborative library projects, in which two separate libraries join forces, have increased dramatically in the last five years. These fall within three distinct categories. The first model is two organizations sharing one larger building divided by main walls or floors. Clientele for each are directed to their institution; library collections are located within the institution's area, and services for each clientele are delivered separately. Little is shared except utilities and possibly maintenance.

The second model is shared use in which two institutions build a single library facility with separate entrances and services but are housed under a single roof, sharing selected spaces. These might include an auditorium, group meeting rooms, computer labs, media viewing areas, exhibit space or lobby.

Joint use is the third model. It has been defined as designing and erecting a single facility, which integrates all patron services, and there are few, if any, institutional distinctions. When San Jose State University's (CA) library joined forces with the City of San Jose's central public library to create the Dr. Martin Luther King, Jr. Library, public planners and the professional library community took notice. The 475,000-square-foot building was named 2004 "Library of the Year" by the *Library Journal*.

CONCLUSION

In summary, the community college library is viewed as all things to all people. "It is a recreational space, a research facility, a gathering place, a cultural facility and, in some cases, it serves as the public library for its surrounding community. How will we continue to do all things well?" (Schweitzer 2005). The redefinition issue is not unique to community colleges but more so than for other academic libraries.

As community colleges seek to invest talent and funding in providing quality academic and service programs, their libraries will be a key ingredient in the delivery of graduates who contribute to the vibrancy of geographic areas and their workforces.

REFERENCES

American Association of Community Colleges (Trends and Statistics). www.aacc.nche.edu/.

"Bearings on the future: The Tidewater Community College strategic plan." Norfolk, VA: Tidewater Community College. www.tcc.edu. (Accessed November 2000).

Berry, John. 2004 "Library of the year: The San Jose model." *Library Journal* 15 (June) www.libraryjournal.com/article/CA42793.html.

Hoachlander, Gary, Anna C. Sikora, and Laura Horn. 2003. "Community college students: Goals, academic preparation, and outcomes." 2003: *Educational Statistics Quarterly* 5, 2 (Tidewater Community College, Portsmouth, VA). www.nces.ed.gov/programs/quarterly/vol_5/5_2/q4_1.asp#H4.

Office of Institutional Effectiveness, Norfolk, Virginia. www.tcc.edu. (Accessed February 2005).

Virginia Community College System. "Statistical Profile 2002–03" (Richmond, Virginia). www.vccs.edu (Accessed February 2005).

Virginia Community College System, Academic and Student Affairs Committee. "Dual Enrollment in the VCCS Report" (Richmond, Virginia). (Report presented March 24, 2005).

Schweitzer, Aileen (Director, Thomas Nelson Community College Library and Resources Center). March 10, 2005 e-mail to author.

SPECIAL LIBRARIES

Richard E. Wallace

DEFINITION

A special library is one that is set up to serve the information needs of a defined set of users by facilitating access to and dissemination of needed information. Its collection of resources is maintained and organized in a manner that enhances (and can be determined by) the way the users access the resources to acquire the information they need.

Many organizations use names other than library for their information unit. Names include variations on information, knowledge, and analysis. For example, information center, knowledge center, market research, and analysis. For purposes of this chapter they are all called *special libraries*.

A special library can be a physical collection of resources, a person with the means (computer, telephone) to access internal or external resources, or something in between. These libraries are found in all types of for-profit and non-profit oganizations, colleges, and universities. They may serve the entire organization or just one of its subunits, or some combination of both. The user group(s) served depends upon who is willing to provide managerial and financial support.

Each library's collections and resources are determined by the interest of the users they serve and the types of resources necessary to provide the needed information. Thus, the collection and resources will change as the parent organization's interests change. The size of the staff varies from one person (solo librarian) to twenty or more.

A special library usually has one or more of these characteristics:

- Subject-oriented staff (by education or training)
- Exists so long as it is considered an asset to an organization's mission

- Subject-specific resource collection—*specific to the parent's needs*
- Usually small and well-defined user group
- Is dependent upon outside resources—*staff will travel*
- *to the resource site*
- Virtual resource collection
- Very current resource collection
- Staff usually knows all their users by name
- Many users may not be in the same physical location as the library
- Collection is organized and defined by the users and their needs
- Staff is highly user oriented
- Staff members usually have more than one of the normal library-related job functions—*the larger the staff the more individual jobs become specialized*
- Size of physical facilities is no indication of resource or staff size

Using the description above means there are a large number of libraries that can be classified as special libraries. However, due to similarities between libraries, special libraries can be broken into a number of classes, including medical, law, church/synagogue, departmental libraries within public and academic libraries, advertising, newspaper, and chemistry. The American Library Association stated that as of December 2003 there were 8,300+ special libraries in the United States. These numbers do not include government and armed forces libraries or those special libraries in public and academic libraries.

OVERVIEW

This chapter covers:

- When the organization is ready to establish a library
- The library as an organizational unit
- Budgeting
- User services
- Acquisitions
- Organization of materials for access
- Challenges facing the special library
- Sources for further study of special libraries

WHEN IS THE ORGANIZATION READY?

For a library to exist within an organization, or one of its subunits, there has to be a recognition of the need for economical, efficient, and effective ways to access and retrieve information. In addition there has to be a willingness and desire to make a direct commitment of some of the organization's, or subunit's, financial and physical resources to achieve this goal.

An information audit should be arranged when someone in authority in an organization without a librarian, and/or library, realizes employees are spending an exorbitant amount of time looking for information to do their jobs. Although this is usually done by an outside consultant, there have been instances where a librarian has been hired and has conducted the audit.

The purpose of the audit is to help determine (1) what internal and external resources are currently available within the organization; (2) what types of resources might be required; (3) how information is used and knowledge shared among the potential users; (4) how and where the users currently acquire such information; and (5) the knowledge and skills the library staff will need to ensure information is effectively and efficiently acquired, organized, and distributed.

Formal and informal user surveys need to be conducted throughout a special library's existence. The data gathered helps the library manager prove the value of his/her unit's contribution to the organization's bottom line.

LIBRARY AS AN ORGANIZATIONAL UNIT

The mission, organization, and structure of a special library are heavily influenced by its parent organization or the subunit of which it is a part. During the life of a special library there will be changes in reporting lines and funding.

The reporting line for special librarians varies widely from directly to the organization's CEO to a department head. The types of departments reported to include R&D (Research and Development), administrative services, personnel, and finance. The reporting line is dependent upon and influenced by who the library serves, how it is funded, the size of its collection of resources, its staff size, and its physical location.

Some special libraries have some form of committee or board

as part of the reporting line. The library manager may or may not have any input into who is appointed to the committee. The committee members are employees of the organization. The committee's authority may be advisory or it may be the final word. For most special libraries it is somewhere in between.

In many cases, the librarian's supervisor is a non-librarian and has little knowledge of how a library functions. The librarian must make an effort to educate him or her. This can be a continuous and sometimes frustrating process because supervisors are often transferred or promoted.

Not only must the librarian educate the supervisor about what the library does, he/she must show why the library is a real asset to the organization or subunit. The library is a service unit and is therefore always subject to closure if it is not proving it is contributing to the bottom line. This aspect of a librarian's job is called "marketing." The selling of the library as a valuable asset goes on continuously and must be done at *all* levels of the organization. A number of books and articles have been written on this.

As part of a marketing strategy vision and mission statements need to be drafted. This requires knowledge and understanding of the parent organization and should take into account its vision and mission statements.

> **Figure 3-1   Recommended Written Policies/Procedures in a Special Library**
>
> Statements
>   Mission
>   Strategic plan
>   Marketing plan
>   Goals and objectives
> Policies
>   User services
>   Collection development (including de-acquisition)
>   Copyright
>   Cataloging/indexing
>   Records management
> Procedures
>   User services (including circulation)
>   Acquisitions
>   Cataloging/indexing
>   Records management
>   Procedures for jobs not covered in the 4 items above
> Other
>   Budget
>   Job descriptions
>   Organization chart with responsibilities
>   Purposes and responsibilities of library committee

STAFF

Although special library staffs vary in size, most are staffed by one professional librarian and sometimes one or two clerks or paraprofessionals to help. This lone professional has become known as a solo librarian. There is a division within the Special Libraries Association devoted to this type of library service.

A solo librarian is responsible for all aspects of the library operation. This position requires the use of time-management and the acceptance of some isolation because there are no colleagues close at hand with whom to collaborate. The solo librarian must be flexible and willing to adjust to the continuously changing demands for service. Deadlines create pressures and long hours because the user requires information, which often impacts directly or indirectly on the organization's bottom line.

Not only must the solo provide service to his/her users, time must be found for training and continuous education: performing the technical functions (cataloging, circulation, shelving) required to keep the library operating; and performing the functions of a manager (preparing budgets, writing monthly reports, marketing, supervising and preparing performance evaluations if lucky enough to have help). Some librarians, including solos, even manage other departments such as mail/receiving, corporate records, reproduction/duplication, or information technology. Several librarians in for-profit organizations have moved up the organizational chart to supervise the library and other departments.

There are special librarians who do not have a physical library to maintain. These librarians use telephones, computers, and the resources of other libraries to obtain the information their users need. They may be employees of the organization, consultants, or contract employees. They may not even be in the same physical location as their users.

Special libraries were the first types of libraries to have staffs who were not employees of the organization served. While the librarian, and other staff, are hired by an employment agency, the library and its resources belong to the organization being served. Difficulties with this situation include time the librarian must spend gaining the trust of the users and the financial safeguards that must be instituted.

Although many special librarians have professional degrees there are instances where persons with subject expertise and/or training have been selected to set up a new library or manage an existing one. This happens because someone in authority knows the library is essential but has no idea how a library functions.

One of the things an experienced librarian can do is take advantage of the special librarians' proclivity to network among themselves. This networking takes place across special libraries regardless of subject or type. The willingness of special librarians to help one another is one of the strengths of special librarianship. A good place to start is by joining one of the local chapters of the Special Library Association.

Another way to get help is to join some of the library-related Internet discussion lists. You do not have to be an active participant to learn about new ideas. However, participation is a good way to obtain input when you would like help with a question or problem. Library-related electronic newsletters also provide a way to stay current.

BUDGET

In order to exist, a special library needs financial resources to pay staff and to acquire the information needed by users. Budgets and funding mechanisms vary widely. The budgeting system and financial record keeping a special library uses is determined by the parent organization.

Staff and information resources cost money. An organization having a good library understands this and is willing to take the expenses from the income or profits every year because the library helps the organization's employees do their jobs better. If the library staff is perceived as not helping the organization achieve its goals (including making a profit) then the library can be discontinued.

The budgets for most for-profit and non-governmental special libraries are not publicly available because it is thought that such data could help competitors determine undisclosed financial information about the parent organization. The actual budget for special libraries varies widely; examples include no formal budget, lump sum spent at the librarian's discretion, and detailed budget similar to those in public and academic libraries.

The size of special libraries' budgets is as varied as the budget systems used. Library budgets can be (1) a percent of the parent's or unit's sales or profits; (2) a percent of the R&D or marketing budgets; and (3) a system of charge backs where each unit using the library pays a percentage of its budget. The percentage may be based on the percent of the library staff time used or on some form of head count.

There are also differences in what line items are included in a special library's budget. For example, some or all of these items may not be included:

- Accounting
- Association memberships
- Computers and peripherals
- Furniture and shelving
- Maintenance
- Postage/shipping
- Property taxes
- Space allocation
- Staff benefits
- Travel
- Utilities

Final authority for purchases (up to some fixed amount) usually rests with the library manager. There are cases where this authority rests with a committee or the library manager's supervisor.

The methods used for ordering and receiving and paying for materials vary also. Methods of ordering and receiving can include one of these or some combination:

- Use of parent organization's purchasing department
- Library generates own purchase orders
- Library orders online or by telephone without a formal purchase order

Payment methods include check, an impress account (usually limited to payments of less than $100), company-issued credit cards, or expense account (librarian uses own money and is repaid).

USER SERVICES

The types of services special librarians offer their users are diverse and many. These services may be determined by formal and informal information audits or surveys. The analysis of the information needs of the users is ongoing and helps the librarian determine the types of services required and how they will be offered.

Because the user group is finite and static, a special librarian can get to know the way individual users work and the types of information required. This gives the librarian an opportunity to provide very customized and personal service, which may be difficult to do in a public or academic library. This knowledge helps the librarian to evaluate current and future services to be offered.

Special librarians do as much of the information work (identify, obtain, analyze) as a user requests. By letting the librarian do the "leg work" the user can utilize his time on other job-related activities. The librarian can do it more efficiently and effectively because he/she knows how to obtain what is needed, and the cost per hour for finding the information will be less.

In addition to the normal user services offered by public and academic libraries, special libraries offer the following:

- Reference referral
- Literature/patent searches of databases
- Current awareness alerts

- Analyses of information found
- Competitive intelligence
- Journal routing
- Answering the request rather than just teaching user to look for answers
- Connecting the user with an outside expert
- Translation of foreign language materials
- Document delivery of even the most obscure material
- Willingness to travel to a resource when necessary

Many special libraries offer their users direct access to online hosts such as DIALOG, STN, QUESTEL/ORBIT, LEXIS/NEXIS, or WESTLAW to do their own database searching. Some librarians still do the actual searches or hire information brokers (expert online database search consultants). There are several reasons for this:

- Librarian is more proficient in database searching
- Librarian may have subject expertise (e.g., patent searches)
- User feels uncomfortable searching because "the clock is ticking" while connected to the database
- Librarian's time is cheaper than the user's time

In addition to the individuals who will do searches, there are companies like Find/SVP, NERAC, and Teltech that have large staffs of subject specialists to conduct searches. These firms work on some form of fee, the fee usually being based on the number and types of searches performed.

Find/SVP, NERAC, and TelTech are companies that will help identify and locate information-related resources in the areas of business and science/technology. Their staffs of experts can provide resources for answering questions, conducting literature/ patent searches, locating experts, or conducting marketing surveys. These are good resources to use when working on requests that are outside the scope of the library's collection or the expertise of the staff.

Find/SVP	www.findsvp.com
NERAC	www.nerac.com
TelTech	www.teltech.com

When a user has an information request, which is beyond the library staff's knowledge or the resources available, special librarians look for help beyond the library. Special librarians tend to have an intimate knowledge of the organization's employees' expertise and interest. Thus, they are often able to refer the user to someone within the organization. If necessary, outside experts or consultants are hired to help.

The existence of a special library within an organization is dependent upon the value of the services offered to users. To maintain this value-added service, special librarians will go all out to find the information the user needs. Librarians seek "the answer" because they are more efficient and effective at locating "the answer" and because in most cases their hourly salary rate is lower than that of the user.

ACQUISITIONS

Special libraries that have physical collections of paper and/or electronic resources need to acquire new materials in order to remain relevant to their users' needs. Like a number of other processes and procedures used by special libraries, the acquisition of resources will follow those of the parent organization. These methods may be totally different from those found in public or academic libraries.

Although a good idea, many special librarians do not have a formal and/or written collection policy. The librarian will acquire material in whatever format will provide the user with the information he requires. The only limitation might be cost or copyright considerations.

Figure 3-2 Copyright

Copyright is an important issue for special librarians, especially those in for-profit organizations, since most of the materials acquired are subject to copyright laws. Staying up-to-date with the law can help prevent the parent organization from being sued for infringement. In many cases the librarian is the most knowledgeable person in the organization about the law and its ramifications.

Copyright topics to be familiar with:
- *Fair use*
- *Licensing*
- *Obtaining permission of copyright owner(s)*
- *Copyright Clearance Center*
- *Resource sharing (including interlibrary loan)*
- *Preservation/archiving*
- *Reproduction rights (paper, electronic, audio/visual)*

Some special libraries act as the total organization's purchasing agent for books, journal and newspaper subscriptions, videos, etc. The item ordered may be outside the scope of the library's collection. There may be a charge back or the library may absorb the cost into its budget. Acting as the central purchasing agent allows the librarian to create bibliographic records in case other employees may want to use the item.

In addition to items regularly acquired by public or academic libraries, special libraries may acquire some of these items:

- Association publications
- Patents
- Sheet maps
- Standards
- Trade journals
- Translations of journal articles and/or patents

Also, an item will be acquired even if it will only be used once.

Special libraries not only use the traditional materials selection tools but also jobbers and publishers' announcements and catalogs, bibliographies, and word of mouth. If an item is on a subject directly pertinent to users it will usually be acquired before reviews are published.

Expediency is the concern when ordering materials. The special librarian will order from whatever source provides the item(s) wanted in the most cost-effective manner. Sources include traditional and non-traditional publishers, bookstores, jobbers, second-hand dealers, or whoever can supply the item. If an item is from an unusual source or hard to find, a jobber will be employed. The special librarian can use some of these unusual sources because he/she is allowed to pay for the item(s) with a credit card and/or without a formal purchase order.

Special libraries cannot acquire all the resources they need because of cost and lack of physical space. Thus, they are dependent upon public and academic libraries and other special libraries for things such as journal articles and electronic databases, as well as books, government reports, etc. Journal article photocopies are one of the most ordered items.

Special libraries will maintain runs of journal titles directly relevant to their users and depend upon other libraries, publishers, and vendors for articles from journals that they do not have. Many small special libraries use the services of vendors or the fee-based services of academic libraries (e.g., Purdue University's Technical Information Service). These usually charge a service fee plus the copyright charge. The charges are usually nominal and are less than if the library subscribed to the journal.

Only the largest special libraries can afford to contract for access to the electronic journal databases of Elsevier, Wiley, ISI Thomson, or Gale. The subject of contracting for database usage is beyond the scope of this chapter. Several books on contracting are listed in the references.

The requirement for currency of resource materials and lack of physical space requires special libraries to continuously review their collections. Weeding, or de-acquisitioning, must be a regular activity. Methods of disposal of the discarded materials depend on the parent organization's policies. The methods used include (1) giving materials to employees; (2) donating to public or academic libraries; (3) selling to secondhand dealers; (4) donating to an organization that will send them to Third World countries; or (5) placing in the trash.

Figure 3-3   What Should Be in a Collection Development/ Acquisitions Procedures Manual

---

While St. Clair and Williamson provide two lists of items to consider in developing a policy[1], this list specifies what should be included in a manual:

- *Organization and library mission statements*
- *Acquisitions policy*
- *Handling user recommendations/requests*
- *Subjects and formats acquired*
- *De-accessioning*
- *Purchase vs. borrow*
- *Chargebacks vs. library pays*
- *Purchase approval procedures*
- *Purchase order procedures*
- *Payment methods (charge card, checks, cash)*
- *Vendor selection criteria*
- *List of vendors currently used*
- *Replacement (new, used)*
- *Gifts (including exchanges)*
- *Journal article photocopies (including who purchases and/ or pays)*
- *Supplies*

1 St. Clair and Williamson (1992, p.106)

ORGANIZATION OF MATERIALS FOR ACCESS

The types of resources housed by special libraries varies from the traditional to the unusual. Types of materials found include:

- Advertisements
- Engineering drawings/models
- Internal reports/documents
- Maps
- Musical scores

- Operator's manuals for machinery
- Patents
- Slides/pictures

The storage, organization of, and access to the library's resources are done with the user in mind and vary from the traditional book classification schemes to systems designed just for a library's collection(s). While computers are the most common tool for accessing the content of non-electronic resources, there are still a number of libraries that use paper-based indexes (including the card catalog). Special libraries tend to provide more comprehensive subject analysis and access methods to their collection(s) than do public or academic libraries.

Also affecting the organization and access methods used is the fact that many of the items housed are generated by the library's parent. The librarian is expected to organize and provide the access that will allow users to easily access and utilize these materials in their daily job-related activities. Since access is usually by electronic means, familiarity with digitization and scanning of older materials is needed.

Most special libraries have some form of library automation software to help organize and maintain the collection. Although this topic is beyond the scope of this chapter, it is important to note that some special libraries participate in the automation systems of consortia or library systems or Web-based systems in order to reduce the cost of acquiring and maintaining the software and equipment needed in a library automation program.

Special libraries even provide access to materials housed elsewhere within the parent organization. Documents and other resources needed by a department to function are housed in the department with subject and content analysis done by library staff so all employees may know of their existence. Methods for organizing and accessing its resources are an essential item for any special library.

CONCLUSION

One of the biggest challenges facing small special libraries is going to be the ubiquity of electronic resources. More and more resources are going to be available only in electronic format. E-books will become more common, journals will be available only in electronic format, and more scientific information is going to be available electronically.

The special librarian will have to provide the right mix of online and paper resources so as to be as comprehensive as possible. This will take ingenuity and resourcefulness because of budgetary restraints and the rising costs of electronic and paper resources. The special librarian's role will continue to involve selection, control, and gatekeeping.

Finding the needed information will continue to play an important role in user services. Special librarians will need to learn and embrace the technology supporting electronic resources and exploit those technologies that will best serve their users. In addition, the Internet and the Web will become more important in the delivery of information. Users will need to be trained to search resources effectively and efficiently and then be able to evaluate what they find.

As electronic resources become even more prevalent, the special library as a physical space will probably decline, with the exception of libraries dealing with certain subjects (e.g., science), because older paper resources contain information needed by users. The digitization of older resources means users will have less need for special libraries but not special librarians. These information gurus will still be needed to help find answers among the trillions of bits of data. Users will find that even though they can find information, good enough will not be acceptable.

To determine what services and resources to provide their users, special librarians must be knowledgeable about the needs and requirements of their users. They must listen and understand the problems and issues users face in doing their work. The special librarian will do this through informal and formal market research methods (surveys, focus groups, and getting out of the office/library for one-on-one meetings). The special librarian will continuously analyze and review the procedures and activities used to meet user information requests. Lack of money, staff, space, and time will require eliminating, or revising, inefficient and ineffective procedures and activities so new services and/or resources can be added.

REFERENCES/FURTHER READING

GENERAL

Reitz, Joan M. 2004. *Dictionary for library and information science*. Westport, CT: Libraries Unlimited.

SPECIAL LIBRARIES

*Managing small special libraries, 1992: An SLA information kit.*1992. Washington, DC: Special Libraries Association.

Berner, Andrew, and Guy St. Clair, eds. 1996. *The best of OPL II: Selected readings from the "One-person library," 1989–1994.* Washington, DC: Special Libraries Association.

Kreizman, Karen. 1999. *Establishing an information center: A practical guide.* London: Bowker-Saur.

Matarazzo, James M., and Suzanne D. Connolly, eds. 1999. *Knowledge and special libraries.* Boston: Butterworth-Heinemann.

Mount, Ellis. 1991. *Special libraries and information centers: An introductory text,* 2nd ed. Washington, DC: Special Libraries Association.

Porter, Cathy A., et al. 1997. Special libraries: A guide for management, 4th ed. Washington, DC: Special Libraries Association.

St. Clair, Guy. 1993. *Customer service in the information environment.* London: Bowker-Saur.

St. Clair, Guy. 1994. *Power and influence: Enhancing information services within the organization.* London: Bowker-Saur.

St. Clair, Guy. 1996. *Entrepreneurial librarianship: The key to effective information services management.* London: Bowker-Saur.

St. Clair, Guy. 1997. *Total quality management in information services.* London: Bowker-Saur.

St. Clair, Guy, and Joan Williamson. 1992. *Managing the new one-person library.* London: Bowker-Saur.

Seiss, Judith A. 1997. *The solo librarian's sourcebook.* Medford, NJ: Information Today.

Seiss, Judith A. 2001. *The OPL sourcebook: A guide for solo and small libraries.* Medford, NJ: Information Today.

Simon, Carol. 2005. "How can you be a manager?: You're a solo." *Information Outlook,* 9, 3 (March): 13–14.

AUDITS AND SURVEYS

Eng, Susanna, and Susan Gardner. 2005. "Conducting surveys on a shoestring budget." *American Libraries,* 36, 2 (February): 38–39.

Glockner, Brigitte. 2004. "Accountability and accreditation for special libraries: It can be done." *Australian Library Journal,* 53, 3 (August): 275–284.

Henczel, Susan. 2001. *The information audit: A practical guide.* Munich: Saur.

Hibberd, Betty Jo, and Allison Evatt. 2004. "Mapping information flows: A practical guide." *Information Management Journal,* 38, 1 (January/February): 58–64.

Wood, Steve. 2004. *Information auditing: A guide for information managers.* Ashford, Middlesex, UK: Free Pint. (Available: www.freepint.com).

MARKETING

Hart, Keith. 1999. *Putting marketing ideas into action.* London: Library Association.

Reed, Sally Gardner. 2001. *Making the case for your library: A how-to-do-it manual.* New York: Neal-Schuman.

Seiss, Judith A. 2003. *The visible librarian: Asserting your value with marketing and advocacy.* Chicago: American Library Association.

Wallace, Linda K. 2004. *Libraries, mission & marketing: Writing mission statements that work.* Chicago: American Library Association.

Walters, Suzanne. 2004. *Library marketing that works.* New York: Neal-Schuman.

BUDGETING

Sellen, Betty-Carol, and Betty J. Turock. 1990. *The Bottom line reader: A financial handbook for librarians.* New York: Neal-Schuman.

Warner, Alice Sizer. 1998. *Budgeting: A how-to-do-it manual for librarians.* New York: Neal-Schuman.

Warner, Alice Sizer. 1992. *Owning your numbers: An introduction to budgeting for special libraries.* Washington: Special Libraries Association.

USER SERVICES

Ross, Catherine Sheldrick, Kirsti Nielsen, and Patricia Dewdney. 2002. *Conducting the reference interview: A how-to-do-it manual for librarians.* New York: Neal-Schuman.

Rugge, Sue, and Alfred Glossbrenner. 1995. *The information broker's handbook,* 2nd ed. New York: McGraw-Hill.

Sacks, Risa. 2005. "Anatomy of a phone search: Primary research using the original 'online'." *Searcher,* 13, 3 (March): 42–47.

Whitlatch, Jo Bell. 2000. *Evaluating reference services: A practical guide.* Chicago: American Library Association.

ACQUISITIONS

Anderson, Rick. 2004. *Buying and contracting for resources and services: A how-to-do-it manual for librarians.* New York: Neal-Schuman.

Chapman, Liz. 2004. *Managing acquisitions in library and information services.* London: Facet.

Chen, Chiou-Sen Dora. 1995. *Serials management: A practical guide.* Chicago: American Library Association.

Curtis, Donnelyn. 2005. *E-journals: A how-to-do-it manual for building, managing and supporting electronic journal collections.* New York: Neal-Schuman.

Eaglen, Audrey. 2000. *Buying books: A how-to-do-it manual for librarians,* 2nd ed. New York: Neal-Schuman.

Kovacs, Dianne K., and Kara L. Robinson. 2004. *The Kovacs guide to electronic library collection development: Essential core subject collections, selection criteria, and guidelines.* New York: Neal-Schuman.

Lee, Stuart D., and Frances Boyle. 2004. *Building an electronic resource collection: A practical guide.* London: Facet.

Osborn, Andrew D. 1980. *Serial publications: Their place and treatment in libraries,* 3rd ed. Chicago: American Library Association.

Slote, Stanley J. 1997. *Weeding library collections: Library weeding methods,* 4th ed. Englewood, CO: Libraries Unlimited.

Tennant, Roy. 2004. *Managing the digital library.* New York: Neal-Schuman.

ORGANIZING MATERIALS

Hsieh-Yee, Ingrid. 2000. *Organizing audiovisual and electronic resources for access.* Englewood, CO: Libraries Unlimited.

Intner, Sheila S., and Jean Weihs. 1998. *Special libraries: A cataloging guide.* Englewood, CO: Libraries Unlimited.

Weber, Mary Beth. 2002. *Cataloging nonprint and internet resources: A how-to-do-it manual for librarians.* New York: Neal-Schuman.

ARCHIVES AND RECORDS MANAGEMENT

Cook, Michael. 1999. *The management of information from archives,* 2nd ed. Brookfield, VT: Gower.

Gill, Suzanne L. 1993. *File management and information retrieval systems: A manual for managers and technicians,* 3rd ed. Englewood, CO: Libraries Unlimited.

Megill, Kenneth A., and Herb Schantz. 1999. *Document management: New technologies for the information services manager.* London: Bowker-Saur.

MISCELLANEOUS SOURCES

ASSOCIATIONS

Association of Independent Information Professionals (www.aiip.org)
Special Libraries Association (www.sla.org)

JOURNALS

Flying Solo (Solo Librarians Division, Special Libraries Association)
Information Outlook (Special Libraries Association)
MLS: Marketing Library Services (Information Outlook)
One-person Library: A Newsletter for Librarians and Management (Information Bridges International)

4 PUBLIC LIBRARIES

John A. Moorman

DEFINITION

The National Center for Education Statistics' definition of a public library is a good starting point for this chapter. A public library is defined as a library that "is established under state enabling laws or regulations to serve a community, district, or region, and provides at least the following: (1) an organized collection of printed or other library materials, or a combination thereof; (2) paid staff; (3) an established schedule in which services of the staff are available to the public; (4) the facilities necessary to support such a collection, staff, and schedule; and (5) is supported in whole or in part with public funds." (www.nces.ed.gov/surveys/libraries).

While this is a good all-purpose definition, there are public libraries that operate with volunteer staff, and a few public libraries (the exception by far) that operate totally off of endowment funds and receive no public support. But for the purposes of this chapter and book the above definition of what is a public library serves as a good basis for outlining what is meant when the term public library is employed.

What makes a public library different from other types of libraries? The main areas of difference are:

- A public library serves all age groups, all economic groups, all racial and gender groups
- A public library is primarily funded by local government

OVERVIEW

This chapter covers:

- Types of public libraries
- Public library governance
- Public library staffing, funding, and services
- Challenges facing the public library

TYPES OF PUBLIC LIBRARIES

There are three main types of public libraries. The most familiar type is the stand-alone public library. By this we mean a public library that is a separate entity not a part of a larger system or regional entity. These libraries go by a variety of names; city library, county library, municipal library, township library, district library. The differentiation here is that the public library is a unit that serves a defined local, single jurisdiction legal entity. Its governance will be discussed later in the chapter as it comes in many forms depending upon the state laws defining its establishment and operation.

> There are 9,211 public libraries in the United States.

A second type of public library is a regional library. This library consists of public library locations serving more than one unit of local government such as a city or county. The degree of independence of the local public library location will vary according to the setup of the regional system. Some public library locations within a regional system have considerable autonomy and depend upon the regional library for specialized services such as materials purchasing and cataloging. Other public library locations are just that and the regional library has total control over local public library location services and programs.

A third type, much smaller in number, is the combined public library. By this we mean that the public library location is in combination with another entity. The most popular combination is the combined school/public library where the public library is connected with a K–12 school, most often a high school. A less popular but growing in number combination is where the public library and a community college library are combined in one facility. A third option is the combined public/university facility. A good example of this is the main library of the San Jose Public Library in San Jose, California, which shares a facility with the University Library of San Jose State University.

PUBLIC LIBRARY GOVERNANCE

Public library governance is also a mixed picture. A Board of Trustees governs most public libraries. This board may be appointed by the local governing entity or elected from the area in which it serves. Most district libraries are self-governing entities with the ability to set tax rates as well as having a governing body elected by the people within their boundaries. The powers of the Board of Trustees vary according to the state, city, or other code under which they were established and operate. Most boards have control over library operations outside of the budget process where they must go to another governmental entity for final funding approval.

In the regional library setting the board may be composed of members from individual political units within the library's area of operation. These may be elected, appointed by local library groups, or appointed by units of government such as cities or counties within the area served by the regional library. As with other types of public libraries, control over operations varies although most have control over all operations outside of the budget process where they must also go to other governmental entities for final funding approval.

In the combined library setting there is generally a public library board for the operations of the public library part of the combined library. The other governmental entity for the library will be the entity for the partner organization be it school or academic. In these cases there is usually a formal signed contract between the unit of government for the public library and the unit of government for the other entity, outlining in detail who is responsible for each aspect of library operation and where the financial responsibility lies for library operations and services. This contract is essential for the continuance of this type of library.

A final type of public library governance occurs when the library has no Board of Trustees but is considered a direct part of local government. In these cases the library administrator reports to an elected or appointed official of city or county government and the library is considered the same as other departments of that unit of government.

All of the above methods of public library governance have their advantages and disadvantages. What makes them work is the people who participate in whatever governance structure is present and the trust and respect that the library has on the local level.

PUBLIC LIBRARY STAFFING

Staffing in the small public library varies considerably. The smaller the library the less likely there will be someone on the staff with a master's degree in library and information science. The smallest public libraries may have only one employee and this individual may be employed for less than 40 hours per week. Some states have specific requirements for educational attainment for directors of public libraries. There may be various levels of public libraries depending upon population served with lower levels only requiring a high school education and some library experience of their director. Other states have a different approach, such as Virginia where all libraries serving a population of over 13,000 must have an ALA MLS degreed librarian as director in order to receive their full state aid allocation.

PUBLIC LIBRARY FUNDING AND BUDGETING

As indicated earlier, local units of government primarily fund public libraries. While most states provide some level of state support in the form of state aid grants or grants through the State Library for a variety of purposes, generally 80–90 percent of the library's operating budget comes from local government sources. Other sources of funding include library revenue from fines, fees, gifts, and grants. Most public libraries receive little or no direct federal funding.

Another, and not to be overlooked, source of funding is that provided by Friends of Library and Foundation groups. These volunteer groups, organized to assist the library in providing services and programs not provided through regular budgeted funds, can be a valuable resource in enriching a library's offerings to the public. One challenge with these groups is in seeing that regular funding bodies do not look upon them as a means to lessen their financial responsibilities for the public library.

The annual process of obtaining funding for library services is a challenge for any public library. Part of this challenge is the relationship that most public libraries have with their local funding entity or entities. As mentioned earlier, while most libraries have a Board of Trustees invested with governing responsibility for library operations, this authority does not extend to the establishment of the budget. With the exception of libraries such as district libraries in Illinois, where the Board of Trustees has taxing and revenue-collecting authority, most libraries have to request their annual funding from either city or county boards. This can be a difficult task as the public library is competing against a wide variety of interests including Public Safety, Parks and Recreation, and Health and Social Services. An important part of successful budget planning is positioning the library in the community as a vital community resource. To do this the library must be more than a passive part of the community and the library director needs to be an active participant in community life. It is important that Board of Trustee members be well connected in the community.

PUBLIC LIBRARY SERVICES

Most public libraries offer a standard list of services which include:

- Materials checkout and return
- Collection Development
- Adult Services
- Children's Services
- Outreach Services

MATERIALS CHECKOUT AND RETURN

This service raises two questions in the public library that are not as prevalent in other library settings.

Who may use your library?

The first question is Who may use the library? At first glance the answer is obvious, those who through their taxes pay for the service. However, it becomes more complex as public libraries deal with individuals who may work in one jurisdiction but live in another, or their library's location may be more convenient to users than the library located in their unit of government, or their library may be better than a neighbor's or worse for that matter. Many public libraries are part of cooperative agreements that allow their residents to use area libraries on the same basis as their library and vice versa. Some are not. This question becomes particularly vexing when use of a public library's services by those outside the jurisdiction covered by the library exceeds a level that is politically comfortable to the funding body. Then the question arises as to whether you charge for this use and if so how much? The author was once director of a public library where almost half of its use came from those outside its geographic boundary. This is not an easy situation to handle. However, this question is one that occurs with frequency in areas of concentrated population growth where library service is uneven in its distribution and level of funding.

The second question deals with material return. As public libraries serve all citizens within their service areas the ability to conveniently return materials is one that is of more concern than it is in special, school, or academic settings. How do you handle the desire for off-site return? This involves questions of where to place these return vehicles, what types of return should be permitted, what staffing is needed to provide transportation of these items back to the library, and how often do these return locations need to be checked?

COLLECTION DEVELOPMENT

In many small public libraries collection development becomes the responsibility of the library director. In some libraries this individual does both the selecting and ordering, and processing of incoming materials. What is ordered depends upon the financial resources available and the demands that the community places upon the library. In recent years the explosion of information in electronic format has placed a significant burden upon the small public library, as these resources are expensive both in licensing cost and in the technology needed to support them. Yet public libraries are expected to have access to these resources. Many state library agencies have statewide database programs, which supply selected databases to all public libraries within their states. These programs are a godsend to the smaller public library.

The public library, as with other types of libraries discussed in this book, places a strong emphasis on obtaining what the user desires. In addition to the purchase of materials for the collection this involves the use of inter-library loan to acquire access to materials that the library does not own outright. Most small public libraries are net borrowers rather than net lenders where inter library loan is concerned. However, many small libraries have items in their collections, particularly where local history or genealogy are concerned, that are desired by users in other communities.

ADULT SERVICES

This service area includes what is commonly called reference service, reader's advisory service, access to the Internet, and a variety of other services including public copy services. Unlike other types of libraries where this service is to limited clientele such as company employees, faculty, or staff, public library adult services includes individuals of all ages and economic, social, and racial backgrounds. The information needs of this wide and varied group pose a challenge to everyday library service. Any hour serving at a reference desk can bring questions ranging from who is the local fire chief, to how to cook frog legs, to what disease do these symptoms correspond, to what are the main factors in the economy of Tanzania. Another challenge in the provision of reference service in the small public library is the increasing presence of technology. All public libraries are expected to provide access to the Internet along with word processing and spreadsheet programs at a minimum. This access requires personal computers, printers, telecommunications and the hardware and software to make this possible. Now more than ever before public librarians are expected to be knowledgeable in the technology of information access as well as the methods of information access.

CHILDREN'S SERVICES

This area of service is one of the first that comes to mind when public libraries are discussed. It is also one that can be used to good effect with the public when discussing financial needs. Even if an individual does not use the public library the inherent goodness of providing access to information and assisting in acquiring and enhancing reading and comprehension skills gives the public library a warm and fuzzy feeling for most citizens.

A major emphasis of this area is on programming. From a variety of story-hour formats including lap-sits, pre-school and elementary, library staff provide children with a personal connection to the world of literature. These programs are highly interactive and use the full complement of audio-visual stimuli. A major emphasis is on the development of language skills and socialization in the young child. In providing story-hour opportunities the public library is working with the school system to enhance the ability of the young child to comprehend and enjoy the printed word. Many libraries have active partnerships with their local school districts and some public libraries receive assistance from the school district for their activities.

A second area of programming that most public libraries do is the summer reading program. Here creativity abounds as all sorts of activities occur during this period, such as visits from local nature centers, programs such as jugglers, musical ensembles, and the creation of story gardens and many craft programs. The challenge facing public libraries with summer reading programs is how competitive should they be and what awards should be given for successful participation or completion. Each library must find its comfort level with this challenge.

OUTREACH SERVICES

Webster's Third New International Dictionary's definition of outreach includes: "to go beyond . . . to go too far . . . to reach out." In the public library setting, outreach usually refers to library services and programs that are held outside of the building(s) that the library occupies. However, some public librarians would be partial to the second definition.

Public library outreach refers to any service or program that is conducted outside the library. These may include bookmobile or mobile service, remote site materials return, and programs such as book-by-mail, and remote access to databases. The author would also include in outreach the activities that library staff carry out in the community whether it be serving as members or on boards of groups such as the United Way, Chamber of Commerce, and Civic Clubs.

CONCLUSION

Public librarianship in the coming years will be full of challenges. The first challenge will be to the very existence of the public library. This is nothing new for as each new technology has arisen since the 1940s there have been those who have stated that it threatens the existence of the public library. However, with the Internet and the arrival of search engines such as Google this is a threat not to be taken lightly. Information is now readily accessible in many homes without the necessity of a public library visit. Music is readily downloadable from Internet sites and the E-book is becoming an easier option to the book format. Furthermore, we see for the first time small communities and larger cities and counties actually closing down their public libraries.

For public libraries to survive in this climate they must follow the planning steps outlined in the planning chapter and make certain that they have defined missions, values, and a vision that reflects the reality of the community they serve and provides a well-defined niche for the library in that community.

A second challenge is the tremendous explosion in both knowledge and the formats in which it is delivered. With limited funding it is a challenge to know which formats have staying power and when to abandon formats that have been superseded by newer and more effective means of information delivery. Another result of the knowledge explosion is the need for more staff training and development to keep current and be able to provide proper service to library users. This again is a financial issue as well as a time issue in libraries with limited staff.

A third challenge is technology itself. Rapidly changing technology is a costly proposition. With new software, expanding databases, advances in printing technology, and information storage and transfer comes a continuing necessity for equipment update and replacement. In the small public library with limited resources this will be a challenge for years to come. While Gates Grants were a godsend, they are expiring and no new funding sources are immediately present.

A fourth challenge is the increasing lack of graduate schools of library and information science. As the current generation of librarians, of which the author is one, reaches retirement in the next ten years there appears to be a shortage of replacements. Public libraries need to look at creative ways of insuring that there will be an adequate supply of trained, qualified librarians in the years to come. Distance education is one answer but not a total solution. Libraries should look at their own staff and encourage and support those who desire graduate education so that they will be ready to take over when retirements occur.

Another challenge has two sides to it: the first is population decline; the second is rapid growth. In the case of population decline, the challenge becomes how to serve an ever-receding population while still existing as a viable entity. This is the situation faced in many rural areas in the United States. The case of rapid growth is the other side of the coin but just as problematic. Growth presents significant challenges, particularly in an era where politicians are elected on the platform of tax cuts. The expectation is that growth will enable enough increased revenues to provide expected services. This is a tenuous expectation at best.

While the public library faces significant challenges in the future the situation is nothing new. In looking to the future we need to remember the past and the people we serve. If we remain attentive to their desires and needs and make our institutions a vital part of the community public libraries will continue to survive.

REFERENCES

National Center for Education Statistics. 2005. *Public libraries in the United States: Fiscal year 2003*. Washington, DC: Department of Education.

FURTHER READING

De La Pena McCook, Kathleen. 2004. *Introduction to public librarianship*. New York: Neal-Schuman.

Greiner, Joy M. 2004. *Exemplary public libraries: Lesions in public library leadership, management, and services*. Westport, CT: Libraries Unlimited.

Janes, Joseph et al. 1999. *The Internet public library handbook*. New York: Neal-Schuman.

Jones, Plummer Alston. 2004. *Still struggling for equality: American public library services with minorities*. Westport, CT: Libraries Unlimited.

La Guardia, Cheryl, and Barbara Mitchell. 1998. *Finding common ground: Creating the library of the future without diminishing the library of the past*. New York: Neal-Schuman.

Matthews, Joseph R. 2003. *Measuring for results: The dimensions of public library effectiveness*. Neal-Schuman.

Go to www.neal-schuman.com and check the titles in their How-To-Do-It Series. Many of these titles deal with specific aspects of public library operation.

5 SCHOOL LIBRARIES

Richard Rubin

DEFINITION

Organizationally, the American Association of School Librarians (AASL/ALA) and the Association of Educational and Communication Technology (AECT) define school library media centers as:

> " . . . an organized collection of printed and/or audiovisual and/or computer resources which (a) is administered as a unit, (b) is located in a designed place or places, (c) makes resources and services accessible and available to students, teachers, and administrators" (Ingersoll and Han 1994, 8).

OVERVIEW

This chapter covers:

- History of school libraries
- Mission of school libraries
- Challenges facing the school library

INTRODUCTION

The school library media center has one central function—to support the curriculum of the school. The fiscal and human resources are directed to this end. There are many secondary, albeit important, functions that the school library media center performs as well. It stimulates the imagination of young people, it promotes critical thinking, it exposes young people to diverse points of view on important topics, it provides exposure to the cultural differences that exist in the world, and it provides some entertaining diversions as well.

School library media centers are embedded in much larger organizations. On one level, although there may be a school librarian who exercises immediate control, ultimate control and supervision of the library is the concern of the school's principal. Alternatively, school library media centers may be governed by a special administrator in charge of curriculum for the entire school system, who may be responsible for selection or approval of materials for all of the schools' library media centers. Finally, because school library media centers exist as part of the entire school system, they are governed by a school board, whose administrative powers are delegated to a school administration. This administration often consists of a superintendent and assistants. Although these individuals seldom get involved in direct supervision or control, they often become involved when there are complaints about materials.

HISTORY

The school library media centers in the United States have nineteenth-century origins, but there were actually very few of them until the twentieth century. Their development was accelerated in the twentieth century by many factors. In the 1920s, impetus for school library media centers grew because of the development of regional accrediting agencies, which promoted the need for trained librarians. At this time, the National Education Association's Committee on Library Organization and Equipment published the first standards for junior and senior high and junior high schools. In 1925, the National Education Association (NEA) created standards for elementary schools. K–12 standards were published in 1945. In the 1950s, another push was given when the Soviet Union launched *Sputnik*. The successful placing of a satellite in space by the United States' rival created considerable social and political upheaval as Americans feared they would soon be militarily inferior to their adversary. The space race thus gave a strategic significance to efforts to improve the American educational system. One of the results was substantial increases in federal funding for elementary and secondary education, especially to improve curricula and the training of teachers. It was a logical extension to provide money to expand the library collections of these schools.

Expansion in the number of school library media center collections began in the 1960s, and additional standards were promulgated in 1960 and 1969 to reflect the library's increasing sophistication. This decade saw the development of strong political support. This political support was expressed primarily through the passage of the Elementary and Secondary Education Act (ESEA) in 1965, which provided federal support to purchase materials for schools and libraries, and which in turn resulted in a tremendous expansion of school library media center collections. The growth of school library collections and the variety of formats collected, including A-V materials, led to the creation of new standards in 1975, emphasizing the importance of a strong media collection.

MISSION

Today, the mission of the school library media center reflects a dynamic and broad perspective of the roles of the librarian and the library. These roles have been emphasized by the American Association of School Librarians (ALA) in its work *Information Power*. First published in 1988, and revised in 1998, *Information Power* shifted the focus on traditional school library practice from the building and management of collections to developing students as lifelong learners. It also created the first nationally published information literacy standards. The philosophy underlying *Information Power* is that the primary mission of the school library media center is "to ensure that students and staff are effective users of ideas and information" (p. 6). This mission is accomplished in three ways: "by providing intellectual and physical access to materials in all formats; by providing instruction to foster competence and stimulate interest in reading, viewing, and using information and ideas; [and] by working with other educators to design learning strategies to meet the needs of individual students" (p. 6). In turn, the role of the library media specialist is four-fold: (1) to serve as a teacher, collaborating with students and teachers to evaluate the learning and information needs of all; to instruct students and assist in curriculum development; (2) to serve as an instructional partner, developing policies and curricula that improve the information literacy skills of students and collaborating with teachers to design meaningful learning activities that involve the development of information skills; (3) to serve as an information specialist by evaluating, acquiring, and making available information resources and by modeling strategies for effective information seeking; and (4) to serve as a program administrator helping to create and implement policies for the library media center, to manage library staff, and serve as an advocate for the program to others. Eisenberg has concisely summarized the school library media specialist's role in the following way:

> School librarians *teach* meaningful information and technology skills that can be fully integrated with the regular classroom curriculum. They *advocate* reading through guiding and promoting it. And they *manage* information services, technologies, resources and facilities.

Today, it is estimated that there are more that 94,000 school library and media centers located in 95 percent of public schools and 86 percent of private schools. The size of the workforce in these libraries is considerable. More than 66,000 librarians and 99,000 support staff work in school library media centers alone. But the picture is not entirely bright. For example, a quarter of all schools have no school librarian. In addition, the average age of a librarian is 45 with 50 percent planning to retire in the next 12 years. In schools, there is only one school librarian for every 953 students (Minkel 2003). The potential shortage of school library media specialists could have significant and unfortunate consequences.

CHALLENGES

The contemporary school library media center faces many challenges. These include the following:

- Ensuring that the library plays an integral role in the functioning of the school
- Dealing with increases in technology
- Dealing with declining funds in schools
- Addressing the shortage of certified media specialists
- Dealing with censorship of library materials

ENSURING THAT THE LIBRARY PLAYS AN INTEGRAL ROLE IN THE FUNCTION OF THE SCHOOL

Central to the philosophy of *Information Power* is that the librarian and the library be perceived as central features of the school and that the librarian be seen as a collaborator in developing effective learning strategies. If school library media centers are to thrive in the future, they must be recognized for their importance to the function of the school. Too often, the library is considered an expensive appendage to the educational process rather than an integral part, which is especially ironic, given the evidence of the relationship of school library media centers to academic achievement. It has been shown that students who score higher on norm-referenced tests tend to come from schools with larger library staff and larger school library media collections. In addition, high academic performance of students has also been correlated with school library media centers in which librarians served in an instructional and collaborative role. The size of the library staff and the collection were the best predictors of academic performance, with the exception of the presence of at-risk conditions such as poverty.

These facts highlight the reality that school librarians need to communicate clearly and cooperate closely with teachers, principals, and administrators. By demonstrating the importance of the library and its ability to contribute to the school's mission, greater political and fiscal support is more likely to follow. Fortunately, there is some evidence that library media specialists are having an impact. Lau (2002) reports that in a survey conducted by *School Library Journal*, 66 percent of the school librarians responded that their principals are very supportive of library collaborations with teachers, 46 percent of librarians teach classes; 95 percent instruct students on how to use print and online resources, and 30 percent recommend and evaluate vendors for potential classroom textbook purchases. Ninety percent report that they are satisfied with their jobs and the amount of respect they receive.

DEALING WITH INCREASES IN TECHNOLOGY

Schools have devoted considerable resources to educational technologies. In many ways they are leaders in this area. They have incorporated television as a part of classroom teaching for years. To this they have added laser discs, videocassettes, CD-ROMs, DVDs, and computers. Of course, the impact of access to the Internet has been dramatic and rapid. The number of public school and private school classrooms with access to the Internet increased from 77,853 in 1995 to 82,232 in 2003. In addition, the proportion of elementary and secondary school students using computers at school rose from 70 percent in 1997 to 91 percent in 2003 (U.S. Department of Education 2004). As technologies and technological use increase, the school library media center will have to respond in kind, meaning increasing demands in terms of costs, staffing, training, equipment, and physical facilities. In addition, as students increasingly view the Web as the most common channel to obtain information, librarians play a special role in identifying the many resources that are available in the Web environment, and in training and educating both students and teachers on how to locate and evaluate Web sites. Similarly, librarians must be able to organize Web sites for local access.

THE IMPORTANCE OF INFORMATION LITERACY

With the increasing use of technologies in the classroom and the media center, it is clear that students need to be well educated on how to locate and evaluate information. The underlying rationale for this education, however, has been broadened in recent years. The purpose is not only to develop these skills so that students can be more proficient academically, but also lifelong learners. As the American Association of School Librarians has noted in its latest version of *Information Power:*

> Central to this new context is the idea of the "learning community." This phrase suggests that all of us—students, teachers, administrators, and parents as well as our local, regional, state, national, and international communities—are interconnected in a lifelong quest to understand and meet our constantly changing information needs. (p. 2)

Such a perspective places information acquisition, dissemination, and use in the broader context of social responsibility. It is not enough to be a good locater and evaluator of information; it is the responsibility of all to continue to learn and to contribute what we have learned to our society in a beneficial manner. As a consequence, The American Library Association has created nine information literacy standards that all students should meet. These standards actually involve not only how to access, evaluate, and use information, but also define what it means to be an independent, lifelong learner, and what responsibilities we have to contribute to the learning community in a responsible manner.

Figure 5-1 Information Literacy Standards for Students
Standard 1: The student who is information literate accesses information efficiently and effectively. Standard 2: The student who is information literate evaluates information critically and competently. Standard 3: The student who is information literate uses information accurately and creatively. Standard 4: The student who is an independent learner is information literate and pursues information related to personal interests. Standard 5: The student who is an independent learner is information literate and appreciates literature and other creative expressions of information. Standard 6: The student who is an independent learner is information literate and strives for excellence, information seeking, and knowledge generation. Standard 7: The student who contributes positively to the learning community and to society is information literate and recognizes the importance of information to a democratic society. Standard 8: The student who contributes positively to the learning community and to society is information literate and practices ethical behavior in regard to information and information technology. Standard 9: The student who contributes positively to the learning community and to society is information literate and participates effectively in groups to pursue and generate information. (pp. 8–9)

DEALING WITH DECLINING FUNDS IN SCHOOLS

There is little doubt that some citizens have limited confidence in their school systems. This, coupled with a general feeling among taxpayers that they have been taxed enough, has led to a resistance to increasing their tax burden for the public schools. The damage to schools from this trend is magnified by the need for additional monies to accommodate the rapid changes in learning technologies and the proliferation of excellent print materials published today for young people. Some urban school districts have been hit particularly hard. Because schools are undergoing financial strains, there is an understandable temptation to place existing resources directly into teaching along with classroom materials and activities. Such a reallocation merely increases the drain on dwindling school library media center financial resources and diminishes the opportunity for the libraries to assist effectively teachers in the learning process.

ADDRESSING THE SHORTAGE OF CERTIFIED LIBRARY MEDIA SPECIALISTS

For some years, it has become clear that the labor force of librarians, including those working in schools, is aging. Everhart (2002) reports that in the next 12 years, approximately 68 percent of school librarians will leave their profession. Already, this has resulted in a severe shortage of certified media specialists nationwide. A recent survey has suggested that the number of states experiencing severe shortages has increased from 12 states in 2000 to 30 in 2002. Previously, these shortages appeared to concentrate in inner cities and rural areas, but now the problem has spread to suburban areas as well. The American Library Association is now actively developing strategies to assist in the recruitment of certified media specialists, and schools of library and information science are beginning to respond by offering more school library media programs, some using online and interactive video delivery systems. In addition, the Institute for Museum and Library Services is developing initiatives to help alleviate the shortage as well. If professional programs are unable to respond quickly to this pressing need, more and more individuals without the necessary training will be hired by school systems that are already tempted to replace certified media specialists with paraprofessionals to meet the pressing fiscal demands of their school systems. The resulting loss in quality and vitality of the media center would be a disturbing result.

DEALING WITH CENSORSHIP OF LIBRARY MATERIALS

There are few issues in librarianship that generate so much heat and so little light. Schools have traditionally been vulnerable to censorship attempts, especially because they are supposed to serve *in loco parentis*. Among the crucial issues that define school censorship problems are

- the differing views of the function of schools and school library media centers
- the rights and powers of school boards versus the rights of students and parents

These issues have been battled out in years of court cases, many of which have resulted in unclear or contradictory conclusions. This judicial ambivalence was highlighted in one of the most important school library media center cases, which reached the United States Supreme Court. This case is now referred to as the "Island Trees" case, or "Pico," named after Stephen Pico, the student who filed the complaint (Board of Education 1982). The following is a brief discussion of some of the fundamental issues raised by the legal and philosophical arguments found in the various cases. Awareness of these issues is important to any understanding of this situation for today's school media center.

The functions of schools and school library media centers. Defining the functions of schools can have profound consequences on how one perceives the functions of school library media centers.

There are at least two fundamentally differing accounts. One perspective is view the schools as a place to inculcate the values of the local community—the majority values. Such a view perceives the school as an instrument of particular values. Children, in this sense, are perceived as highly vulnerable to outside influences and need protection until they are old enough to know that these influences are problematic. Such a view is, in itself, not wholly unreasonable. It seems obvious that children do need protection from physical abuse, and some might argue that this is easily extended to intellectual harm as well. The purpose of schools is to inculcate the students with specific orthodox attitudes as well as basic knowledge. Exposure to unorthodox points of view would be undertaken only under conditions in which substantial control is exercised to ensure that the views are not mistakenly understood as acceptable or reasonable alternatives.

From this perspective, the school library media center represents a potential problem. Most obvious is that the school library media center has traditionally been a place of voluntary attendance, where the materials are voluntarily selected by the student. Some guidance may be involved, but as a rule, there is considerably less guidance and control over exposure and interpretation of materials in the library than in the classroom. If the inculcation of values is to be effected, one function of the librarian or library worker would be to monitor each student's selections. In many cases, this is a practical impossibility. The alternative is that the library exercises very careful and restrictive selection of materials and, most likely, restrictive access to materials for some, usually younger, children.

The second perspective is to view the school as a place where students are exposed to a wide variety of points of view. The function of the school is to familiarize students with many perspectives, emphasize critical thinking skills and judgment-making skills. It is not the school's place, however, to assert a particular perspective or attempt to inculcate the specific values of the local or majority community. It attempts to prepare students to discriminate among ideas so they can make future judgments on important issues in which there are many differing opinions.

The school library media center in this setting would likely function quite differently. The library collection would likely contain many perspectives, some unorthodox as well as orthodox, and the librarian's function would be less supervisory and controlling. Access would tend to be unrestricted.

These two perspectives have been painted here as polar opposites, although there are certainly many gradations that reflect the realities of school library media centers. All schools inculcate values, and all try to get students to think, more or less. But how one perceives a school's primary purpose is likely to affect one's attitude seriously when one hears that a book on suicide, one by a revolutionary, or books that contain explicit language about sex are part of the library collection. Those who subscribe to the former view are much more likely to restrict or control materials. Similarly, even in schools in which the inculcation of local or majority values is paramount, a more subtle distinction might be made regarding its school library media center. One can perceive, for example, that the function of the classroom is different from the function of the school library media center. One can argue that the classroom is the place where values are inculcated and still believe that the school library media center's purpose is different, a place for exposure to a wide array of ideas, even those that are unorthodox. In this sense, the concept of the library carries with it the supposition that it is a special forum—a place where many different, even controversial and subversive ideas may co-exist. In this way, a distinction between classroom purposes and library purposes is possible. Obviously, if one perceives the library as a special forum for ideas, the library collection would predictably be more catholic in perspective, no matter what the defined purpose of the classroom.

The rights of school boards and students (and parents?). Censorship problems in schools also arise from the friction created by the conflicting authority of the school board and the rights of young people. Traditionally, school boards have exercised considerable legal authority and power in the United States. Generally, education falls primarily within the province of the states. States have delegated the authority to local school boards that have been given broad authority to run their school systems, including the selection of teachers, curricular materials, and materials for the school library media center.

There is little doubt that school boards are responsible for school library media centers, but it is seldom their central focus. From time to time, school boards are surprised to discover that some of the materials on the school library media center shelf are not to their liking or the liking of parents. Problems usually arise when parents file objections to materials their children have selected from the school library media center. But objections also arise from principals, teachers, students, and school board members themselves. When challenges occur there is a tendency in many cases to restrict or withdraw the material, especially when there are no formal policies for selection and reconsideration of these materials.

The actions of school boards to remove or restrict materials may often go unchallenged. Although the rights of young people may be limited, the courts have recognized that students do not give up First Amendment rights and due-process rights just because they are in school. This highlights the delicate balance that must be struck in schools concerning the rights of school boards to run their schools as they see fit and the individual rights of citizens, including young people, to First Amendment and due-process protection. The balance is dynamic.

The lack of clarity regarding the legal rights of boards, the place of the school library media center, and the rights of students literally ensure that more problems await on the horizon. The problem will be magnified as the library media center collections expand to include resources on the Internet. There is certainly plenty of dissent in our society regarding what is suitable material for young people, and the school library media center will remain a lightning rod of political controversy in this arena.

CONCLUSION

While there are many challenges facing school libraries and school librarians in the coming years, the overall picture remains optimistic. With the increasing use of technology in the classroom and dependence on sources such as the Internet for curriculum enhancement, there is an ever increasing need for the skills that the school library media specialist brings to the school setting.

To make sure that the school library remains an integral part of the educational operation, it is imperative that school library media specialists continually work to upgrade their skills and work collaboratively with teachers and administrators to see that all information resources are used to their fullest extent in the instructional process.

REFERENCES

American Association of School Librarians and Association for Educational Communications and Technology. 1998. *Information power: Building partnerships for learning.* Chicago: American Library Association.

Board of Education, Island Trees Union Free School District V. Pico. [42 CCH S.CT. Bull] (1982).

Eisenberg, Mike. "This Man Wants to Change Your Job." *School Library Journal.* 48 (September 2002):47–49.

Everhart, Nancy. "Filling the Void." *School Library Journal.* 48 (June 2002): 44–49.

Ingersoll, Richard, and Mei Han. 1994. *School library media centers in the United States, 1990–1991.* Washington, DC: U.S. Department of Education.

Lau, Debra. "Got Clout?" *School Library Journal.* 48 (May 2002):40–45.

Minkel, Walter. "The Year in K–12 Libraries: School Librarians Redefine Themselves." *In the Bowker Annual Library and Book Trade Almanac.* 48th Edition. Medford, NJ: Information Today, 2003. 10–15.

United States Department of Education, National Center for Education Statistics. 2005. *Digest of education statistics, 2004.* Washington, DC: U.S. Department of Education.

FURTHER READING

Martin, Ann. 2005. *Seven steps to an award-winning school library program.* Westport, CT: Libraries Unlimited.

Snyder, Timothy. 2000. *Getting lead-bottomed administrators excited about school library media centers.* Westport, CT: Libraries Unlimited.

Stein, Barbara L., and Risa W. Brown. 2002. *Running a school library media center: A how-to-do it manual, 2nd ed.* New York: Neal-Schuman.

Part II

Administration in the Small Library

BUDGETING

John A. Moorman

DEFINITION

A budget takes the library's planning and puts it into a revenue and expenditure picture. A budget is also the operating plan for allocating resources among priorities within the library.

OVERVIEW:

This chapter covers:

- Basic outline of the budget process
- Basic formats for budget preparation
- How budgets are prepared
- Suggestions on budget preparation
- Additional resources for further study

INTRODUCTION

Before discussing the budget process it is necessary to make general comments about budgeting in libraries. While the information presented below describes the budgeting process and gives pointers on how to prepare and present budgets, it may not fully relate to the situation found in many libraries. The budget that the library prepares may only deal with certain aspects of library service. For example, a college, special, or community college library may have personnel funding as a part of the institution's general personnel budget, or may have certain building functions such as maintenance and utilities coming under another part of the institution's budget. Some libraries do not even know the total expenditures for library services, as they are not broken out of the institution's general budget.

BUDGET TYPES

There are two types of budgets, capital budgets and operating budgets.

> **Tip**—If the expense is major and nonrecurring it is a capital expense. If the expense is normal and reoccurring it is an operating expense.

CAPITAL BUDGETS

A capital budget is for major, nonrecurring items that have long life spans and may require multiyear planning. Capital budgets may be projected out over a period of three to ten years or more. Many libraries or the institutional entity providing funding have a dollar amount before an item may be considered for inclusion in a capital budget, that is, anything over $25,000 is considered for inclusion in a capital budget. What goes into a capital budget? Major equipment purchases such as vehicles, heating and air-conditioning equipment, building renovation, new building planning, construction and furnishing, automation upgrades or migration. Any item that is not a normal operating expenditure or normal maintenance of equipment and building is a candidate for the capital budget.

In selecting items for a capital budget, a planning document is an important tool. What does the library's plan indicate will be done for the next several years? What needs are implied that do not fit into an operating budget? To prepare for a capital budget, examine current building and operations to see what items have a limited expected life span or will likely need replacement sooner rather than later. Working with staff and appropriate governing entities, gather information on costs, decide when in the budget time frame this item or project best fits and place it there. Remember that like an operating budget, a capital budget is a plan and a proposal of accomplishment. It will likely change over time but serves as a planning tool for expenditures that are major in nature and have a higher initial cost than what is normally placed in the operating budget.

OPERATING BUDGET

> The line item budget is the most used budget process in libraries.

The most common way of developing an annual operating budget is the line item budget. Other approaches to budget preparation include the zero-based budget and the program budget.

LINE ITEM BUDGET

The line item budget focuses on what is bought, whether it is staff services, equipment, supplies, books, materials or electronic databases, or utilities. See Figure 6-1 for a sample work form.

Figure 6-1 Line Item Budget				
Item	Current Fiscal Year	Next Fiscal Year	Dollar Change from Current Fiscal Year	Per Cent Change
Revenue				
Local Government				
State Government				
Federal Government				
Library Sources				
Other				
Total Revenue				
Expenditures				
Compensation				
Salaries and Wages				
Retirement				
Health Insurance				
Workers Compensation				
Other				
Total Compensation				
Collections				
Books				
Audio-Visual				
Databases				
Other				
Total Collections				
Operations				
Building Maintenance				
Communications				
Contractural Services				
Insurance				
Maintenance				
Supplies				
Miscellaneous				
Postage				
Printing				
Travel and Training				
Utilities				
Total Operations				
Total Expenditures				

Each major expenditure and revenue category receives a line in the budget. Depending upon library needs, or the requirements of funding entities, the line item budget may have more or fewer lines within it. When a line item budget is the basis for library operations, the annual budget process is based upon suggested changes in each line item within the budget and requests for changes must be justified accordingly.

ZERO-BASED BUDGET

The zero-based budget is a totally different approach to the provision of library services. Unlike the line item budget that uses as its base the previous year's budget, zero-based budgeting is a process of preparing an operating budget that starts with no authorized funds, thus the name for the process. Each activity to be funded must be justified in its totality. In the preparation of a zero-based budget each major area to be funded becomes a decision unit and decision packets are prepared. Library decision units could include:

- Circulation
- Adult Services
- Children's Services
- Technical Services
- Facilities
- Administration

These packets usually contain several alternatives for achieving service objectives. The selection is made between alternatives within each budget unit and the budget is put in its final form for consideration.

The zero-based budget is a more time- and resource-consuming process than either line item budgeting or program budgeting. For it to work properly it requires a detailed consideration of the mission and goals of operations, identification of decision units and decision packages, analysis of decision packages, development of measurable performance and service objectives for each decision unit, and monitoring performance accordingly. This method is seldom used by library or governmental units for ongoing annual budget preparation. What is more common in practice is that some aspects of a library's service may be selected on an annual basis for this approach, or the library as a whole will be considered for zero-based budgeting on a regular basis such as every five to ten years.

PROGRAM BUDGET

A program budget defines library services by what service is being given. All aspects of that individual service, that is circulation, youth adult, and so on are presented in a budget for that service. The library's budget becomes a series of program statements combined into a total budget reflecting library operations. Another budgeting term is performance budgeting. The goal of performance budgeting is to describe in measurable units the outcomes desired for the funding expended. Performance budgeting is possible using any of the budgeting methods described above. What is unique about this type of budgeting is that the budget is directly connected to specific goals of the organization. An example of this would be if one goal of the library were to have one-day return of materials to the shelf after check-in. The total costs of this objective would be directly related to the goal in the budget preparation.

BUDGET PREPARATION

Tip—Communication is essential to the budget process. Make sure that the following are always kept informed:
- Appropriate staff
- Individuals, or board, to whom you report
- Officials of government funding entities.

Budget preparation and development are an ongoing process. Work on next year's budget is beginning as approval is received for the current year's budget. A library director is continually looking at library operations, and discussing library needs with staff, Board of Trustees, academic deans, provosts, and local officials. Awareness of library services and needs is essential to budget development and approval. This awareness is not accomplished by an annual presentation to a board or governing body, but by continual exposure to library services, programs, and needs.

In preparing a budget the following items are essential:

- Have accurate and detailed information on library operations and services.
  It is essential to have in-depth and accurate information on the library. Without it success in any request for increases in services, staff, or programs is highly unlikely.

- Have a plan for what is desired to be accomplished with the budget.
  A plan is essential if an effective, understood budget is to be prepared, a budget that stands a chance of approval by the library's governing board and funding entities.
- Understand the political situation in which the library operates.
  What are the plans and goals of the funding entity(s) for the coming year? In academic and special library settings, what is the library's position within the institution and how do faculty, business associates, and administration view it? In the public library setting, how strong politically is the library board and support base? A year with tight resources, or when the entity is looking at a tax-rate reduction, may not be the year to ask for a substantial increase in library funding. Know when it is good to be a team player for long-term benefits or when it is opportune to ask for new programs or services. Sometimes it is time to fight no matter what, but at least be aware of what the library is facing.
- Know and follow the time frame of the funding entity(s) for budget preparation and submission.
  There are few things worse than missing deadlines for budget submission. Make sure that there is knowledge of all deadlines. If due to circumstances beyond control, that is, conflicting deadlines from other funding entities, or lack of information on resources due to legislative slowness in determining state aid monies, and deadlines will be unable to be met, notify appropriate officials immediately. Generally they will be accommodating.

In presenting a budget request to any group the following points are important:

- Keep the presentation clear, short, and simple.
  Avoid the tendency to use library jargon and have too many charts, graphs or PowerPoint examples. Present highlights only and give emphasis to those areas that are proposed for changes from the current budget.
- Give one individual the responsibility for overall budget presentation.
  It is easier for individuals to understand a presentation when they are dealing with one individual rather than three or four. Have others available to answer questions but do not employ a team approach to the basic presentation.

- Have a thorough understanding of the budget and be prepared for questions on all aspects of it.
  There will always be unanticipated questions. Be knowledgeable in all aspects of the budget. Have others on the faculty/staff/board of trustees/friends of the library/higher administration available as needed to elaborate on sections of the budget where appropriate.
- Go into each session with a positive approach.
  This is as important as any of the above.

BUDGET TRACKING

> Tip—It is good to have a separate page in monthly budget reports to highlight unusual occurrences in spending or revenue.

An important element of the budgetary process is budget tracking. This is an ongoing process. It is an expected part of library operations that the library's governing entities, or administrative units to which the library reports, will require monthly reports on how the budget is being spent. These reports should include what revenue has been received, what has been spent, what has been encumbered, and the percentage of the total year's budget that has been used to date. An encumbrance is simply the anticipated cost of items for which purchase authorization has been given to a supplier but the product or service has not yet been received. This enables the library to have a more accurate picture of where its expenditures stand at any one time. See Figure 6-2 for a condensed example of the form used to present this report.

Figure 6-2 Budget Report Form

	Budget	Actual	Encumbered	Total	% Spent and Encumbered
Compensation	1,200,000	395,250	-0-	395,250	32.9%
Collections	220,000	105,324	15,443	120,767	54.9%
Supplies	43,000	19,342	4,249	23,591	54.8%
Per Cent of Budget Year Completed	41.6				

In its completed state the form would also indicate what percentage of the total budget had been spent during this time period. There would also be as many line items on the form as there are line items in the budget.

Budget tracking is also an important component of budget preparation as it serves to indicate areas where expenditures are exceeding expectations and line items must be accordingly increased in next year's budget or where expenditures are not as high as expected and line items could be decreased in next year's budget.

CONCLUSION

Budgeting is the process whereby a library's resources are distributed to provide the services and programs approved by the institution's governing body. How it is accomplished varies from library to library. Many factors play a role in the process including the type of library, its governance structure, and, in the case of academic and special libraries, how the parent institution allocates resources.

FURTHER READING

Hallam, Arlita W. and Teresa R. Dalston. 2005. *Managing budgets and finances, A how-to-do-it manual*. New York: Neal-Schuman.

Miller, Gerald J. et al. 2001. *Performance based budgeting*. Boulder, CO: Westview Press.

Rubin, Jack, ed. 1992. *Handbook of public budgeting*. New York: Marcel Dekker.

Smith, G. Stevenson. 1999. *Accounting for libraries and other not-for-profit organizations, 2nd Edition*. Chicago: American Library Association.

7 POLICIES AND PROCEDURES

John A. Moorman

Policies and procedures are at the heart of any library's operation. Without properly developed policies and procedures an institution will flounder and both users and staff will be unclear as to what they are to do and how they are to respond to everyday questions and situations.

POLICY DEFINITION

The *Concise Oxford English Dictionary* defines policy as "a course or principle of action adopted or proposed by an organization or individual." It defines procedure as "an established or official way of doing something." The core difference is that policy is a statement approved by the governing body of the organization that indicates how the organization will respond to a certain situation or event.

PROCEDURE DEFINITION

A procedure is a statement that describes how a certain activity or function is to be carried out. It is often tied to policy in that it describes how a specific policy is to be carried out. Procedure, unlike policy, does not require action from a governing body to be in effect.

OVERVIEW

This chapter covers:

- Policy development
- Procedure development
- Examples of procedures and policies
- Policies for libraries to consider

POLICY DEVELOPMENT

In developing policy, the administrator and staff should play an important role. While it is the governing entity, whether board of trustees, school board, county or city government, or the organization's board of directors that has the final say in the development and approval of any policy statement, it is important that as much input as possible be brought into the development of each policy statement. Good policy is the result of much thought, examination of the library's experience, knowledge of the community in which the library operates, and examination of how other libraries in similar settings have dealt with the situation being considered. The more minds that can be brought to the matter the better the end policy will be. However, it is not the role of the library administrator to make policy. The library administrator only recommends policy to the governing board of the institution, or to the person to whom he/she reports. If the library administrator does not agree with the policy developed by his/her governing entity then he/she has choices to make as to his/her future with the organization.

Players in policy development
- Staff
- Director
- Individual to whom director reports
- Governing body

PROCEDURE DEVELOPMENT

Procedure is a different matter. This is the responsibility of the library staff. While it is good to let governing boards know about library procedures and even to share procedure documents with them it is not their area of responsibility.

In procedure development the more minds employed the better, particularly those who will be in the direct line of its implementation. Procedure should be in simple language, without nuances, covering the *major* points of how a specific policy or activity is to be accomplished.

POLICIES NEEDED

What policies are needed to operate a library properly? This depends upon the size of the library, its relationship to the larger units of which it may be a part, and whether it has any contractual relationships with other entities. For example, if your library is part of a corporate business entity, or is a division of a city or county, then you may not need a personnel policy because that will be covered by the policies of the larger unit. Look at your operations and determine what authority you have over them. The areas where you have operational control are candidates for policy statements. See Figure 7-1 for a list from *A Pocket Reference Manual for Public Library Trustees,* published by the South Carolina State Library, which describes major areas to consider when developing a policy manual for your library.

Figure 7-1   Policy List for Public Libraries

The following list of policies may be relevant to the library's need. Every library does not necessarily require every policy on the list. It is provided here to help boards check their policy accomplishments and needs. The list is arranged in the form of an outline to underscore how policies relate to one another. Listed under each policy are items that may be considered and covered when making policy.

I. Mission and Role Statement

II. Library Board By-Laws

III.Public Library Service Policies

   A. Eligibility for borrowing and services

      1. Resident and non-resident

      2. Programming and outreach

   B. Collection Development Policy

      1. Mission and goals with community description

      2. Responsibility for selection

      3. Selection criteria for each format

      4. Scope and priorities of collection

      5. Selection procedures and vendor relations

      6. Evaluation, weeding, and maintenance

      7. Censorship, access, and challenged materials procedure

      8. Intellectual Freedom Statement, Library Bill of Rights

      9. Gifts and donations

   C. Circulation Policy

      1. Loan period and renewal

      2. Confidentiality

      3. Reserved material

      4. Fines, damages

      5. Interlibrary loan

      6. Special collections

      7. Audiovisual equipment

   D. Reference Policy

   E. Facilities Policy

      1. Hours of operation

      2. Americans with Disabilities compliance

      3. Security

      4. Meeting room use

      5. Exhibits and displays

      6. Copiers and other equipment use

(continued)

```
Figure 7-1   Policy List for Public Libraries (Continued)
```

F. Community Relations Policy
  1. Cooperative borrowing policy
  2. Relations with Schools
  3. Volunteers
  4. Friends Groups
G. Patron Behavior Policy
  1. Unattended children
  2. Respect for staff, users and library property
H. Internet Use Policy
IV. Management Policies
A. General
  1. Responsibility and authority
  2. Budget accounting and financial management
  3. Procurement, including gifts
B. Personnel
  1. Responsibility and authority
  2. Job descriptions and classifications
  3. Salaries and benefits
  4. Hours, annual and sick leave, overtime, holidays
  5. Hiring, termination, resignations and nepotism
  6. Performance evaluation and promotion
  7. Continuing education/professional development
  8. Discipline and grievances
  9. Americans with Disabilities Act compliance
  10. Fair Labor Standards Act compliance
  11. Sexual harassment
  12. Personnel records
C. Facilities
  1. Responsibility and procedure for maintenance
  2. Acquisition and ownership
  3. Insurance and liability
  4. Emergency preparedness
  5. Americans with Disabilities Act compliance
  6. Use of equipment, vehicles, etc.

Source: *A Pocket Reference Manual for Public Library Trustees*, 1999.
(pp 65–68)
Permission received from the South Carolina State Library

Figure 7-1 is not an all-inclusive list, but an example of the many areas where policies will be necessary for the successful operation of the library. How do you go about developing successful policies? The first step is to look at what you currently have, what has worked, what is not working, and where you see gaps.

In policy development look at/for:

- What you currently have
- What has worked
- What is not working
- Where you see gaps

There are books, that contain sample policy statements, some of which are listed in the bibliography. Examine these, contact librarians in like institutions and ask for copies of their policy statements. Many libraries now have their policy statements available on their Web sites. Remember you are not the first institution to deal with this issue, take advantage of what others have done and modify it to fit your specific situation or need. It is advisable in any policy development to run your policy past an attorney before finalizing it. It may be common sense to you and your board, but the law may think differently and a little legal advice up front can save a large amount of legal time and cost later.

WHAT IS A GOOD POLICY?

A good policy is succinct and clear yet gives room for staff to interpret. Good policy, like good literature, is hard to write. It is also open to continual revision and examination. See Figure 7-2, for example:

Figure 7-2   Policies Governing Use of Library

The following rules have been established by the Williamsburg Regional Library Board of Trustees to ensure that use of library facilities is as pleasant and free from distractions as possible.

The following are not allowed in the library:

1. Willful damage to or unauthorized removal of library property.
2. Disorderly conduct, creating a nuisance, or unreasonably disturbing or offending those in the library.
3. Extreme body odor or other strong smells.
4. Children six and under without adequate supervision.
5. Unattended children seventeen and under left on library grounds at closing.
6. Animals other than service animals.
7. Abusive, loud, or obscene language.
8. Smoking.
9. Open food or beverage containers or the consumption of food or beverages without authorization from the library. (Beverages in bottles, cups with lids, or cans are acceptable unless otherwise posted.)
10. Soliciting, selling, distributing leaflets, or posting notices not authorized by the library.

Continued failure to follow library rules will be grounds for denial of library privileges. Police will be called when a patron refuses to leave the library after being asked to do so, or when a person in the library or on library grounds is engaging in unlawful behavior.

[Approved by WRL Board of Trustees May 11, 1994. Approved as amended by WRL Board of Trustees October 19, 1999. Approved as amended by WRL Board of Trustees March 27, 2002. Approved as amended by WRL Board of Trustees October 23, 2002. Approved as amended by WRL Board of Trustees April 28, 2004.]

Figure 7-2 shows a policy that deals with the use of a public library. It gives general guidance to staff and the public as to what is permitted in library facilities. But it is not detailed in its description of what is or is not permitted. For example, there can be different interpretations of what "extreme body odor or other strong smells" or "abusive, loud, or obscene language" may be. This gives staff latitude to deal with each situation in its context rather than being held to one strict standard.

Figure 7-3 is an example of an academic library policy:

Figure 7-3   General Building Policies
General Building Policies **No Food or Beverages are to be consumed/used in public areas of Ladd Library. Use of Tobacco Products is prohibited.** Exceptions: beverages in spill-proof containers, water in clear containers with covers, gum, and small candies which stay in the mouth. Reasons: • Custodians have to clean up the mess. • Food, etc., attracts bugs which eat paper. • Beverages can spill onto equipment and/or books. • Moisture spilled on books, carpets, or furniture promotes growth of mold, which is harmful to books and people alike. **No rollerblades or skateboarding.** **No pets are allowed in the Library, with the exception of guide/therapy dogs for patrons with special needs.** Source: Bates College Web Site. Used with permission.

The public library policy (Fig. 7-1) was first approved in 1994 but has had four amended versions since then. This indicates that it has been examined on a regular basis and hopefully refined at each examination. It is important that the governing body of your library regularly examines policy statements. This is important for two reasons. The first is that regular reviews enable all board members to become familiar with library policies and with the reasons for their existence. The second is that it requires the library to regularly examine its policies to see if changes are needed.

Figure 7-4 is an example of a policy dealing with a specific situation. It states the reason for the policy and outlines what is permitted and what is not permitted. Again it indicates that it has been examined on a regular basis.

Figure 7-4 Animals in the Library

To prevent possible injury to library patrons and staff, and to prevent possible damage to library property:

1. Animals are not permitted in any Williamsburg Regional Library facilities, except:
    *   Trained guide-animals or service-animals that are leashed or harnessed may accompany individuals in libraries. (See Code of Virginia 51.5-44 E.)
    *   Animals that are part of a library-sponsored program may be allowed, but must be leashed, harnessed, or caged, or at all times under the supervision/control of an owner or trainer.
2. On library grounds (the entries, sidewalks, and parking lots adjacent to the building), animals must be leashed, harnessed, or caged; under their owners' control; and not left unattended by their owners.

[Approved by WRL Board of Trustees February 14, 1990. Approved as amended by WRL Board of Trustees March 27, 2002. Approved as amended by WRL Board of Trustees December 1, 2004.]

WHAT IS A GOOD PROCEDURE?

Writing procedures is similar to writing policy in that good procedures are clear and should be able to be easily followed. While procedures should be as concise as possible they should be long enough to describe adequately what is desired. As Figure 7-5 demonstrates any procedure should also cover the basic steps of how an activity, or action, should be accomplished.

Figure 7-5   Procedure—Accounts Receivable

A. Accounts Receivable

Any monies due to the library are billed and accounted for by the finance office. This includes funds to be reimbursed by the Friends of the Library, WRL Foundation, and grants; meeting room and theater usage fees not collected, co-sponsored program expenses with other agencies and credits for returned materials.

1. Procedure

a) Send the original and a duplicate copy of any invoices or paid receipts to the finance office. The finance office will match invoices with any purchase orders and reconcile monthly expenditures. The finance office will prepare a bill and send it to the individual or group responsible for payment. When a check is received for payment, the bill will be dated and marked paid by the finance office.

b) Theater and room use fees are typically paid in advance. If overtime charges or additional expenses are incurred, program services staff will provide an invoice to the finance office. This invoice will include a summary of hours and facilities used, the date and amount of any prepaid credits, and the balance due.

(1) The finance office will bill the patron and file a copy in the Finance Office accounts receivable file. The Program Services department will submit invoices to the Finance Office at month's end.

(2) When payment is received, the check will be given to program services staff to ring into the cash register, mark paid in full on the room reservation form and the duplicate invoice, and forwarded to the finance office with the daily cash register reconciliation.

(3) Other: Credits in lieu of a check reimbursement on some accounts, such as regular book vendors, simplifies the accounting process and is acceptable. The finance office handles credits of an unusual nature such as inadvertent overpayment credits and monies due from limited use vendors.

In writing a procedure first examine what it is that you are describing. Then break it down to its component parts, indicating what steps or actions are first, what comes second, and so on through the completion of the task or action. Procedures are not a place to tell you why you are doing something, but only what you are doing and in which order it should be accomplished. Notice in Figure 7-5 that procedures do not have to be specific to individuals. It tells you that the finance office does this and the program services department does that, not who in each area is responsible for performing the work.

There is a tendency in writing procedures to be too specific and too detailed. While sufficient specificity and detail are needed to enable individuals to perform what is desired, too much of either can have a counter effect and hinder efficient library operations.

CONCLUSION

Policies and procedures are an essential part of any library operation. However, there is the tendency to overdo both. Not every action needs a policy statement nor does every step in your operation need a procedure outlining how it is to be performed. A second problem in this area is the tendency to make procedures into policy statements. Before making a policy statement examine it thoroughly. Is a course of action being stated or a principle by which the library will operate? If so, it is policy. Is a way of doing a task or an operation within the library being described? If so, then it is procedure.

REFERENCES

A Pocket Reference Manual for Public Library Trustees. 1999. Columbia: South Carolina State Library.
Library Policies. 2005. Williamsburg, VA: Williamsburg Regional Library.

FURTHER READING

Brumley, Rebecca. 2004. *The public library manager's forms, policies, and procedures handbook with CD-ROM.* New York: Neal-Schuman.

Brumley, Rebecca. 2006. *The reference librarian's policies, forms, guidelines, and procedures handbook with CD-ROM.* New York: Neal-Schuman.

State Library of Ohio. Policies of Public Libraries. Located at winslo.oh.us/publib/policies.html. Other state libraries also have similar sites.

8 STAFFING

John A. Moorman

DEFINITION

Staffing deals with individuals who are paid employees of the library.

OVERVIEW

This chapter covers:

- Hiring
- Training
- Scheduling
- Supervising
- Evaluating
- Dismissing

> A good staff is the core of any library operation.

Personnel administration, which covers all of the above, is an area where knowledge of current laws is essential. If the library is part of a larger unit such as a school district, corporation, or entity of local government, that organization will have a human resources or personnel department. This department will work with the library and handle, or coordinate, most of the above activities. If this is not the case, it is essential that the library staff working in these areas have a detailed knowledge of personnel law and also have an attorney skilled in this area available for consultation.

HIRING

The employment of individuals to fill positions within the library is the most important part of the staffing process. If it is done poorly, or without proper attention being paid to what the law requires, it can cause tremendous waste of staff and money.

> Do not start the hiring process until you know exactly what you need.

The first step in the hiring process is to determine exactly what is needed. This step is often overlooked amid the rush to hire that librarian, shelver, cataloger, or even library director. Before beginning the process, make sure that there is agreement on what it is desired that the new employee will do. Examine in detail the current job description, or if a new position, make sure that a job description is developed that accurately reflects the tasks and duties that will be expected of the person in this position. There are many types of job descriptions but all should cover the basics; what they are expected to do, where they are expected to do it, to whom they report, necessary qualifications for the position, and any requirements such as drug testing and background checks that will be necessary before employment. The job description for a senior library clerk (Fig. 8-1) is a good example of what should be found in a job description.

Figure 8-1   Job Description

DEPARTMENT:
Williamsburg Regional Library/Circulation Services

NATURE OF WORK:
Under the supervision of the Circulation Services Director, the Circulation Services Senior Clerk is responsible for processing the incoming library materials on an automated system; keeping the library shelves in order; retrieving reference materials; handling simple clerical duties; changing the status of items needing mending; and performing other duties as requested by supervisor.

ESSENTIAL FUNCTIONS OF THE JOB:
Checks in library materials on automated system; changes the status of items on computer as needed.

Checks and empties all book and video drops.
Sorts and shelves library materials; shelfreads daily to maintain shelf order. Adjusts collection as needed to relieve overcrowding.

Assists in the opening and closing of the library.
Assists in maintaining neatness, order and repair of periodical collection.
Assists in maintaining neatness and order of CD collection.
Assists the reference department by checking in, taping, stamping, and routing periodicals.

Assists with implementing new procedures.
Assists supervisor with training of new shelver/clerks.
Assists in maintaining neatness of public areas of library.
Performs general clerical duties such as making copies of handouts and other materials as needed.

Assists administration staff with copier maintenance.
May participate in library-wide committees or projects.
Performs other duties as needed.

JOB LOCATION AND EQUIPMENT OPERATED:
The job is located in two libraries; also in the bookmobile as needed. Work involves bending, lifting up to 25 pounds, and pushing and maneuvering bookcarts filled with library materials. Administers work typically standing at a counter with regular walking, light to medium lifting and other limited physical activities; regular operation of computer and scanning equipment is required; other office equipment as required. Regular contact is made with employees and the general public.

(continued)

Figure 8-1 Job Description (*Continued*)

REQUIRED KNOWLEDGE, SKILLS, AND ABILITIES:
Ability to compare names and numbers quickly, resulting in a working knowledge of the Dewey Decimal System.

Ability and willingness to understand and carry out oral and written instructions efficiently. Ability to work under minimal supervision.

Ability to work well with other employees and maintain good work habits in an open space.

Ability to follow through on numerous details and work well under pressure.
Ability to learn and work with the library's automated system.
Ability to lift up to 25 pounds.

MINIMUM QUALIFICATIONS:
Minimum age: 16. High school diploma or equivalent preferred. Experience as a shelver/clerk.

NECESSARY SPECIAL QUALIFICATIONS:
Requires the ability to travel among various library sites.
****

WORK SCHEDULE:
Full-time, non-exempt position; 40 hours per week; includes some evenings and weekends.
DEPARTMENT: Circulation Services
SUPERVISOR: Circulation Services Director
DATE PREPARED: June 20, 1990
REVISED: December 1992; October 1993; August 1995; January 1996; April 1996; April 1999; July 2001; October 2001; July 2002
Williamsburg Regional Library, Used with permission.

Make sure in the job description that requirements are for what is needed, not what is desired. As an example, only specify the amount of education needed for the position in question.

Once the job description is completed and approved, then comes the process of seeking applicants. Where should it be advertised; locally, regionally, nationally, or only through in-house sources? This depends on the job, and whether there are in-house candidates that would adequately fill the position. If serious consideration will not be given to candidates outside of the general area, then only advertise in local sources.

The job advertisement is important. It should be a summary of the duties and requirements of the position with either a salary range or beginning salary indicated. Give enough information so that only those who are qualified or willing to come for that salary should be applying (this doesn't guarantee this though). If forms have to be filled out by all applicants indicate so and where they can receive these forms. Indicate if a resume is required. Make sure that a closing date for the receipt of applications is indicated. If there is none indicate "open until filled."

Once the applications have been received, it is good practice to acknowledge to the applicants that they have been received. In deciding which candidates to interview, first examine all applications to make sure that necessary qualifications are met. In most cases, several applications can be winnowed out at this time. Hopefully, there will be at least three individuals who meet enough of the job criteria to be seriously considered for the opening. Generally, it is good to interview no more than 5–7 individuals for any single opening.

Prior to the interview session develop a list of questions to ask of each interviewee. The questions should be the same for each person interviewed. Figure 8-2 shows a set of interview questions used in Librarian I interviews.

Figure 8-2   Interview Questions

1. Please tell us about how your education and work experience have prepared you for this position in these areas:
   a. Reference and Readers' Advisory Service
   b. Collection Development
   c. Programming/Outreach
2. Public Libraries, like many institutions, are currently in a period of great change. How do you deal with change?
3. What interests you most about the position of Reference Librarian?
4. Considering your accomplishments, what are some of the reasons for your successes?
5. What do you like most about library work? What do you like least?
6. What do you see as the role of the public library in the community?
7. What are your strengths?
8. What are your weaknesses?
9. Describe your ideal workplace, colleagues, and management.
10. The Internet and electronic resources are an increasingly important part of library services. What is your experience with these sorts of resources, and what do you think is the role of these resources in the public library?
11. The Library is looking for staff that has a commitment to working here at the library. How does this fit into your plans over the next couple of years? Where do you see your career in five years?
12. Why should we hire you for this position?

Williamsburg Regional Library. Used with permission.

Make sure all interview questions are legal.

Make sure that the questions asked are legal and will give enough information about the individuals, their skills and experience to enable a wise final selection to be made. It is important to check references for finalists for positions. Although most references have been pre-selected to tell nothing but the best about the individual in question, there are times when voice and response can give insights that would not have been able to be obtained otherwise.

Before making a job offer make sure that the final choice understands what the job requires, what benefits and salary he/she will receive, what schedule he/she will work, and when and where he/she is expected to report. Ask the candidate if there are any final questions and be sure to let him/her know whom to contact if additional questions occur prior to start date. A written letter should follow up any job offer so that there are no questions about the job offer. Request a written acceptance from the individual. It is good practice for a member of the interview team to personally call all those interviewed to let them know of the employment final decision.

TRAINING

See Figure 8-3 for a sample of a new employee checklist.

Figure 8-3   New Employee Checklist

New Employee Checklist

NAME:

_____

DEPARTMENT:

_____

JOB   TITLE:

_____

SUPERVISOR:

_____

IMPORTANT DATES

_____ Start Date

MANDATORY TRAINING

Date	Training	Time	Location
	Benefits Orientation	9:00 a.m.	Building A
	Customer Service Training		Fire Training Center
	Substance Abuse Training	2:00 p.m. – Mandated Employees 1:00 p.m. – 4:00 p.m. - Supervisors	
	New Employee Orientation Tour	8:30 a.m. – 3:30 p.m.	Building C

DEPARTMENT INFORMATION   **Date Completed By**

Please review with new employee & initial

Tour of work location

_____   _____

Introduction to co-workers

_____   _____

Work hours/lunch times

_____   _____

Time/Leave accrual sheet completion

_____   _____

Reporting absences/lateness

_____   _____

Organizational Structure of Department

_____   _____

(continued)

Figure 8-3 New Employee Checklist (*Continued*)

Expectations of new employee   _____

_____

Telephone Usage   _____

_____

Employee Performance/Development   _____

_____

Overtime Policy   _____

_____

Internet Usage   _____

_____

E-Mail Usage   _____

_____

County Property/Equipment Use   _____

_____

    Uniforms (if applicable)   _____

_____

    Tool/Clothing Allowance (if applicable)   _____

_____

Outside Employment   _____

_____

Emergency Conditions
& Unexpected Closings Policy (AR–10)   _____

_____

EVALUATION INFORMATION
_____ Probationary Review Due to Human Resources
_____ Annual Performance Evaluation Date
Return this form to HR with the Probationary Review Form.

_____   _____

Supervisor's Signature   Date

James City County, Virginia. Used with permission.

As this example indicates, the employee checklist should provide a thorough introduction to the job and the entity for which the individual now works.

Continued job training is a mixture of on the job experience, in-house workshops conducted by library staff or individuals brought in from the outside, and attendance at outside workshops and conferences. Excellent resources for these training opportunities are regional, state, and national library associations, organizations such as OCLC and regional networks such as SOLINET, AMIGOS, and PALINET. Other sources for excellent training opportunities are state library agencies and their respective library development divisions. A list of these resources will be found at the end of this book.

SCHEDULING

Scheduling of staff is always a challenge. Factors involved in scheduling include hours of operation, number of staff, including how many are full-time and part-time, needs of the institution, any limitations placed upon scheduling by previous practice, agreements or labor contracts, and how many locations are involved. This does not include factors such as illnesses, maternity and family leaves, and educational class or workshop attendance. How is a good work schedule prepared? There are basically two ways. The first is to prepare a grid chart with times needed and then place individuals in the chart until the schedule is filled. The second is to purchase scheduling software. With this software you can input names, hours of employment, and other factors and the software will come up with a work schedule. The way to locate good scheduling software is to check with other libraries, place informational requests on list serv, or to contact the library development division of your state library agency.

Factors to remember in developing any work schedule are: be fair, be consistent, follow all regulations imposed by personnel policies or labor contracts, and schedule according to library needs, not staff desires. It is important to communicate regularly with staff during all phases of work scheduling.

SUPERVISING

Employees need supervision to see that tasks are accomplished in a timely and appropriate manner and that policies and regulations are followed in the performance of their work. Good supervision is an art as much as it is a science. It involves knowledge of human behavior, good communication skills, knowledge of the work that is to be accomplished, flexibility, a good sense of humor, and the ability to control ego and feelings. The best supervisor is one that appears not to be supervising, but simply observing and encouraging his/her employees in their daily activities.

The following are the ten bes of good supervision:

- Be available
- Be aware
- Be clear
- Be concise
- Be fair
- Be flexible
- Be firm
- Be patient
- Be supportive
- Be understanding

These are easy to say but hard to accomplish. All individuals are good at some of them but few, if any, are good at all of them. How are skills improved in this important and essential area? There are books and articles that assist in focusing attention on aspects of good supervision. They will be found in the bibliography at the end of the book. Other sources are workshops put on by various associations including chambers of commerces, community colleges and universities, state library agencies, or by consultants who specialize in this area.

Remember that in supervision as in other areas of work, whether dealing with staff, board, governing officials, or the general public, people like to be treated with respect and fairness. Before acting as a supervisor always ask, "Is this the way I would like to be treated?" If the answer is no, then why take this course of action?

EVALUATING

Evaluation is a yearlong process not just the week before the evaluation is due.

Regular evaluation is an essential part of effective personnel management. All individuals need regular feedback to know if they are performing tasks at the expected level. Supervisors need to communicate to those they supervise about successes or failures in job performance. Evaluation often becomes a chore when communication about job performance is not done on a regular basis and there is not an ongoing flow of information from supervisor to employee as well as employee to supervisor about work and the setting within which it is accomplished. A good evaluation process is a summary of conversations held during the time period since the last evaluation and holds no surprises for either party.

The most often used time frame between evaluations is one year. Some institutions conduct evaluations on a six-month basis or when problems are occurring for which correction is needed if employment is to continue.

Evaluations come in all shapes and sizes. There are check-the-block-evaluations where individuals are rated on a variety of workplace behaviors and job performance standards. There are modifications of this approach where room is given for comments. There are written evaluations where specific job performance questions are used. There are also as many variations of the above as there are evaluators. Use what works best in your situation and serves the purpose of recording job performance and giving expectations for future performance.

Another important aspect of the evaluation process is whether the evaluation is directly linked to any pay adjustment or is separate from any consideration of employee pay. Each approach comes with its advantages and problems. If an evaluation is linked to pay there can be an immediate positive reinforcement of work accomplishments. However, it can also be a negative factor if good performance is not sufficiently rewarded from a financial standpoint. If the evaluation is not linked with any pay adjustment, it might not be given sufficient weight by either the employee or the individual giving the evaluation.

No matter what form of evaluation is employed, there will always be a subjective element involved. The goal of any evaluation will be to remove as much as possible any subjectivity from the evaluation process and to provide each employee with as fair and objective an evaluation as possible. A good evaluation is:

- Fair
- Objective
- Reflects actual performance during the time covered by the review
- Measures work performance against job expectations
- Allows for employee input
- Gives expectations for the next evaluation period

Sufficient time should be set aside for discussing the evaluation with the employee. It is advisable to share a copy of the evaluation with the employee prior to this meeting so that the employee comes prepared to discuss the evaluation. Points of disagreement can be noted in the final review. It is general practice to have the employee sign an acknowledgment that he/she has seen the evaluation and has discussed the evaluation with the supervisor.

DISMISSING

Dismissing an individual from employment is never an easy task and is a step that should only be taken after all other measures have been tried. It is vitally important that the library has a detailed personnel policy, which has thorough disciplinary policy sections outlining what offenses will result in personnel actions being taken. Generally, a personnel policy will have step penalties for various job offenses, with most offenses resulting in warnings and suspensions. However, for some serious offenses the immediate penalty is dismissal from employment.

The goal of any employer is to keep employees in employment. Much time and effort has been spent in hiring, equipping, and training these individuals and the best course is to work with individuals to see if their work performance or job behavior can be brought up to an acceptable standard. Thus, in most cases, it is important to work with the individual, using whatever personnel resources available to counsel the individual prior to seeking to dismiss the individual from employment.

The importance of documentation in the employment process cannot be emphasized enough. In dismissing an employee there will need to be sufficient documentation of the work performance or behavior in question to pass muster with any agency to which the employee might go for redress in the case of dismissal. This is vitally important. This documentation should be substantial, indicate that the performance in question has arisen over a period of time, and outline what steps have been taken to correct the work performance/behavior prior to dismissal taking place. It should also indicate that the library's personnel policy has been followed and that there are no special exceptions in the case under consideration. It is important here to consult with the library's governing body's human resource department or library attorney to make certain that no steps have been omitted or not properly followed.

When the time comes to dismiss an employee make sure that another individual is present as a witness to the dismissal. This person can be another staff member or a member of the human resource department of the city, county, or larger entity of which your library is a part. Make the presentation brief stating only the reason for the dismissal. Do not get into an argument with the individual being dismissed. Make them aware of what benefits will be coming to them and how they will receive them. Have someone observe them as they take their belongings from the library and make sure that they have turned in all library property before they leave. Notify library staff that the individual is no longer an employee of the library and is not to be allowed in non-public areas of the library.

Dismissing an employee from the library is never an easy task, nor should it be. However, it is one that a library administrator will do more than once during his/her career. The rules to remember are—do it fairly and firmly and with consideration for all involved.

CONCLUSION

Staffing is one of the most challenging aspects of library operations. In hiring, training, scheduling, supervising, evaluating, and dismissing library employees the librarian is dealing with individual human beings and all that they bring to the table. To be successful the librarian needs to make sure that actions are legal, follow policy and procedure, and are done fairly and in a consistent manner.

REFERENCES

James City County, Virginia. *Human Resources Forms.*
Williamsburg Regional Library, Williamsburg, Virginia. *Interview Questions.*
Williamsburg Regional Library, Williamsburg, Virginia. *Job Description.*

FURTHER READING

Baldwin, David A. 2003. *The library compensation handbook: A guide for administrators, librarians, and staff.* Westport, CT: Libraries Unlimited.
Giesecke, Joan, and Beth McNeil. 2005. *Fundamentals of library supervision.* Chicago: American Library Association.
Simmons-Welburn, Janice and Beth McNeil. 2004. *Human resource management in today's academic library.* Westport, CT: Libraries Unlimited.
Van Zant, Nancy Patton. 1980. *Personnel policies in libraries.* New York: Neal-Schuman.
Yesner, Bernice L., and Hilda L. Jay. 1998. *Operating and evaluating school media programs: A handbook for administrators and librarians.* New York: Neal-Schuman.

9 BUILDINGS

Frederick A. Schlipf

DEFINITION

A building is the structure that houses the library.

This chapter is concerned with how libraries occupy space and with how we can work to be sure that the spaces created for our libraries to occupy truly meet our needs.

OVERVIEW

The chapter covers:

- Steps in the library planning and construction process
- Basic requirements of library buildings
- Typical library contents
- Major design problems to avoid
- Effective floor plan for a small public library

WHY PLANNING LIBRARY BUILDINGS IS IMPORTANT

Providing proper space is a problem for most libraries. Many libraries are too small, and in addition many librarians struggle with ineffective room arrangement, poor lighting, inadequate air-conditioning, insufficient wiring, poor security, annoying acoustics, and other common problems. Library buildings are not as important to long-term success as is friendly, competent staff or strong collections, but bad buildings can totally hamstring library operations, alienate users, damage collections, and cost far too much to operate.

Buildings are also a problem because of their initial cost. Librarians can undertake many projects piecemeal. Collections and computer services can be developed over many years, but buildings usually require onetime expenditures of large sums of money, far more than libraries can set aside from operating funds.

Due to their cost and permanence, buildings also require extremely careful planning. Badly chosen books and equipment can usually be replaced fairly easily, but buildings are so expensive that they usually must be used for many decades. The architectural choices of one generation are visited upon successive generations like family blessings or curses.

Although planning and building new library spaces is a complex undertaking, it actually consists of a number of individual steps. If you don't skip essential steps, if you spell out your needs clearly, and if you take time to learn what works and what doesn't work, everything should turn out well.

STEPS IN PLANNING AND CONSTRUCTING LIBRARIES

Good library construction is a very straightforward undertaking. The major steps include:

1. Decide what kinds of services your library needs to provide.
2. Determine the kinds of spaces you need in order to provide those services.
3. Hire an architect to design a library with the spaces you need.
4. Find the money to construct the library.
5. Build the library.

DECIDE WHAT KINDS OF SERVICES YOUR LIBRARY NEEDS TO PROVIDE

It is difficult to design a library until you've made a number of decisions about services. Some decisions have little impact on buildings, but it is surprising how many decisions have a direct impact on the kind of structure you need. For example, the maximum size of your collection and the formats of materials in your collection will determine the number of shelving sections and other storage units. How your customers use your library (or *would* use your library if you had the correct space) will affect the number and size of study tables and armchairs. The types of programs and other events you want to house will affect the size and placement of meeting rooms. The decision to let people drink coffee in the library will affect your choice of carpeting. All of these decisions—and often hundreds of others—will directly determine the spaces, room arrangement, and finishes of your library.

Deciding on the services you need to offer is primarily a job for you and your board or administrator. Often you can do this by working your way through a comprehensive list of decisions, but you will need to keep in mind and pay special attention to your users' needs and interests.

When planning services, many libraries simply rely on input from staff and users. If you listen to the people who use the library, or simply watch them at work, you can learn a good deal about what they want and do not want. The danger, of course, is that we all have a tendency to filter out unconsciously things we don't really want to hear. For example, if I am personally opposed to coffee in libraries, I may simply ignore suggestions from my patrons.

Carefully constructed surveys offer a chance to gather more unbiased data. It's fairly easy to survey library users. This is particularly true for most small academic, school, and special libraries, since they have limited user groups.

In the case of public libraries, things get more difficult, since a substantial number of residents in many communities almost never use the library. When public libraries survey users in the library, they don't learn anything about the people who do not use the libraries and the services those people would like to see. To learn about the entire community's interests, you may have to talk with people who never use your library, or who use other libraries in preference to their home library.

One easy way to find out what your citizens find lacking in your public library is to survey them when they use neighboring libraries. (Obviously this can take place only in situations where nearby libraries honor each other's borrower's cards.) By finding out what leads your citizens to prefer other libraries, you can find out what can be improved in your library. An example of such a survey appears in Appendix 8 of *Serving Our Public: Standards for Illinois Public Libraries*.

Once you try to survey the entire user population of a public library, things can get a great deal more difficult. Most librarians who feel this is essential will want to consult a professional (and ideally evaluate at the outset whether the cost of the survey justifies its findings). Unfortunately, one of the main reasons for undertaking surveys is to prove to the people who are providing the funds that what you have been saying all along is correct. In situations like this, librarians sometimes end up doing surveys just to demonstrate by more acceptable methods what it is that citizens want.

In much of the planning these days, one of the most frequent problems is dealing with campus planners or civic leaders who contend that the digital revolution has made libraries obsolete—usually because they have other plans for the money. You will need to be prepared for this contention and know how to deal with it.

DETERMINE THE KINDS OF SPACES YOU NEED IN ORDER TO PROVIDE THOSE SERVICES

This step is called "programming." When you have completed this step, you should have a very detailed list of all the spaces you need in your new library, the physical characteristics of those spaces (such as square footage, ceiling height, and so on), the contents of those spaces (such as the number and types of shelving units or tables), and the physical relationship between the spaces. For example, the description of a quiet reading room for adults might specify the number and types of seating, whether parts of the collection will be stored in the room, the type of atmosphere, special features like fireplaces, the room's location with regard to the rest of the library, and so on. The size estimate should reflect the amount of space required for each item in the room, to be sure the room will be neither too large nor too small.

> Even if your proposed library is no larger than a Porta Potty, someone will call it a Taj Mahal.

If you have experience with programming or have taken an extensive course, you may want to prepare your own building program, but most libraries are better off hiring building consultants.

When you hire a consultant, you will add more depth to your planning team if you hire a librarian with a broad range of experience with library design rather than an architect, since the combination of a librarian and an architect will give your planning team greater depth.

In addition, if your consultants work for you rather than for your architect, they're much more likely to give you the unbiased second opinion you need. For this reason, hiring a "team" consisting of an architect and consultant is a poorer choice than hiring individuals as separate entities.

When you hire a library building consultant, look for someone with work experience in real libraries and a track history of consulting on other projects. And look for someone whose company you enjoy. You will spend a great deal of planning time with your consultants and architects, and if they drive you up the wall socially, you are in for a number of seasons of discontent. If you can find a good consultant, you will be better off keeping that person on your project until construction is ready to begin, for you will need someone who knows how libraries occupy space and who has experience with good and bad buildings to react to design ideas. Programs can be surprisingly detailed and correspondingly long, ranging from about 50 to 200 pages, single-spaced.

HIRE AN ARCHITECT TO DESIGN A LIBRARY WITH THE SPACES YOU NEED

Public libraries almost always hire their own architects, and most academic libraries are large enough to justify hiring architects for those projects alone. But if you run a corporate or school library, someone else may hire the architect for an entire building. When you are unable to choose your own architect, having a building program and making sure the proper administrators are familiar with it is tremendously important.

If you cannot choose your own architect, it is even more important that you keep your consultant on the job. You need to be sure that someone with experience speaks up for your needs. Sometimes you need someone who can simply disagree with powerful people on your behalf, for you may not always find it comfortable to point out that a really stupid idea is in fact a really stupid idea. When your architect wants to place your school library next to the band practice room or the weight training room, or when your architect proposes a new college library based on the principle of the chambered nautilus, you need someone with a loud and independent voice to say "no."

Public libraries are usually independent agencies and hire their own architects. When you do this, you have a much better chance of having a library design that responds to your specific needs, but there are still many badly designed public libraries out there. For this reason, it is important that you select an architect with a track record of designing functional and effective library buildings.

Laws concerning hiring architects vary from state to state, but, generally speaking, you will have tremendous leeway in picking the firm you want. The main thing you may be barred from doing is picking a firm by low bid, but that is a very bad practice for projects as complex as libraries.

Most libraries begin looking for an architect by sending out RFI (requests for information) letters to likely firms. Architects who are interested in the job will respond with elaborate submissions, including lists of key personnel, information on prior work, and so on. In soliciting information, it is important to require unambiguous detail on the number of completed library projects and on the specific scope of the architect's work in each project. Before selecting a group of three or four architects to interview, always talk with people in the libraries that the architects designed, to be sure that they are happy with the relationship and the resulting library.

When the time comes for interviews, specify that each firm's proposed "project architect" (the person you will work with most of the time) make the presentation for the firm, and that you know about that person's specific expertise. Some architectural firms practice "bait and switch," sending to interviews charming and inspiring sales architects that you may never see again.

In most cases, you will want to have your architect develop the "schematic design" for your library before you begin a major fundraising campaign or schedule a bond referendum. The AIA (American Institute of Architects) standard contract forms specify five stages in the design and construction process. The first is schematic design. In this stage, the architect and client review a wide variety of design options, select the one the client prefers, and create a basic building design. By the end of this process, you should know how the library will be laid out (floor plans) and what it will look like seen straight on (elevations). You should also have a preliminary budget. In order to raise money for construction, you need the information in the schematic design, so you can show donors or voters what the completed library will look like and tell them how much it is likely to cost.

FIND THE MONEY TO CONSTRUCT THE LIBRARY

For many library construction projects, finding money is the crucial step and sometimes the hardest one. An old saw in the architecture business states that the single most important construction material is money.

Schematic designs and the cost estimates that accompany them are essential for fundraising, but in many cases you will also need renderings (attractive pictures of the completed building) or models. Renderings and models of buildings that do not yet exist require extremely skilled work and are not the kind of undertaking you can do at home. They are also expensive, and you will need to decide what level of investment is best for your library.

Fiscal pressures frequently tempt libraries to save money through cut-rate construction. However, throughout the 25- to 100-year-life of a building, initial construction costs are a minor component of total lifetime operating costs. A small savings effected during construction can cost a library many times that amount in extra costs over the life of the building.

CONSTRUCT THE BUILDING

The remaining four stages from the architectural perspective come after you have located money for the project: They include:

- **Design development.** In this stage, the general schematic designs are refined and expanded to provide information on how the entire building will work, including heating, lighting, and other essential mechanical systems. (Some architects regard furniture placement as part of design development, but you will want these decisions made as part of the schematic design and furniture shown on your floor plans.)
- **Bid documents.** Bid documents are the incredibly detailed drawings and specifications necessary to construct a high-quality building by low bid. Even for a small library, they can run to dozens of large sheets of drawings and hundreds of pages of specifications.
- **Bidding.** Your architect will manage the bidding process for you. Obviously, you hope that the low bid is within your projected cost. If bids are lower than you expect, it gives you a chance to improve your library with "add alternates," which are included in the bid requirements. If bids are too high, your contract with your architects may require that they redesign and rebid the project at their cost. It is important to be sure that individual construction firms—in addition to providing attractive bids—have the necessary "horsepower" to do the job.
- **Construction.** Typically, constructing a small library building takes about nine months to a year, although remodeling and expansion can take twice as long if you do not move out. If your library is part of a larger structure, construction time may depend on the schedule for the entire building.

> Delay means a smaller, cheaper building. Construction costs always increase faster than the value of money in the bank.

GROUND BREAKING AND RIBBON CUTTING

Most libraries—particularly public libraries—benefit from ceremonies to celebrate the beginning and completion of the work. Be sure to invite all the right people, get the media to attend, keep speeches short (and audible), involve cute children, and feed everyone.

This is the briefest possible review of the construction process. For much more detail, check the sources listed at the end of this chapter.

BASIC REQUIREMENTS OF LIBRARY BUILDINGS

All small libraries have somewhat similar architectural requirements, whether they are located in separate buildings or in rooms in larger buildings. Some of the most important requirements include:

- **The right amount of space of the right type in the right arrangement.** This is where a building program is essential, for it gives you a yardstick for evaluating proposed designs.
- **Strong floors.** Books are extremely heavy, and floors designed for typical office use are seldom strong enough for book storage. For this reason, many small corporate libraries end up in basements, where floor strength is less of a problem. Libraries are usually designed to hold a minimum of 150 pounds of contents ("live load") per square foot. Compact shelving running on rails requires substantially more floor strength.
- **High-quality light.** Libraries require bright, even, low-glare lighting. Usually this means careful control of daylight (north light is best and west light worst) and the use of lighting systems specially designed to reduce glare. As a general rule, the best results are obtained by using reflected uplight, bouncing all light off white ceilings. Some workable quick specifications include (a) fluorescent fixtures using 4-foot T-5 or T-8 tubes with a CRI (color rendering index) of at least 85 and a color temperature of 3500° Kelvin, (b) electronic ballasts, (c) strip fixtures directing 100 percent of light upwards, and (d) fixtures spaced to provide at least 60 footcandles of illumination at table-top. Unfortunately, bad lighting is common in even new

libraries. Among the things to avoid are recessed down lights (can lights), skylights, and task lighting.

Creating excitement with light in a library is like creating excitement with steps in a nursing home.

- **High-quality HVAC (heating, ventilating, and air-conditioning) systems.** HVAC systems should meet current standards for air exchange and efficiency of operations. They should keep the meeting room comfortable when it has 20 people and when it has 100. HVAC systems also need to control relative humidity. Humidity in libraries should not greatly exceed 50 percent. Except in old buildings, where condensation from humidification can be a problem in very dry weather, humidity should not fall below 30 percent. Because relative humidity changes as temperatures fluctuate, HVAC systems designed to lower temperatures at night can lead to destructive levels of humidity if they do not include humidity sensors. For example, if temperatures are lowered from 70 to 60 degrees Fahrenheit—just 10 degrees—and the moisture content of the air does not change, relative humidity can increase from a book-friendly 50 percent to a mold-friendly 70 percent. Far too many libraries have seen mold develop on books when temperatures are lowered. Mold also flourishes happily in school libraries when carpets are steam cleaned just before buildings are shut down for the summer.
- **Pleasant acoustics.** Libraries that echo or reverberate are unpleasant to occupy. Library rooms that transmit sound easily can lead to serious compromises with user confidentiality. And library offices that fail to provide a place for private conversations can cause major problems. Among the worst sources of acoustic problems in libraries are hard-surfaced ceilings and floors, large areas of glass, and office walls that do not continue past suspended ceilings. Cathedral or barrel vault ceilings (or any other shapes that are not flat) often transmit sound in impressively distressing ways, but they are usually acceptable if they have acoustic surfaces. If your suspended ceilings are installed before partitions between rooms are built, conversations in one room can frequently be heard in the room next door. Architects frequently do not hire acoustical engineers to review designs, and clients sometimes need to insist that they do. The list of readings at the end of the chapter includes an excellent review of library acoustics.

- **Adequate ceiling height.** Most book shelves are high (typically 7' or 7'6"), and 8' ceilings are almost always too low. Suspended uplights (the only satisfactory way to light small libraries) usually hang down at least two feet from the ceiling, so ceilings need to be a minimum of 10 feet high to keep the lights 8 feet off the floor. Most libraries do better with ceilings 11 or 12 feet high.
- **Good sightlines.** The easiest way to maintain good security in libraries is to maintain good sightlines. If a single staff member at the service desk can see all areas of the library (including the front door and the entrances to the restrooms) operating the library will be far easier. (In an effort to provide the best possible sightlines, a number of libraries have been designed with stack aisles radiating from service desks like the spokes of wheels. This has proven to be a disastrous idea.) One of the best ways to improve sightlines is through internal windows and glass walls. It helps to provide windows between offices and public areas, and to create study rooms that are essentially fish tanks. (It's also a good idea to watch out for unfortunate sightlines, particularly when restroom doors are open.)
- **Clear internal arrangement.** As libraries grow larger and more complex, keeping their floor plans simple and straightforward becomes more and more difficult, but small libraries should be easy to understand. The floor plan discussed at the end of this chapter provides an example of a clear and straightforward design.
- **Pleasant internal spaces.** Most libraries want to encourage users to stay in the library to read, use computers, consult library staff, and (increasingly) socialize with other library users. To be successful, therefore, libraries need comfortable, well-lighted spaces with good acoustics and—wherever possible—views of the outside world. One of the great challenges in library design is providing cozy spaces that do not lead to supervision problems. Interestingly, one of the most successful solutions has been to install a few diner-style booths, which appeal to people who come to the library in pairs or groups, and which feel far more private than they really are.
- **Parking.** School libraries and corporate libraries usually rely on parking provided for the entire building, and libraries on small residential campuses may expect students to arrive on foot, but all public libraries need to be concerned about where people will park. Local codes may

specify minimum off-street parking. A good first rule of thumb is that your parking lot should be at least as large as the floor area of your library.

- **Provision for after-hours return of materials.** Every library needs to provide a way for users to return books and recordings when the library is closed. A wide variety of return bins is available. Library users particularly like bins that they can reach from the windows of their cars; this requires one-way driveways, heavy bollards to protect bins from collisions with cars, and a long, straight run that allows drivers to pull up closely to the bins. Return slots can also be built into walls, but the receiving bins must be in fireproof spaces. (In many new libraries, return bins or wall slots are located on driveways that curve too much to allow users to pull sufficiently close.)

- **Good sites.** All libraries need convenient sites. For public libraries, this means sites next to other destinations, such as stores. Most campuses seek central locations for their libraries. For corporate and school libraries, this means sites in the middle of buildings, not in remote locations. There are also sites you may not want. If you build a new public library across the street from a homeless shelter, you can expect that all of your comfortable chairs will be occupied by sleeping non-readers much of the day. If you build a school library next to the gym, you can expect to have problems with noise. Most good sites, of course, are sought after by other organizations or departments in addition to yours, and you may need to be very aggressive to protect workable turf.

- **Provision for expansion.** No matter what people say, all libraries run out of space sooner or later. For this reason, all separate library buildings should be designed for later expansion. However, corporate libraries that require more space may be easier to relocate to larger areas in the building than to expand in their original quarters.

- **Inexpensive maintenance.** Some buildings can be extraordinarily difficult (and therefore expensive) to maintain. Keep your life simple (and inexpensive) by avoiding light fixtures you cannot reach (or that fill with visibly dead bugs), wall surfaces that are hard to clean, light-colored grout in ceramic tile floors (when you say "dark grout," be sure your designer doesn't decide that means "pastel grout"), cut pile (rather than tightly woven loop) carpeting, high-maintenance exteriors (such as wood or EIFS [External Insulating Finishing System] rather than brick), highly complex mechanical systems, etc. (See the section below on "Major Design Problems to Avoid: Difficult Maintenance" for detailed suggestions.)

- **Good security.** Security needs vary with the type and size of the library, but all libraries have security concerns. Among the issues you will need to confront are limiting the number of entrances, providing alarms with time delays on fire exits, installing appropriate systems for fire detection and control, supervising restrooms, controlling who can open windows, providing panic buttons for staff members at service desks, and determining whether you need a theft control system. Each of these issues has design and space implications. For example, the security gates for magnetic theft control systems cannot be directly adjacent to door hardware, computers, or bookshelves.

TYPICAL LIBRARY CONTENTS

Almost all libraries have similar needs for interior contents:

- **Service desks.** Most small libraries have single, multipurpose desks. Even if several people must be on duty at busy times, there will be other times when a single person is sufficient to meet users' needs. By limiting your library to a single desk, you can correspondingly limit the number of people it takes to operate the library. Service desks need extraordinarily good sightlines. As the plan at the end of this chapter demonstrates, it is possible to set up a 6,000-square-foot library so a single person can oversee the entrance to the building, the entrances to the restrooms, reader seating, stack aisles, and people using the program room.
- **Shelving.** Most libraries use steel cantilever shelving with decorative end panels. Cantilever shelves hook onto support posts. They are more sturdy and reliable than shelves supported by pins at their ends, and vastly better than shelves that slide into slots. Cantilever shelving for libraries is made by half a dozen specialty manufacturers, and you are always better off sticking with one of them. Libraries that purchase low-cost shelving designed for other purposes quickly regret the decision. Many libraries purchase shelf end panels with slat wall sections to enable displays of books at the end of stack ranges.

- **Storage for other parts of the collection.** Hardbound books are easy to store if they are not too large, but everything else is challenging. Library furniture and shelving catalogs are full of special equipment for storing atlases, unabridged dictionaries, newspapers, paperbacks, graphic novels, CDs, DVDs, kits (book/cassette sets and all sorts of other combinations), and so on. Librarians tend to have strong opinions on much of this equipment, so you will be better off watching it in use in other libraries before making a selection.
- **Reader seating.** Most libraries provide a mixture of seating at tables and in upholstered chairs. Tables come in a variety of sizes. I prefer four-person tables, because they work for both groups of students and for individual users who like to spread out their work, but some libraries purchase smaller tables for two readers or even for one. (Single-person tables are called "carrels.") Upholstered furniture is essential if you want to encourage people to linger in the library, but avoid couches in any area except children's departments. (Adults aren't comfortable sharing couches unless they know each other, teenagers are occasionally too eager to share, and you probably have some adult users who are eager to turn your couches into beds.) Furniture varies tremendously in quality, and library furniture is more expensive primarily because it is sturdier. If you buy your reading tables and chairs from a discount furniture store, they may not last out the year. Placement of furniture also matters. By and large, for example, users do not like sitting with their backs to the action.
- **Program rooms.** Most libraries have spaces for programs or for meetings. In a public library, a program room will be much more successful if it and the restrooms can be reached directly from the entry foyer, enabling the program room to be used when the rest of the library is closed. For this arrangement to take place, it must be part of the building planning from the very beginning. (Be sure that fire exits from the program room lead to the outside world and not into other areas of the library, or your plan to separate programs from the rest of the library will be defeated.)
- **Restrooms.** Public restrooms are essential in many libraries, but they can be a royal pain. Be sure your restrooms have floor drains and that all surfaces are easy to clean. It helps if the entrances to the restrooms are clearly visible

from the service desk. Unless you plan to keep restrooms locked at all times, issuing keys to your users as needed, you will be better off with restrooms with stalls and with outer doors that do not lock. For all but one-person restrooms, be sure that the fixtures and their users are not on proud display to patrons of the opposite sex who happen to be walking by when the door opens. (Check your plans for both direct views and views reflected in mirrors.) Many larger libraries have installed airport-style restrooms, with zigzag entry passages rather than doors.

- **Staff workrooms.** All libraries need staff workrooms with doors that lock. Even if staff members do most of their work at the service desk at slow moments, they still need a place to store materials in process, leave complex projects spread out, keep purses, coats, and belongings. One of the sad mistakes many libraries make when money is tighter than they hoped is to begin space reduction by eliminating staff workspaces.
- **Storage.** Most libraries have massive quantities of stuff that needs to be stored somewhere. If you build a new library without a good-size storeroom, you will be in the market for a large garden shed within a few months.
- **Circulation space.** In architectural language, "circulation space" is walking around space, not space for lending and receiving books. (To avoid confusion when you speak with your architect, you may want to use the term "lending" for the latter.) All libraries need open space for people to move about. Fitting in all the tables and chairs and desks isn't enough.
- **Support spaces.** All libraries require hallways, entryways, electrical rooms, mechanical rooms, and custodial spaces, and two-story libraries devote a substantial amount of space to stairways and elevators. For many school and corporate libraries, these spaces are not part of the library itself, but almost all academic and public libraries need to plan for them.

MAJOR DESIGN PROBLEMS TO AVOID

The library world is full of bad design decisions. Some of the most frequently encountered bad ideas include:

TOO MANY ENTRANCES

The only way to keep an eye on the contents of your library is to have a single entrance near the service desk. You will frequently be under pressure to maintain more than one entrance, but if you let this happen you will tie up expensive staff members watching doorways. If people push them on you, remind them of how having to watch more than one door will drive up your staffing costs, and ask them if they are prepared to provide the extra operating money every year.

Some very common situations leading to multiple entrances are:

- **Public libraries in converted commercial buildings on town squares, with front doors facing the square or courthouse and back doors (*far* to the rear) facing parking areas.** In addition to being almost impossible to watch, back doors will spook your staff when they hear unknown people fumbling around after dark.
- **School libraries with entrances from more than one part of the school.** This concept may appeal to people who want the convenience of multiple entrances, or who want to funnel different age groups through different entrances, but you may have major supervision problems.
- **Historic libraries with inaccessible front entrances.** Buildings of this type (which include most Carnegie buildings) can be made accessible only by providing a new entrance and an elevator connecting the basement and upper floor or floors. Unless you are lucky enough to have a library built on sloping land, where people entering a new addition can simply walk into either the basement or main floor, you will end up with many ways into the building. Such buildings are also a problem because their architecture frequently indicates the location of the main entrance. If you close the main entrance and bring everyone in through a new, accessible entrance, you will destroy part of what you are trying to save.

BAD LIGHTING AND GLARE

More libraries suffer from bad lighting than almost any other problem, but avoiding it is fairly easy. The worst sources of glare are skylights (which are always a really bad idea), western windows without blinds (modern glass helps, but you still need blinds), and highly direct artificial lights. For small libraries, always stick with high-quality fluorescent uplight. Strips of suspended fluorescent uplight fixtures (without "perforations," which display all the dead bugs) work extremely well. Tell your designer you want no can lights ("recessed down lights") or task lights.

BAD SECURITY

A wide variety of situations can undermine security. For example, if users can open the windows in your library, they can pitch your books into the bushes outside and retrieve them later. If book aisles have dead ends, people can be cornered by users they are not eager to meet. The sources of security problems in libraries are many and are frequently not understood by architects who do not specialize in libraries. Ask your consultant to list the features you need and then look at your plans.

INADEQUATE STAFF WORKSPACE AND STORAGE SPACE

When cost becomes an issue (as it almost always does) the first thing superintendents or corporate managers or mayors or library boards want to cut is staff and storage space. As a result:

- **Many libraries are planned to handle 20 years of growth in collection sizes, but they have no space for even one additional employee.**
- **Many libraries have virtually no place to store anything.**

DANGEROUS FEATURES

A number of clever architectural design features have caused problems in libraries. Among some common ones are:

- **Balustrades with horizontal bars.** Bars (banisters) are vertical for good reason, because small children can climb horizontal bars and be up and over the barricade in seconds.
- **Indoor water features.** Libraries with indoor water features have trouble with users falling in, kids dropping books into the water, leakage into lower floors, coins clogging drains, and staff members constantly running to the restroom in response to the encouraging sound of running water.
- **Staircases without risers.** A riser is the vertical panel that connects two treads. Some designers like to omit them because it creates an open and airy look, but users with acrophobia panic when they can see through stairs, and objects fall through the openings. In general, libraries work best with as few steps as possible. And they should never (ever) have "cute" steps.

FUNNY SHAPED BUILDINGS

Some designers love curved and diagonal walls. Unfortunately, all too often such walls lead to interior spaces that are hard to use. Almost everything libraries own is rectangular and fits rectangular spaces. Diagonal walls lead to funny corners, and curved walls are expensive. (Years ago, promoters of round or even hemispherical buildings talked about how such shapes used the least amount of surface to enclose the maximum amount of space, but most of them were practical failures because so much of the space was unusable. Rectangular buildings are easier—and much cheaper—to build, and it's hard to hang pictures in an A-frame, let alone in a geodesic dome.)

TOO MANY BUILT-INS

Long before library buildings wear out, their owners change their way of doing business. The more that spaces are designed to work in only one way, the sooner librarians find they don't work at all. Libraries are full of abandoned niches for card catalogs that no longer exist, special provisions for 16mm film projectors, and other well-designed places for long-forgotten gadgets. The way to avoid this is to never send architecture to do the job of furniture. If your spaces are clean, open, well-lighted, and heavily wired, you stand the best possible chance of having them work for decades to come.

One bad idea in the same family as built-in furniture is so-called "task lighting," lighting carefully positioned to light specific work areas or objects. The trouble with task lighting is that—long before the light fixtures wear out—librarians move the things the lights illuminate, and too many libraries end up with special light fixtures lighting not much of anything.

RADIAL STACKS

A number of libraries have been built with stacks arranged like spokes of a wheel, usually to allow someone seated at a service desk to see down multiple aisles at the same time. This is an unbelievably awful idea, but for some reason people keep reinventing it.

REMODELING UGLY BUILDINGS

Remodeling is surprisingly expensive, about two-thirds the cost of new construction per square foot. Some libraries buy secondhand buildings thinking they can save money by remodeling them, but usually the only way to save much money is to purchase the building for about the value of the land or to use it just as it comes. If the building does not meet all the criteria listed under *Basic Requirements of Library Building*, and it cannot be easily converted to meet the criteria, run away. Remember also that the cost of dealing with EPA issues such as asbestos, lead paint, and buried fuel tanks can be incredibly high, and that any library that requires ramps or steps to enter will always cause accessibility problems. Unfortunately, every time a town needs a new public library, someone who has been trying for years to ditch a dog of a building suddenly sees his rescuers riding over the horizon like the Seventh Cavalry, with bugles blaring in the afternoon and public money fluttering like guidons.

> A contemporary addition to a historic building eventually becomes a painfully dated addition to a historic building.

ATRIUMS

Atriums are large open spaces that connect two or more floors. Often they are topped with skylights. Atriums look elegant, and in large buildings they sometimes help people get their bearings. But they take up immense amounts of expensive space, transmit noise, encourage children on upper levels to experiment with gravity, cause temperature control problems, interrupt traffic flow, and usually have light fixtures that are difficult to maintain. Few small libraries have enough space for designers to suggest atriums, but it is worthwhile being forearmed.

DIFFICULT MAINTENANCE

Libraries by and large receive extremely heavy use, and the building that looks elegant and handsome on opening day may be difficult to keep that way over the years. Some designers are very conscious of which materials are the easiest to keep looking good, but others are motivated more by vogues and costs. Among the most important questions to ask at the beginning of planning are:

- **What is the life span of the carpeting?** Many kinds of carpet (such as cut pile) are too fragile for institutional use.
- **If carpet tile is chosen to allow replacement of stained or damaged areas, how many years will pass before the replaced tiles stand out prominently from the older, faded tiles?**
- **How will you change your lightbulbs?** Many fixtures are almost impossible to reach once construction scaffolding has been removed. Although we have been aware of the problem for years, new libraries open all the time with lights no one can reach.

- **Will your light fixtures quickly fill with visible handfuls of deceased insects?** Chandeliers shaped like hanging bowls pose particular problems. This is one additional strong argument for uplighting—dead bugs don't show.
- **Are your wall surfaces sufficiently washable?** Latex paints are very much in vogue now because they do not emit solvents while they dry, but they are harder to keep clean. Ask your designers to provide names of heavily used institutions with the kind of paint they are recommending. Instead of paint, many libraries use vinyl wall coverings.
- **Where will you store your ladders?** Many public libraries find they have no place for ladders, but so do academic libraries, which may find that campus operations and maintenance departments expect every building to provide spaces for its ladders.
- **Where will you store your lawnmower and snowblower?** This question is a particular concern of public libraries, which frequently find they have no legal space to store gasoline-powered equipment.
- **How will you maintain resilient flooring?** Many standard types of flooring—such as vinyl tile—require frequent stripping, waxing, and buffing. Other types—such as rubber tile—can be maintained by damp mopping.
- **How will you maintain ceramic tile flooring?** Actually, washing tile is easy. The problem is the grout, which is virtually impossible to clean. Unless you start out with very dark grout, most of the grout—but unfortunately not all—will soon be permanently dark. There are lots of pastel colors that don't qualify as dark but are frequently suggested.
- **Is your furniture easy to maintain?** Tabletops need to be made of strong laminates—linoleum and (particularly) wood are far too fragile, no matter how elegant they look when they're new. Service desktops in turn need to be made of materials stronger than everyday laminates—try solid core laminates, Corian, or stone. Upholstery needs to withstand 100,000 or more "double rubs." (Some libraries with fragile tabletops or countertops end up covering them with glass, which is fragile and causes glare by reflecting light.)
- **Is the exterior of the building sheathed in durable material, such as brick or stone?** Wood, EIFS (External Insulating Finishing System), and some other materials may be initially attractive, but they tend to lead to very high long-term maintenance costs. EIFS is very popular for commercial storefronts these days, but it consists of just a skim

coat of stucco over plastic foam. It is easily dented or damaged, has to be repainted, costs nearly as much as brick, and when water gets in behind it, tremendous structural damage can result.)

EXAMPLE OF AN EFFECTIVE LIBRARY FLOOR PLAN

The floor plan that accompanies this chapter was developed for the public library of Tolono, a small town in central Illinois. The library was completed in 1997 and measures about 6,000 square feet. The architect was Gary Olsen of Champaign, Illinois, who has an extensive track record designing successful small public libraries. The floor plan illustrates a number of excellent design features, including:

- **Oversight.** A single staff member standing at the service desk can see almost the entire building by simply looking around. He/She can see people arriving and leaving, including people entering the program room and the restrooms. He/She can see down all the book aisles, he/she can see what's going on in the program room by looking through the windows. He/She can see children on the reading structure by looking through the two glass walls in the director's office. About the only area hidden is the adult reading space with soft seating, because the view is blocked by shelving.
- **Wayfinding.** People entering the library find it easy to orient themselves. The service desk is the first thing they encounter, enabling them to ask for help immediately. Children's services are located on one side of the desk and adult services on the other, which means that collections can be grouped logically. The same good sightlines that serve the staff serve users, who can see almost everything in the library while standing at the service desk.
- **Program room usable after hours.** The library is designed so that the program room can be used when the building is closed. People using the room have necessary access to the restrooms, but not to the rest of the library.
- **Quiet reading space.** By isolating adult soft seating in one corner, the library has protected adults who want to be as

Figure 9-1 Library Floor Plan

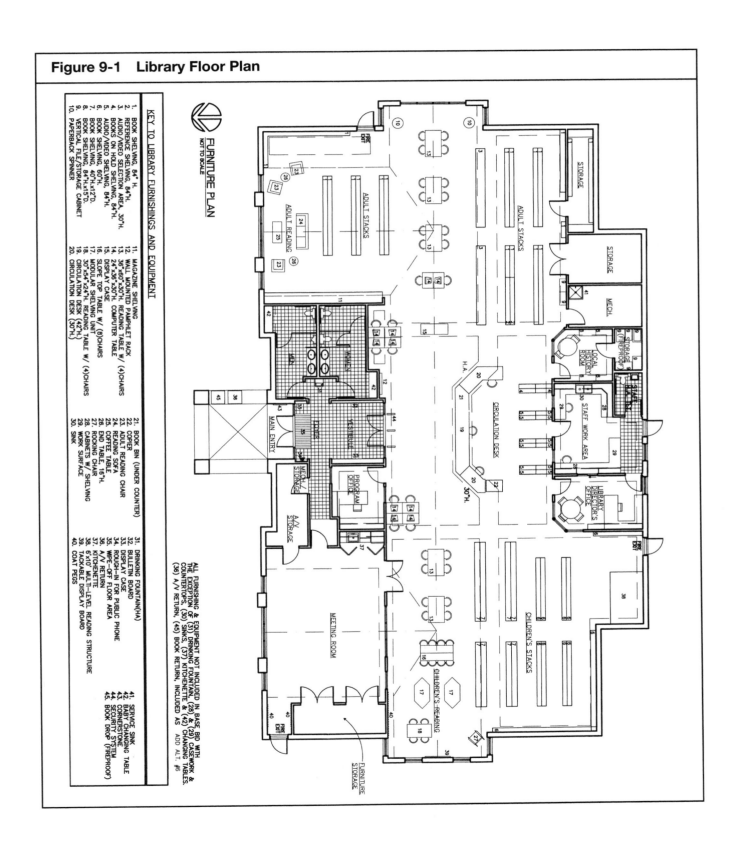

KEY TO LIBRARY FURNISHINGS AND EQUIPMENT

1. BOOK SHELVING, 84" H.
2. REFERENCE SHELVING, 84"H.
3. AUDIO/VIDEO SELECTION AREA, 30"H.
4. BOOKS ON HOLD SHELVING, 84"H.
5. AUDIO/VIDEO SHELVING, 84"H.
6. BOOK SHELVING, 60"H.
7. BOOK SHELVING, 40"H.x12"D.
8. BOOK SHELVING, 84"H.x15"D.
9. VERTICAL FILE/STORAGE CABINET
10. PAPERBACK SPINNER

11. MAGAZINE SHELVING
12. WALL MOUNTED PAMPHLET RACK
13. 36"x60"x30"H. READING TABLE W/ (4)CHAIRS
14. 24"x36"x30"H. COMPUTER TABLE
15. DISPLAY CASE
16. SLOPE TOP TABLE W/ (8)CHAIRS
17. MODULAR SHELVING UNIT
18. 30"x54"x24"H. READING TABLE W/ (4)CHAIRS
19. CIRCULATION DESK (42"H.)
20. CIRCULATION DESK (30"H.)

21. BOOK BIN (UNDER COUNTER)
22. COPIER
23. ADULT READING CHAIR
24. READING SOFA
25. COFFEE TABLE
26. END TABLE, 16"H.
27. ROCKING CHAIR
28. CABINETS W/ SHELVING
29. WORK SURFACE
30. SINK

31. DRINKING FOUNTAIN(HA)
32. BULLETIN BOARD
33. DISPLAY CASE
34. ROUGH-IN FOR PUBLIC PHONE
35. WIPE-OFF FLOOR AREA
36. A/V RETURN
37. KITCHENETTE
38. 6'x10' MULTI-LEVEL READING STRUCTURE
39. TACKABLE DISPLAY BOARD
40. COAT PEGS

41. SERVICE SINK
42. BABY CHANGING TABLE
43. CORNERSTONE
44. SECURITY SYSTEM
45. BOOK DROP (FIREPROOF)

ALL FURNISHING & EQUIPMENT NOT INCLUDED IN BASE BID WITH
THE EXCEPTION OF (31) DRINKING FOUNTAIN, (28) & (29) CASEWORK &
COUNTERTOPS, (30) SINKS, (37) KITCHENETTE & (42) CHANGING TABLES.
(36) A/V RETURN, INCLUDED AS ADD ALT. #6

FURNITURE PLAN
NOT TO SCALE

far as possible from the noise of children. The seating also offers north light and a view of the main street in front of the library.

- **Computers.** Computers are high-maintenance devices. Patrons using computers need more help than patrons reading books, and some libraries want to oversee the use of the Internet. Of all library furniture and equipment, computers need to be closest to service desks. In this library, computers are clustered near the service desk. To make this work, the library needed space, electrical wiring, and data connections.

The following three points are important ones, but they are not revealed by the floor plan.

- **Indirect lighting.** Almost all of the library's lighting is bounced off the ceiling.
- **Attractive architecture.** The building is a handsome structure with interestingly complex cathedral ceilings.
- **Modest cost.** Because the architect was able to create a striking design while employing standard construction techniques, the building was constructed of durable materials at a very reasonable cost.

This library was the result of extensive staff input, a carefully written building program, and an architect who had the skill and library knowledge to combine function and good design.

CONCLUSION

If all of this sounds complex, that's because it is. Unless you already have two or three library building projects under your belt, you will be much better off if you start out with experienced assistance. If you're a public librarian, try your state library development office. If you run a school library or corporate library, talk with your facilities managers, but don't expect them to understand the special space needs of libraries without indoctrination or outside assistance. Similarly, expect campus architects to bring great strengths in terms of planning, campus standards, and quality construction, but sometimes to have little knowledge of the practical needs of library buildings.

Hiring an experienced building consultant to prepare a program (and preferably to stay on the design team to forestall bad design ideas and to walk you through the steps of the process) will always help and will frequently prevent serious errors. And be sure the architect selected for your specific project has a track record of designing libraries that work.

Finally, remind your employer that building libraries is exhausting for librarians, and that you will need all kinds of special consideration and loving care during the entire process.

FURTHER READING

American Library Association, Library Administration and Management Association, Buildings and Equipment Section, Functional Space Requirements Committee. 2001. *Building blocks for planning functional library space.* Lanham, MD: Scarecrow.

Dahlgren, Anders C. 1996. *Planning the small library facility.* LAMA Small Libraries Publications Series, (2nd ed.) Chicago: American Library Association, Library Administration and Management Association.

McCarthy, Richard C. 1999. *Designing better libraries: Selecting and working with building professionals,* 2nd ed. Fort Atkinson, WI: Highsmith Press.

"Sample Surveys," in *Serving our public: standards for Illinois public libraries.* Rev. ed. Chicago: Illinois Library Association. (pp. 74–88.) 1997.

Sannwald, William W. 2001. *Checklist of library building design considerations.* 4th ed. Chicago: American Library Association.

Schlipf, Frederick A., and John A. Moorman. *From problem recognition to ribbon cutting: The public library construction process.* Available online at www.urbanafreelibrary.org.

_____. *Let there be at least half-way decent light: How library illumination systems work—And don't work.* Available online at www.urbanafree library.org.

Wrightson, Denelle, and John M. Wrightson. 1999. "Acoustical considerations in planning and design of library facilities," *Library Hi Tech,* 17: 349–57.

10 PLANNING

Nelson Worley

No amount of planning will ever replace dumb luck!
—Slogan seen on a coffee mug

DEFINITION

Planning is the process by which the library determines its course. Planning results in a time-specific plan document, which is used as the basis for library operations.

OVERVIEW

This chapter will cover:

- Why plan?
- The planning cycle
- Several PLA planning models
- Other planning methodologies
- Sources for information necessary for planning
- Essential components of a plan

WHY PLAN?

Planning is an ongoing, cyclical process of assessment, forecasting, goal setting, implementation, and evaluation. The planning process typically asks four questions:

- What is the library's current condition?
- What do you want the library to be?
- How does the library get there?
- Did the library get there?

The planning process offers several opportunities for the library:

- Considers the needs of the community
- Identifies trends
- Identifies options and possibilities
- Encourages creative thinking
- Provides direction to library services
- Sets priorities
- Focuses attention on effectiveness and efficiency
- Provides feedback for learning, adapting, and improving library services
- Encourages library and individual accountability
- Orients the library and library staff members toward the future

For all these opportunities that the planning process presents for the library, it is likely that the most important reason for planning is that it is a requirement, either of the library's governing body, the locality, and/or the state. In fact, it is quite likely that having an up-to-date plan is a requirement for receiving funding.

THE PLANNING CYCLE

Regardless of the planning model or methodology chosen, the process is cyclical in nature. The basic steps are:

- Planning to plan
- Determining where the library is currently
- Deciding where you want the library to be
- Setting goals, objectives, and activities
- Implementing the plan
- Evaluating

PLANNING APPROACHES

The Public Library Association (PLA) and the American Library Association (ALA) have developed manuals and tools to help libraries assess the needs of communities and set goals and objectives for future development. Although the models and tools cited in this chapter are designed for public libraries, elements may be adapted to other types of libraries. Also, other types of libraries may have their planning process dictated by how the larger unit plans as a whole. In any case, the principles discussed in the model apply to planning in all types of libraries. John Ulmschneider, executive director of libraries at Virginia Commonwealth University, has prepared the following summary of academic library planning which will be of assistance to librarians in the small academic library.

STRATEGIC PLANNING IN ACADEMIC LIBRARIES

Libraries at academic institutions, like libraries everywhere, face a "perfect storm" of challenges that will converge in the near to medium-term future. Chief among those challenges are

- *Changes in funding.* Higher education institutions, especially public colleges and universities, are in the midst of a long-term, permanent decline in public fund support and growing pressure to develop other revenue streams. Consequently, academic libraries must themselves develop new funding sources, while also demonstrating tangible benefit from parent institution investment by planning carefully for maximum impact from every new dollar.
- *Headline-grabbing competition.* Services such as Google Scholar and Amazon.com have created a startlingly new skepticism for senior academic leaders: why should the parent institution invest in its library when "everything, including books, is going to be free through Google?" Academic librarians must plan a multitier response to such misconceptions, rather than react to them as they occur. A high priority for such a response is a well-planned program for building and maintaining digital collections and services.

- *Recruiting and retaining staff.* All libraries share the challenging demographics of the graying library profession. There are simply too many pending retirements and not enough librarians in the career pipeline. Academic libraries need a planned response that anticipates approaching staff shortages, especially shortages of professional librarians.
- *The image of libraries.* While very few libraries anywhere fit the stereotypical image of a quiet place for reading books, academic libraries perhaps have departed furthest from such a traditional model. Contemporary academic libraries are abuzz with group study, coffee shops, computers, snack food, and conversation (although all still provide some places for quiet study and intellectual retreat.) Yet a just-released study from Online Computer Library Center (OCLC) shows that library users still hold a long-outdated image of libraries as quiet places with stern female librarians. Academic libraries require a serious marketing plan that displaces stereotypical concepts held by students and faculty with the reality of their very active role in the academic and social life of their institutions.

How should academic librarians approach planning in this challenging environment? First and foremost, it is no longer sufficient to conduct occasional planning exercises that lay out long-term internal goals. Formal planning exercises must be more frequent, and the focus must be on results that are visible to constituencies and advance overall institutional goals in teaching and learning, research, and student life. Furthermore, the pace of change in higher education is such that long-term planning has questionable value. Planning horizons should be scaled back to no more than 2–3 years, which also encourages more frequent planning cycles. Longer-term goals should be relegated to a mission/vision/values statement, development of which forms the essential first step and foundation for near-horizon strategic planning. Finally, it is no longer sufficient simply to create a document expressing a hierarchy of strategies, objectives, and tasks that incorporates the contributions of each operational area within a library. Planners should adopt formal methodologies for planning that concentrate institutional efforts and speed up the planning process. An important emerging element in such methodologies is integrating a focus on evidence-based results as captured through quantified measures.

Those charged with initiating or leading a planning effort in an academic library have easily at hand the most valuable of resources: examples! Many academic libraries place their strategic plans on their Web sites, and will readily share internal planning documents upon request. The richness of methodologies and processes in these examples provides invaluable guidance for nearly any academic library. Furthermore, examples of powerful alternative planning methodologies that are relatively new to academe and to academic libraries, such as Balanced Scorecard and Compact Planning, have outstanding exemplars on the Web. Librarians can consult excellent plans at libraries ranging from Association of Research Libraries (ARL) institutions to libraries at elite, undergraduate-focused institutions for instructive examples.

Smart planners at academic libraries will start with three fundamental steps. First, if the library does not have one, a mission/vision/values statement must be developed that expresses and captures the culture of the library. Many examples of such statements from academic libraries are available on the Web. Second, leaders of the planning effort will carry out a detailed review of plans and planning methodologies at peer institutions and other related institutions. The result will be a clearly defined planning discipline that accelerates the planning process and creates quantifiable goals or targets. Finally, every aspect of the plan will be tied to the parent institution's goals and ambitions, and demonstrate bottom-line value to the parent institution through quantifiable evidence as well as quantifiable results. Only a library plan that advances the academic institution as a whole will have a compelling place in the institution's vision of its future.

PLANNING MODELS

Since the publication of *A Planning Process* in 1977, two other PLA models have been issued—*Planning and Role Setting for Public Libraries: A Manual of Options and Procedures* (McClure et al., 1987) and *Planning for Results: A Public Library Transformation Process* (Himmel and Wilson., 1998). Each publication has introduced new aspects to the planning model.

Planning and Role Setting introduced the notion of role selection for the public library, defining eight representative role profiles that could be used by library planners to describe the essential priorities of the library and guide the allocation of budget, staffing, and energies. The roles from *Planning and Role Setting* are:

- **Community Activities Center:** The library is a central focus point for community activities, meetings, and services.
- **Community Information Center:** The library is a clearinghouse for current information on community organizations, issues, and services.
- **Formal Education Support Center:** The library assists students of all ages in meeting educational objectives established during their formal course of study.
- **Independent Learning Center:** The library supports individuals of all ages pursuing a sustained program of learning independent of any educational provider.
- **Popular Materials Library:** The library features current, high-demand, high-interest materials in a variety of formats for persons of all ages.
- **Preschoolers Door to Learning:** The library encourages young children to develop an interest in reading and learning through services for children, and for parents and children together.
- **Reference Library:** The library actively provides timely, accurate, and useful information for community residents.
- **Research Library:** The library assists scholars and researchers to conduct in-depth studies, investigate specific areas of knowledge, and create new knowledge.

Libraries using this planning model tend to select three, perhaps four, roles as top priorities for service.

Planning for Results, among other changes, introduced the idea of "visioning"—a concise expression of what is envisioned for the community or how the community will benefit from having a successful library. Previous planning models had been institution-centered, and this new step in the process seeks to create a stronger connection between the library and its community. *Planning for Results* also recast the eight role profiles from the previous planning model into thirteen responses (see Fig. 10-1). This change incorporates libraries' experience in using the original roles and reflects the growing application of technology in the library environment.

Figure 10-1   Service Responses

The **Service Responses** are:

- **Basic Literacy:** A library that offers Basic Literacy service addresses the need to read and perform other essential daily tasks.
- **Business and Career Information:** A library that offers Business and Career Information services addresses a need for information related to business, careers, work, entrepreneurship, personal finances, and obtaining employment.
- **Commons:** A library that provides a Commons environment helps address the need of people to meet and interact with others in their community and to participate in public discourse about community issues.
- **Community Referral:** A library that offers Community Referral addresses the need for information related to services provided by community agencies and organizations.
- **Consumer Information:** A library that provides Community Information service addresses the need for information to make informed consumer decisions and helps residents become more self-sufficient.
- **Cultural Awareness:** A library that offers Cultural Awareness service helps satisfy the desire of community residents to gain an understanding of their own cultural heritage and the cultural heritage of others.
- **Current Topics/Titles:** A library that provides Current Topics and Titles helps to fulfill community residents' appetite for information about popular cultural and social trends and their desire for satisfying recreational experiences.
- **Formal Learning Support:** A library that offers Formal Learning Support helps students who are enrolled in a formal program of education or who are pursuing their education through a program of home schooling to attain their educational goals.
- **General Information:** A library that offers General Information helps meet the need for information and answers to questions on a broad array of topics related to work, school, and personal life.
- **Government Information:** A library that offers Government Information service helps satisfy the needs for information about elected officials and governmental agencies that enables people to participate in the democratic process.
- **Information Literacy:** A library that provides Information Literacy service helps address the need for skills related to finding, evaluating, and using information effectively.
- **Lifelong Learning:** A library that provides Lifelong Learning service helps address the desire for self-directed personal growth and development opportunities.
- **Local History and Genealogy:** A library that offers Local History and Genealogy service addresses the desire of community residents to know and better understand personal or community heritage.

Planning for Results, originally published in two volumes, provides very detailed information on planning steps, tasks, and the service responses. Based on feedback from librarians who used the process in the original version, a more simplified revision, *The New Planning for Results: A Streamlined Approach* (Sandra Nelson et al. 2001), was published. *The New Planning for Results,* with a different format, contains the basic elements of *Planning for Results* while simplifying many of the steps in the planning process. Two examples: In *The New Planning for Results* the planning tasks are reduced in number (from 23 to 12), and the timeline is 4–5 months instead of 8–10 months.

COMPANION VOLUMES TO THE PLA MODELS

There are several companion volumes published by ALA/PLA that may be of assistance in the planning process.

Output Measures for Public Libraries: A Manual of Standardized Procedures (Van House, 1987) was developed to assist public libraries in the areas of planning, measurement, and evaluation. The volume describes measures to be used in assessing common public library services. Suggestions are provided for managing the measurement effort; collecting, analyzing, and reporting data; and interpreting and using the result. Please note that *Output Measures for Public Libraries* and *Planning and Role Setting* are older publications and do not reflect the increased use of technology in public libraries. *Output Measures for Public Libraries* is more useful in measuring the more traditional library services. Other more recent measurement guidelines and tools will be needed for more technologically based library services.

There are several companion volumes, the PLA *Results Series,* for *Planning for Results* and *The New Planning for Results* that are useful for more specific planning activities:

- *Managing for Results: Effective Resource Allocation for Public Libraries* (Nelson et al., 2000) is a resource allocation model based on the service responses in *Planning for Results*; however, it may be used with other planning models. The primary topics are managing staff, collections, facilities, and technology. Work forms are included. One word of caution—some librarians consider some of the activities and tasks very labor intensive.
- *Wired for the Future: Developing Your Library Technology Plan* (Mayo and Nelson, 1998) provides in-depth coverage of the technology planning process. Topics covered include identifying needs; discovering options; selecting an infrastructure, products and services; and

developing and managing implementation. Worksheets are included.

- *Staffing for Results: A Guide to Working Smarter* (Mayo and Goodrich, 2002) provides more in-depth coverage of staffing issues. *Managing for Results* assists in identifying staffing required and the abilities needed for the library to accomplish identified service goals, objectives, and tasks. If the library's planning process indicates that large-scale staff adjustments are needed, *Staffing for Results* provides tools to decide what changes to make and what the possible implications of the changes might be. Worksheets are included.

- *Creating Policies for Results: From Chaos to Clarity* (Nelson et al., 2003) is a tool to assist library directors and trustees in adopting policies that support the library in its efforts to achieve its goals in meeting the needs and priorities of the community. Changes in the library priorities as a result of the planning process will have an impact on library policies. As a result of the planning process, it is necessary to review, revise, and develop policies, regulations, guidelines, and procedures that support the library's efforts to implement its plan. Worksheets are included.

OTHER METHODOLOGIES

The models included above have been developed over the years by PLA specifically to provide tools and training for public library planners in their efforts to improve planning and implementation of public library services. There are other planning methodologies, models, or techniques that may be used. Planning activities are known by numerous terms and varying definitions —long-range planning, short-range planning, strategic planning, reengineering, and crisis management, among others. Management trends such as total quality management and continuous improvement initiatives are also used in planning.

- **City/County Planning Processes.** Depending on your library's governance structure, the library's planning process may be a part of the broader framework of the local jurisdiction's planning. While these processes can and do work, the challenge is to ensure that whatever the planning process used it is meaningful and useful as it pertains to the library.

- **Scenario Planning.** As outlined in *Scenario Planning for Libraries* (Giesecke, 1998), scenario planning focuses on the uncertainty of the environment and urges library planners to take a flexible approach to viewing the future. By playing, "What if . . . ?," different futures are developed. For example, "What if a new library branch is planned and . . .

  o . . . the branch opens with additional staff and resources?
  o . . . the branch opens without any additional staff and resources?
  o . . . the branch's opening is delayed and additional staff have been hired and resources have already been purchased?
  o . . . the branch is delayed and there are no additional staff or resources?

  Considering the scenarios helps planners design strategies to help the library move forward regardless which scenario occurs. An additional benefit of scenario planning is it helps prepare the library staff psychologically for various possibilities.

- **Peer Comparison.** While assessing the library's current situation and creating a vision and goals are important, an equally important aspect of planning may be comparing the library to peer libraries. Peer comparison enhances effective planning. It provides an opportunity to see the library's strengths and weaknesses vis-à-vis comparable libraries in size, type, locale, and so on. In comparing the libraries with neighboring ones, areas of cooperation and collaboration among libraries may be identified. Peer comparison is aided in some states through the adoption of standards, sometimes in formats by levels or profiles that assist in comparison activities. The state library agency may be helpful in providing comparison assistance. A number of states provide access to a statistical collection and analysis tool, *Bibliostat*. More information on this tool is below.

  At the national level comparison has been assisted through the development of the Hennen American Public Library Ratings (HALPR). These ratings are published annually using an index devised by Thomas J. Hennen,

Jr. Additionally, there is *Hennen's Public Library Planner: A Manual and Interactive CD-Rom* (Hennen, 2004), which provides an extensive planning guide with electronic work forms. Hennen's work has a strong emphasis on the use of peer comparison in the planning process.

- **Outcome-Based Evaluation.** While outcome-based evaluation (OBE) is by name an evaluation tool, to some extent it is a misnomer; there is much emphasis on planning. While there needs to be an awareness of OBE because of increasing emphasis on program outcomes by funding authorities, it should be noted that the process is very labor intensive and may be better utilized for specific projects where specific changes in knowledge, skills, and behaviors may be tracked. Drawing upon the model from the United Way of America book titled *Measuring Program Outcomes: A Practical Approach* (United Way, 1996), OBE looks at the impacts, benefits, changes to library users as a result of their participation in library's programs. OBE is effective as a planning tool because in addition to outcomes, the process also focuses on inputs, activities, and outputs. In addition to identifying desired outcomes, outcome targets (numbers and percentages) and indicators (milestones) are also identified. As mentioned, implementing OBE is very labor intensive. It might be wise to consider attending OBE training before attempting to implement it.

OTHER PLANNING AIDS

- Measurement and Evaluation Tools

  o *The TELL IT! Manual: The Complete Program for Evaluating Library Performance* (Zweizig et al., 1996) is a simple, straightforward process for libraries to set goals, to make plans, to monitor progress, to determine the effects and to incorporate what is learned. It can be used by small libraries in a simplified long-range planning process or by medium and larger libraries to focus on a particular project or service. The process helps libraries to demonstrate that the programs and services offered make a positive difference in the lives of the people in the community.

o In 2001, ALA published *Statistics and Performance Measures for Public Library Networked Services.* Charles McClure, John Bertot, and Joe Ryan spent many years researching the impact of networked resources in public libraries and they have developed and field-tested a number of measures for evaluating the use of these resources. The book will assist in:

- Establishing a core set of performance measures that will capture and describe patron use of online resources.
- Collecting and organizing hard statistics based on the measures set.
- Assessing the services the library is providing and identify potential areas of growth.
- Understanding how the library's services are being used by patrons.
- Using the reproducible forms, developing a specific picture of the library's network service and usage that can be communicated to staff, community, and new funding streams.
- Developing financial reports and cost-benefit analysis to support budget increases and reallocate resources.

Recently, Florida State University School of Information Studies received a National Leadership Grant from the Institute of Museums and Library Services to develop a means to provide assistance and continuing education for practitioners wanting to use measures of library electronic resources and services. A Web site is under development, www.ii.fsu.edu/EMIS.

- **State Library Requirements, Standards, and Guidelines**
  Many state library agencies have established requirements, standards, and/or guidelines for public libraries to use in planning. Often the state agency requires that requirements and standards must be included in the library's planning document, and must be met, in order to receive state funding. Some states also provide tools to assist the libraries in planning. Contact the state library agency to identify what requirements, standards, and guidelines are applicable, and to determine what planning tools may be available. Additionally, planning information and tools from other states may also be helpful. The Chief Officers of

State Library Agencies (COSLA) maintains a Web site at www.cosla.org that provides basic information about COSLA and the individual state library agencies.

LIBRARY STATISTICAL INFORMATION

o **State and National Statistical Information**

There are more than 8,900 public libraries in the 50 states and the District of Columbia. Each state has a designated State Data Coordinator, usually appointed by the state librarian, or head of the state's library agency, to gather data on its public libraries and submit to the National Center for Educational Statistics (NCES), "http:// nces.ed.gov./" Through the Federal State Cooperative System (FSCS) for Public Library Data, www.nclis.gov/ statsurv/surveys/fscs/fscs.html, NCES works with State Data Coordinators, COSLA, the National Commission on Libraries and Information Science (NCLIS), the Institute of Museum and Library Services, and ALA in designing and conducting the annual surveys.

NCES releases an annual data file and report based on the survey. This survey is the only national data on public libraries. The data are used by federal, state, and local officials, professional associations, researchers, educators, and local practitioners for planning, research, evaluation, and policy making.

The state data coordinator can be an invaluable resource person by providing more information about the annual FSCS data collection, and using the data more effectively in the library planning and evaluation process.

o *Bibliostat Collect* and *Bibliostat Connect*

A number of state library agencies maintain subscriptions to Internet-based data collection and data analysis tools, *Bibliostat Collect* and *Bibliostat Connect.*

Bibliostat Collect is a customized Internet-based tool that allows for a more complete, accurate, and timely data-collection process for annual public library reports. State library agencies that have a subscription for *Collect* use this tool for collecting data for the FSCS survey as well as state-specific public library data.

A companion application, *Bibliostat Connect,* that is also Internet-based, allows libraries to conduct quick, easy, statistical, and graphical comparisons. A current *Bibliostat Connect* subscription provides access to the most current versions of FSCS, PLA, and state data. In addition to using *Connect* for planning purposes, such as identifying strengths and weaknesses, the peer comparisons can be used in budget proposals and presentations to protect existing, or to secure additional, resources.

Statewide subscriptions to both tools include unlimited software access, toll-free technical support, online help, tutorials, and documentation. To find out if these tools are available, contact the state library agency.

o **Public Library Data Service**
Annually, PLA publishes the *Public Library Data Service Statistical Report* which may be ordered at www.pla.org/ala/pla/pla.htm. As previously mentioned, data from the PLA report is included in *Bibliostat Connect*.

OTHER INFORMATION RESOURCES

o **Federal**
Additional useful data may be available from the U.S. Bureau of the Census www.census.gov/ and the U.S. Bureau of Labor Statistics www.bls.gov/

o **State and Local**
At the state and local level there are a number of sources of data you might find useful in your planning process:
- The Employment Commission
- State and local departments of education
- Economic development departments
- University centers for public service
- State and local chambers of commerce
- Planning commissions

KEY COMPONENTS OF THE PLAN

Regardless of the planning model used, there are several key components that you will need to include in your plan, as outlined in Figure 10-2.

Figure 10-2   Plan Components

- **Mission Statement.** The purpose of the mission statement is to inform the community about the library's priorities. Mission statements should be written clearly and concisely, in terms that are easily understood. A brief, to-the-point mission statement is more easily conveyed and remembered. The mission statement is written later in the planning process, after roles and service responses have been selected; it is somewhat analogous to a brief executive summary of the plan.
- **Vision Statement.** The vision statement describes what the library is to be. What will the future look like? How will the library's future contribute to the community's vision? By comparing the library's vision statement with the existing situation of the library, planners can determine what steps need to be taken. The library plan provides the guide to fulfilling the vision.
- **Goals.** Goals are general statements that describe a desired long—range (usually 3–5 years) achievement. Goals may be service goals or management goals. Service goals directly reflect the roles or service responses selected in the planning process. Management goals which may support service goals are concerned with resources, staffing, funding, or other management issues. Goals should logically follow the library's vision and mission and provide a framework for developing objectives.
- **Objectives.** Objectives are more specific statements that describe a measurable result to be accomplished in a specific period of time. Objectives are written for each goal, although some objectives may overlap goals. Types of objectives include those that:
  o   Develop new services or management operations.
  o   Maintain or improve the quality of a service or management operation.
  o   Reduce or eliminate a service or management operation.
- **Strategies, Activities, Tasks.** Strategies, activities, or tasks are the specific actions that the library will carry out to achieve its goals and objectives.

Level of Effort

After deciding what planning model to use, determining the level of effort to be used in the planning process is an extremely important decision, one that is usually made by you and/or the library board/governing authority. Level of effort is usually described as basic, moderate, or extensive and characterized as follows:

- **Basic**
  o   Process: Informal
  o   Indicators: This level of effort may be appropriate if a good plan already exists that may be adapted and if there are no major external or internal factors that may affect the library.
  o   Who: Library Director, Library Board, Library Staff
  o   Decisions: Based on the committee's working knowledge and review of existing demographic and library data.
  o   Activities: Most of the planning work is completed within the committee.
  o   Time line: Weeks

(continued)

Figure 10-2   Plan Components (*Continued*)

- **Moderate**
  - o   Process: More Formal
  - o   Indicators: This level of effort may be appropriate when a library senses that a complete re-work of its plan is needed and /or the library faces internal or external changes (funding increases or reductions, community growth or decline, etc.).
  - o   Who: Library Director, Library Board, Library Staff, Community Representatives
  - o   Decisions: Based on a thorough review of demographic and library data as well as information from surveys, focus groups, and similar activities.
  - o   Activities: Community input through focus groups, surveys, etc.
  - o   Timeline: Months
- **Extensive**
  - o   Process: Very Formal
  - o   Indicators: This level of effort may be appropriate if the library desires to conduct an extensive planning process, the library is faced with a crisis, the previous planning effort was not successful, and/or the library is facing significant community change.
  - o   Who: The planning committee includes representatives from all identified stakeholders. Additional consulting and/or project support staff may be needed.
  - o   Decisions: Based on extensive review of library and demographic data, information from surveys, focus groups, interviews. etc., with stakeholders and with nonusers.
  - o   Activities: Extensive data collection and stakeholder input through surveys, focus groups, interviews, public hearings, review by other governing bodies.
  - o   Timeline: Several months to a year

PLANNING TO PLAN

Deciding upon the planning model and the level of effort are two of the more important decisions in planning to plan and basically answer the questions "What?" and "How?" The decision about "Who?" is influenced by the level of effort. Moderate and extensive planning efforts call for more community and stakeholder participation. Staff and the library board should give careful consideration when deciding which community representatives and stakeholders are asked to join the planning effort. A collaborative approach to selecting the planning committee is suggested. The question of "When?" to conduct the planning process will be determined by the library's situation. Requirements to submit a long-range plan and updates to the state library agency will be a factor in determining when to initiate the planning process. A library facing a crisis or significant change in the community will be more pressured to initiate the planning process sooner rather than later. If possible, the planning process should be scheduled to allow for maximum participation. The summer months may not be the best time for planning activities.

DETERMINING WHERE THE LIBRARY IS CURRENTLY

There are several important issues to be addressed as library planners begin this phase of the planning process. What information about the library needs to be reviewed? Likewise, what information about the community should be reviewed? What current library services focus on community needs and with what success? Which libraries should be identified as peer libraries? Who will be responsible for reviewing the information and how will it be presented to library planners? SWOT Analysis (Strengths, Weaknesses, Opportunities, Threats) is a planning tool for examining internal and external conditions. What are the current strengths and weaknesses of the library? In the community, the region, the state, and perhaps nationally, what are the opportunities and threats that may affect the library? SWOT Analysis is also a technique that may be used with other groups, such as library staff, Friends of the Library, focus groups, and community groups.

DECIDING WHERE YOU WANT THE LIBRARY TO BE

When deciding where the library should be, give consideration to the community's vision and that of the library. Where is the library compared to the community vision? What are the community needs? Specifically, which community needs will the library help meet? How will the library through its selected roles or service responses connect with the community needs?

SETTING GOALS, OBJECTIVES, ACTIVITIES

The purpose of goals, objectives, and activities is to provide a guide to get the library from its current status to where you want the library to be. Goals, objectives, and activities should address selected roles or service responses and the community needs that the library has chosen to help meet. Again, goals are general statements that state a desired long-range achievement; objectives describe a measurable result to be accomplished in a specified period of time, activities are specifics that identify how the library will achieve its goals and objectives.

IMPLEMENTING THE PLAN

The basic components in implementing the plan are writing, communicating, and utilizing. In writing the plan, it might be advisable to have a smaller, select number of planners to do the drafting. Keep the audience in mind. If the audience includes the general public, extra effort is needed to be sure the plan is clear, concise, and logical. Library terms that may be unfamiliar should be defined. As the written plan progresses, it is advisable to have the drafts reviewed by the planners, the library staff, and the library board. The final document should be accepted by all the planners and presented to the library board and/or other governing bodies for approval.

In communicating the plan, decide to whom and why. When communicating with internal audiences such as the library staff, the intent may be to persuade and/or direct. With external audiences care should be given to match the communication to the audience. A particular audience may be interested in specific goals and objectives rather than the plan as a whole. When communicating to an audience, give consideration to the amount of information needed, how the message might be tailored to that individual or group, the format to be used—electronic, print, presentation, and the right language.

The plan needs to be used, not placed on a shelf to collect dust. A plan should be the foundation for all library activity—strategic planning, technology planning, business plans, budgeting, employee work plans and evaluations. The planning process involves a major investment of time and resources; use the result effectively.

EVALUATING

Just as planning is an ongoing process, so is evaluation. Periodic evaluation of the plan's effectiveness is desirable and useful in both keeping the library on track with the plan and in making any course adjustments. Things change and as things change it may be necessary to adapt the library plan. Flexibility may be needed. In addition to scheduling formal evaluations through numbers-gathering, surveys, focus groups, interviews, and observation, it may be desirable to schedule periodic informal assessments with key individuals from the library board, library staff, and the community.

CONCLUSION

There is no best way to plan. Differences in communities, libraries, and types of libraries will be reflected in the process, in the strategies and techniques used, and in the final written document. Some libraries will undertake a rigorous planning process; others will pursue a simpler one. An individual library can set its own pace for the planning process. The process is flexible so all libraries can plan for improved services. Each user community deserves the good service that results from effective planning. All libraries, regardless of size, need to plan.

REFERENCES

Giesecke, Joan, ed. 1988. *Scenario planning for libraries.* Chicago: American Library Association.

Hennen, Thomas J. Jr. 2004. *Hennen's public library planner: A manual and interactive CD-ROM.* New York: Neal-Schuman.

Himmel, Ethel, and Bill Wilson. 1998. *Planning for results: A public library transformation process.* Chicago: American Library Association.

Mayo, Dianne, and Jeanne Goodrich. 2002. *Staffing for results: A guide to working smarter.* Chicago: Public Library Association.

Mayo, Dianne, and Sandra Nelson. 1998. *Wired for the future: Developing your library technology plan.* Chicago: Public Library Association.

McClure, Charles et al. 1987. *Planning and role setting for public libraries: A manual of options and procedures.* Chicago: Public Library Association.

Nelson, Sandra et al. 2003. *Creating policies for results: From chaos to clarity.* Chicago: Public Library Association.

Nelson, Sandra et al. 2000. *Managing for results: Effective resource allocation for public libraries.* Chicago: Public Library Association.

Nelson, Sandra et al. 2001. *The new planning for results: A streamlined approach.* Chicago: Public Library Association.

OCLC. 2003 *OCLC Environmental Scan:* Pattern Recognition. Dublin, Ohio: OCLC, 2003.

United Way of America. 1987. *Measuring program outcomes: A practical approach.* New York: United Way of America.

Van House, Nancy. 1987. *Output measures for public libraries: A manual of standardized procedures.* Chicago: American Library Association.

Zweizig, Douglas et al. 1996. *The TELL IT! manual: The complete program for evaluating library performance.* Madison, WI: School of Library and Information Studies.

FURTHER READING

Bremer, Suzanne W. 1994. *Long range planning: A how-to-do-it manual for public libraries.* New York: Neal-Schuman.

Hernon, Peter, and John R. Whitman. 2004. *Delivering satisfaction and service quality: A customer based approach for libraries.* Chicago: American Library Association.

Nelson, William Neal, and Robert Feneches. 2002. *Standards and assessment for academic libraries: A workbook.* Chicago: American Library Association.

11 GOVERNING BOARDS AND GOVERNMENTAL RELATIONS

John A. Moorman

DEFINITION

A governing board is the entity responsible for the operation of the library. Governmental relations refer to the process whereby the library deals with entities that have funding or governing relationships with it.

OVERVIEW

The chapter covers:

- Types of governing boards
- Roles of the director and the governing board in library operations
- Examples of board and director evaluation documents
- Ideas for good governmental relations

TYPES OF GOVERNING BOARDS

Libraries have many different types of governing boards.

- School librarians generally report to the principal of the school they serve. In turn, the school board governs the school.
- Special libraries usually report to someone within the hierarchy of the entity of which they are a part. This individual, in turn, reports to the entity's board. It could be a for-profit company's board of directors, a legal firm's partnership board, or a hospital's board of directors.
- Public libraries have a wide variety of governance. Some libraries report directly to the governmental entity, be it a city or county without any sort of an advisory board. Other libraries have a board of trustees, which may have full or partial governing authority for the operation of the library. These boards may be appointed or elected. A third type of public library governance is the district library where the library serves a legally defined area and the board is elected with taxing and full governing authority.
- Academic libraries generally report to an institutional administrator who, in turn, reports to the board of the institution.

ROLES

The relationship between the library's governing body and the director of the library is a major determining factor in how successful the operation of the library will be. It is important that each party understands its role in the operation of the library and adheres to that role in library operations.

> Role of board:
> - Set policy
> - Hire director
> - Determine budget
> - Other duties as specified by company policy or law

A good board member will also have a working knowledge of all laws applicable to the library, be well acquainted with the community, have a working relationship with those who serve on municipal and county councils, regularly attend meetings of the board and participate in regional and national conferences and workshops to enhance his/her knowledge and skills.

The director's role is to operate the library under the guidance of thepolicy established by the board. He/She should have final authority over who is hired to staff the library, set procedures based upon board policy for library operations, and represent the library on local, state, and national levels. A good director, like a board member, should know the local and state officials with whom he/she needs to come into contact in the course of operating a library. The director should actively seek out opportunities through workshop and conference attendance to upgrade and enhance his/her skills.

Any successful library operation requires a partnership between the director and the board. While policy determination is the role of the board, the director and staff need to play an advisory role in the setting of any board policy. Good policy is the result of staff experience and knowledge, coupled with the board's understanding of and appreciation for the community the library serves.

ESSENTIALS FOR A GOOD BOARD-DIRECTOR RELATIONSHIP

What are the essentials for a good board-director relationship? There are six factors that are core to establishing and maintaining a good relationship. These are:

- Hiring process
- Trust
- Respect
- Honesty
- Communication
- Accountability

In hiring a director, the board must take the time to make certain that the individual chosen for the position is the one that best fits the needs of the institution and the community that the library serves. Sometimes in the desire to complete the search process the board may select an individual who does not quite fit the needs of the library or with whom the board does not have a level of comfort. The concept that "Oh well, she/he will grow into the position" is a very dangerous one and usually does not work.

Do not take a job about which you have doubts.

Likewise, before accepting an offer to become a director of a library, the individual needs to look closely at the board as well as at the institution, its staff, and the community it serves. If there is doubt that the board is one that the individual can work with, the individual should heed his/her instincts and look elsewhere for employment.

Trust is the key to any successful board-director relationship. There has to be trust by both the board and the director that each will act within acceptable boundaries, that each has the best interests of the library in mind, and that each can be counted upon to act wisely when any situation arises.

How is trust established? It is the end result of the final four factors. There must be respect by each party for the other party. The board must respect the director for his/her skills and knowledge and likewise the director must respect board members for what they bring to their role as board members. Respect is shown by how each is addressed both in public and in private and how well ideas and concerns are received, listened to, and acted on.

Without honesty no successful board-director relationship can endure. Sometimes honesty is painful and can hurt, but it is essential to establishing and maintaining any successful relationship and the board-director relationship is no different. Both parties need to be honest about their perceptions of library operations, services, relationships with the community and its leaders, and how they perceive each other. Both the board and the director need to be able to accept that neither is perfect and acknowledge when mistakes are made (as they always will be). Sometimes the hardest thing to say is, " I made a mistake on this one," but that acknowledgment is an essential part of any successful relationship.

Communication is at the core of developing and continuing this positive relationship. There are many means of communication, some better than others. Good communication contains several core elements: it is regular, operates through agreed upon channels, is done in a respectful manner, and takes into consideration the needs of the institution and the time needs and expectations of both the board and the director. Both the board and the director should work diligently to see that neither is caught by surprise over any action or event. If either is blindsided by something then it is time to seriously examine the channels and methods of communication. The ability to disagree civilly and with respect for each other is a skill that is often lacking but is an essential part of the communication process.

Accountability is the final factor in the establishment of a good board-director relationship. There are two elements to this factor. The first is that the board and the director both must accept accountability for their actions. It is easy to blame the other party for what went wrong and it might work for a short time, but in the long run it is fatal for the relationship. The second is that both parties must continually look at themselves and evaluate their performance and progress.

I believe that it is just as important for the board to evaluate itself as it is for it to evaluate the librarian. A good tool for a board to use to evaluate themselves is the following document: Figure 11-1 offers a few questions that will help you focus on how well your board is doing.

Figure 11-1   Evaluating the Board

---

1. Do we as a library board meet regularly and have a written agenda distributed in advance?
2. Do all of our board members attend the meetings regularly?
3. Does each member actively participate in the discussion and decisions?
4. As a board do we plan an orientation program for new members?
5. Has the library adopted a written statement of clear and specific objectives, which serves as a basis of services and activities?
6. Is there a written policy manual?
7. Are the statements of objectives reviewed every year and revised if necessary?
8. Is our librarian included in board meetings and expected to present a monthly report to the board, either written or oral?
9. Does our board report regularly to the appropriating body and to the community with statistical, financial and human interest facts?
10. Do members of the board and staff attend system and state library meetings?
11. Does the library provide funds to pay expenses of such meetings?
12. Are you familiar with the state statutes and city ordinances that govern your library operation?
13. Are you familiar with local library history?
14. If all the other trustees were to resign tomorrow, would you be prepared to take over, at least temporarily, as president?
15. When visiting another town, do you ever go to its library to look around?
16. Do you attend all meetings of the board?
17. Do you do your library homework?
18. Are you courteous to fellow trustees, even when you disagree with them?
19. Does the librarian, after gathering the appropriate information, meet with the board or a committee of the board to determine budget needs?
20. Is our budget estimate based on the current year's expenditures plus cost changes, expanded service, standards of good services, and the library's objectives?
21. Does the board formally adopt the budget at an official meeting before submitting it to the governing body?
22. Do members of the board participate in the presentation of the budget to the governing body?

(continued)

Figure 11-1   Evaluating the Board (*Continued*)

---

23. Do you have a policy for accepting gifts, monetary as well as real property?
24. Are you taking full advantage of all existing funding programs—local, system, and state?
25. Is a systematic accounting of funds maintained by the librarian or someone delegated to this particular job?
26. Do all board members receive monthly financial statements that include the budget, current, and year-to-date expenditures with balances for each line item?
27. Do you have written, up-to-date job descriptions for all positions?
28. Are your salaries comparable to those paid in your community for comparable work, and also to the scale of other libraries of comparable size?
29. Does your staff have vacation and sick leave with pay, and an opportunity to participate in Social Security, retirement, and health insurance?
30. Does your staff have comfortable working conditions such as adequate light, heat, ventilation, and work- and restrooms?
31. Is your staff encouraged and helped to get in-service training through paid time and travel expenses to attend professional meetings and workshops?
32. Does your library service all parts of the community: geographic, economic, educational, occupational, social, retired, etc.?
33. Is the library dedicated to real service rather than to mere storage of books?
34. Does your collection meet the needs of the entire community?
35. Does the library take full advantage of the services offered by the library system?
36. Do you visit your library regularly?
37. Do you let your librarian administer the policies you make?

Source: Swan, James. *Working Together: A How-To-Do-It Manual for Trustees and Librarians.* New York: Neal-Schuman, 1992, pp. 37–39. Used with permission.

This document should be looked at on an annual basis and the results of the evaluation used in planning board activities and training. The director is the hire of the board and should be evaluated by the board on an annual basis. Several approaches can be used for this evaluation; see Figure 11-2 for an example.

Figure 11–2   Director Performance Appraisal

**Board of Trustees
Annual Performance Appraisal
Library Director**

Colleagues:

Please complete this form with a numerical rating and comments that support your rating:

5 = Outstanding. Performance exceeds performance standard to a significant degree.

4 = Exceeds Performance Standard. Performance goes beyond performance standard to some degree.

3 = Fully Meets Performance Standard. Performance completely meets performance standard.

2 = Partially Meets Performance Standard. Performance needs improvement to meet performance standard.

1 = Below Performance Standard. Performance fails to meet performance standard.

<u>**Ongoing responsibilities:**</u>

1. Administers the library according to approved Board policies. _____.
2. Provides an adequate number of highly qualified staff members necessary to meet the needs of library patrons in a professional manner _____.
3. Prepares the budget in consultation with the Board and regularly updates the Board on current expenditures. _____
4. Communicates his vision for the development and improvement of the library to his staff, the Board and the community through the establishment of short- and long-range strategic planning goals for the library. _____
5. Oversees the library's program of public relations, including, but not limited to, active participation in community groups, such as Rotary, Chamber of Commerce, local newspapers, willingness to speak to community groups, etc., to inform and promote library services and activities. _____
6. Keeps abreast of advances in library service, is active in library organizations, and attends appropriate meetings, workshops, and conferences. _____
7. Develops and maintains professional working relationships with city and county officials and staff and local state legislators that are beneficial to the operation of the library. _____

(continued)

Figure 11–2   Director Performance Appraisal (*Continued*)

Board relations:

8. Facilitates open and honest communication between administration, staff and Board. _____
9. Regularly reviews and updates policies for adoption/revision by the Board. _____
10. Implements Board decisions in a timely manner. _____
11. Acts as technical advisor to the Board and keeps them informed of changes in library legislation and standards.

Staff relations:

12. Delegate's responsibility and authority to staff members in a way that empowers them to do their jobs well and is perceived as fair and equitable. _____
13. Encourages and offers regular opportunities for training and development. _____
14. Sets an example for the staff by exhibiting integrity, honesty, dependability in dealing with staff, public and Board. _____.

Specific goals for Current Year:

List goals developed at the last evaluation with space for individual comment after each goal.

How would you rate the overall job performance of the Library Director (taking into consideration your own assessment and the assessment of his performance by his department heads? _____

What suggestions for improvement would you offer?

Please consider the following question that we will discuss in CLOSED MEETING:

What suggestion would you make for a salary adjustment (e.g., county cost-of-living increase? An amount or percentage beyond that?

Williamsburg Regional Library, 2005. Used with permission.

Whatever approach used should be consistent, fair, and useful and a tool for further growth and development.

What causes a board-director relationship to go sour? Usually it is the result of one or more of the factors above becoming absent. Communication is poor, respect nonexistent, trust is lacking, honesty gone or expressed in counterproductive ways, and accountability for actions has vanished from the scene. How can the situation be corrected? Depending upon the severity, several steps are possible. If it is minor, the board and director can sit down and work through their differences and hopefully reestablish a good working relationship. However, in many cases the rupture is beyond simple repair and other remedies are needed. These vary from calling in local individuals skilled in conflict resolution to work with the board and director to hiring special consultants who have experience working with board and directors in such settings, or to request the help of outside agencies with experience in board-director relationships. One good source for locating assistance would be the library development department of your state library. This entity should have a variety of resources available to consult.

If all else fails then there are two options, neither one easy nor pleasant. The director is the employee of the board and usually serves at its pleasure, particularly in the public library setting. However, the director may have a contract, which specifies certain obligations on the part of both parties and outlines how the contract may be terminated. Thus, the first option is that the director is fired or asked to resign. The second is that the director resigns, as he/she cannot fire the board. Sometimes one or the other is the only result possible. If either happens it should be handled in a respectful manner by both parties, although that is often not the case.

GOVERNMENTAL RELATIONS

The secret to establishing a successful working relationship with local government entities is much the same as that for working successfully with a library board. There must be trust, respect, and good communication for the relationship to succeed.

The working relationship between the board and local government is a cooperative venture between the board and the director. Hopefully, the library board contains individuals that have friendships or good working relationships with members of the local governing boards, whether they are city or county. Always make good use of these relationships. Also understand if there are difficulties between certain board members and certain members of either city or county governing bodies.

The library director should work to establish good working relationships between him/her and the administrative heads of local government. In some instances, the relationship will of necessity be closer than others as the library director may be considered a department of the local entity and the library board only an advisory one. Again, the skills to work on are good communication, respect for each other, and honesty. A good understanding of the local political scene and how it operates is essential to working with local government. Without that any library director will never be successful in his/her relationship with local government.

In working with library directors, boards, local government, and administration at all levels it is essential that the individual or the entity as a collective body give whomever they are dealing with the same respect, honesty, trust, and communication that they expect to receive. The whole of this chapter can be summed up succinctly in the phrase "Do unto others as you would have them do unto you." All the rest is but icing on the cake.

CONCLUSION

There are three essential elements to any successful working relationship, including the ones discussed in this chapter. These elements are respect, trust, and good communication. While good communication can begin at the start of any relationship, trust and respect must be earned, which takes time and effort, but their accomplishment is at the core of good library relationships.

REFERENCES

Swan, James. 1992. *Working together: A how-to-do-it manual for trustees and librarians*. New York: Neal-Schuman.

Williamsburg Regional Library. 2005. *Director's evaluation form*. Williamsburg, VA. Williamsburg Regional Library.

FURTHER READING

Bielefield, Arlene and Lawrence Cheeseman. 2002. *Trustees, friends, and the law*. New York: Neal-Schuman.

Matthews, Joseph R. 2002. *The bottom line: determining and communicating the value of the special library*. Westport, Conn: Libraries Unlimited.

Moore, Mary Y. 2004. *The successful library trustee handbook*. Chicago: American Library Association.

Reed, Sally Gardner. 2001. *Making the case for your library: a how-to-do-it manual*. New York: Neal-Schuman.

Wade, Gordon S. 1991. *Working with library boards: a how-to-do-it manual*. New York: Neal-Schuman.

12 FRIENDS GROUPS AND FOUNDATIONS

John A. Moorman

DEFINITION

Friends of the Library and Library Foundations are organizations that exist solely to support the library with which they are affiliated. They are 501-C3 non-profit entities as recognized by the Internal Revenue Service.

OVERVIEW

If the funds available to the small library from its funding sources were adequate to cover all library needs as well as providing for special programs and services there would be no need for either Friends Groups or Foundations. However, that is not the case. While there are a lucky few small libraries with ample resources, they are the rare exception. For the rest, dependence on Friends Groups and/or Foundations is necessary if that special or enhanced program is to be provided, that new or renovated facility will have all the furnishings desired, or if new or innovative programs or collections will be possible. While there are Friends groups in special and school libraries and Foundations from which they may draw assistance, they are the exception rather than the rule. In discussing Friends groups and Foundations this chapter will be a reflection of the public and academic library experience.

This chapter covers:

- Friends Groups and how they may be started
- Template for Friends Group bylaws

- Friends Group fundraising and contributions to the library
- Foundations and their startup
- Care and feeding of both Friends Groups and Foundations

FRIENDS GROUPS

Friends Groups, commonly referred to as Friends of the Library, are entities whose sole purpose is to support the activities of the library of which they are a part. Through a variety of fundraising activities, to be discussed later, monies are raised that are then made available for library programs, services, or projects.

How are Friends Groups formed? While there may be a group of citizens with interest in the library who come to the director or governing board with the desire to assist the library, in most cases, the library director takes the initiative and works with the Board of Trustees and interested citizens to begin the Friends Group. Before a Friends Group is to be started the following questions need to have a positive answer:

- Is there sufficient interest in forming the Friends Group?
- Are there individuals who are capable of taking a leadership role?
- Do those interested in forming the Friends Group know the role and limitations of a Friends Group?
- Does the formation of the Friends Group have the active support of the Board of Trustees or library governing body?
- Does the Library have projects in mind for the Friends Group?
- Is there sufficient seed money to get the Friends Group started?
- Is the library director willing and able to take the time necessary for the formation of the Friends Group?

Once all these questions have been answered in the affirmative the group is ready to be formed. In addition for a Friends Group to be effectively organized it needs incorporation papers, a set of bylaws, and 501-C3 status with the Internal Revenue Service.

The first step to getting organized is to get the group of interested citizens together, explain to them the purpose and role of the Friends Group and solicit initial volunteers to serve on the organizing board. Generally, the library director working with the Board of Trustees will hand select this first group. This group then becomes those listed in the incorporation papers filed with the office of the Secretary of State. This is a simple process with a small cost involved.

While the library director can manage this step and the other steps of starting a Friends Group it is best to involve an attorney in all steps of the process. This is where seed money comes in. Generally, it is wise to have on hand $1,000 to get the Friends Group started. Some groups will have a local attorney who will be willing to do the work involved pro bono. However, even with this assistance it will cost up to $500 to get 501-C3 status determination from the IRS.

Once the Incorporation papers have been received from the Secretary of State's office the next step is to develop bylaws for the Friends Group. Figure 12-1 is a template for Friends bylaws developed from the author's 30 years of experience with Friends Groups:

Figure 12-1   Friends Bylaws

**Bylaws of
Friends of Any Library**

Article 1   Name

The name of this organization shall be Friends of Anylibrary.

Article II   Purpose

The purpose of this organization is to create public interest in and greater use of the Anytown Library, to provide financial support to the Library, and to sponsor cultural and related programs. The intention is to supplement and encourage the work of the staff of the Library with the Friends, a separate group, supportive rather than authoritative.

Article III   Membership

Membership in this organization shall be open to all individuals, organizations, businesses, and clubs, in sympathy with its purposes.

Each organization or individual member shall be entitled to one vote.

Article IV   Officers

The officers of this organization shall be a President, Vice-President, Secretary, and Treasurer.

Officers shall be recruited and nominated by a committee chosen by the Board defined in Article VI. The nominations shall be submitted in writing to the membership two weeks prior to the annual meeting. Additional nominations may be made from the floor at the annual meeting with the consent of the nominee.

Officers shall be elected by a majority vote of those members in good standing present at the annual meeting. The term of office shall be for one year and shall begin on the first day of January following the annual meeting.

Vacancies shall be filled by appointment by the Board until the next regular election.

Article V   Duties of Officers

The officers shall have the usual duties and authorities customarily exercised by officers of a non-profit organization.

The President shall be an ex-officio member of all committees.

The Vice-President shall succeed to the President's position upon the inability of the President to serve in that office.

The elected officials shall set up the necessary standing committees. The chairs of the committees and at-large members of the Board shall be appointed by the President. Each chair shall select that committee's members.

Article VI   Board

The Board shall consist of the elected officers of the organization, the appointed committee chairs, and members-at-large. The Library Director and the Chair of the Board of Trustees shall serve as ex-officio members of the Board.

(continued)

Figure 12-1   Friends Bylaws (*Continued*)

Meetings of the Board shall be held at least four times a year. The President may call special meetings.

Members of the Board are expected to attend all regular board meetings. Any member of the Board who misses half of the meetings in any calendar year may be asked to resign by a majority decision of the officers of the Board.

One-half of the members of the Board shall constitute a quorum.

Article VII   Meetings

The organization shall hold at least one meeting a year.

The annual meeting shall be held on a date, to be determined by the Board, near the end of the fiscal year. Members shall be notified in writing at least one month prior to the date of the meeting.

The Board may call a special meeting of this organization at any time.

Only those members in good standing shall be allowed to vote at any meeting.

Article VIII   Dues

Dues shall be paid annually and are good for one year's membership from date of payment. The Board shall set the membership contribution schedule and categories.

Article IX   Fiscal Year

The fiscal year shall be from January 1 to December 31. All funds shall be deposited to the account of Friends of Anytown Library and shall be disbursed by the Treasurer as authorized by the elected officers or the Board.

Article X   Disposition of Assets upon Dissolution

In the event that this organization is terminated or dissolved, all assets belonging to the organization will be transferred to the Anytown Library to be disposed of as recommended by the Library Board of Trustees; however, if the named recipient is not then in existence or is no longer a qualified distributee or is unwilling or unable to accept the distribution, the assets of this organization shall be distributed to a fund, foundation, or corporation organized exclusively for purposes specified in Section 501 C3 of the Internal Revenue Code.

Article XI   Amendments

Amendments to these Bylaws may be made at any meeting of the general membership by a two-thirds vote of those present and in good standing. Notification in writing of the proposed amendments shall be given to each member at least two weeks before the meeting at which voting is to take place.

Article XII   Parliamentary Procedure

Roberts Rules of Order for Small Groups, Revised, when not in conflict with these Bylaws shall govern the proceedings of this organization.

Once the bylaws have been approved, then comes the process of obtaining 501-C3 status with the Internal Revenue Service. This can be a lengthy process. In most cases the Friends Group will obtain a preliminary certification from the IRS good for a certain number of years. At the end of this time, paperwork must be filed to show that the Friends Group is doing what was intended in the initial request to obtain permanent certification.

> Besides local attorneys these sources can assist you in filing 501-C3 papers with the IRS, www.foundationgroup.com and www.links2charity.com.

Paperwork for the initial certification is substantial. As mentioned above, it is best to have the assistance of an attorney in completing the paperwork and communicating with the IRS during the process. Information required for this step includes the group's incorporation papers, bylaws, information about the parent organization, and a fundraising plan and budget for several years' operation. The IRS charges for 501-C3 certification and it can cost upwards of $500 to obtain this certification. However, this is an essential step for without it contributors to the Friends Group will not be able to take a tax-deduction for their contribution.

> It is important that the Library Director be an ex-officio member of the Friends Board.

A solid connection between the Friends and the library is important in the establishment and operation of the Friends Group. Some Friends Groups can, due to Board member interests, become disengaged from their purpose and seek to serve other roles such as supporting groups other than the library or become interested in day-to-day library operations. As indicated in the sample bylaws it is important to have the library director and the president of the Board of Trustees as ex-officio members of the Friends Board. This gives the Friends information on wider library operations and helps them to feel more a part of the library's service to the community. The library director needs to work closely with the Friends Board and serve as the point person for the presentation of library needs to the Friends.

FRIENDS FUNDRAISING

In order to support library operations the Friends Group will need a source of income. Many Friends Groups use used book sales as their primary source of income. Whether the sales are annual, semi-annual, monthly, or combined with an ongoing Friends Book Sale in the library these events need a core of volunteers to be successful.

Questions that need to be positively answered prior to conducting a sale include:

- Is there a sufficient source of books and materials for the sale?
- Can weeded library materials be included in the sale?
- Is there adequate storage for materials between sales?
- How willing and able is library staff to assist with sale setup and take down?
- If you are planning an ongoing book sale is there adequate display space for books in the library?
- Does the Friends Group have adequate volunteer labor to conduct the sales?
- Is there committed leadership among the Friends Group to organize and conduct the sale?

Another question that must be faced before starting book sales as a source of revenue is whether this is a niche in your community that is already taken by another group. If so can you work with this group to include the Friends as a part of their operation? If not, it might be best to look at other fundraising opportunities.

What are other fundraising opportunities? They are as many as there are libraries. One popular source is a Friends Gift Shop in the library. This can be a valuable source of revenue. However, before beginning such an operation the following questions need to be addressed:

- Is there space in the library for such an operation?
- Is this space in a prominent location and is there a long-term commitment to use this space for a Friends Gift Shop?
- Are there enough volunteers to keep the shop open on a regular schedule?
- Is there a niche in the community that the Friends Shop could exploit, so that it will provide a unique source of items for sale?

- Does the shop have the support of the library director and the Board of Trustees?
- Is there a business plan for the shop's operation that indicates its viability?

If these questions have positive answers then this could be a good source of income as well as a way to inform the community about the Friends Group and garner additional members.

FRIENDS ROLE

The sole purpose of the Friends as indicated in the bylaws above should be to assist the library in improving its services and programs. It is important that the library director has a strong voice in selecting the ways that the Friends assist the library. He/She knows the library needs and can prioritize them for the Friends and suggest ways in which their funds could be best used.

Some Friends groups place limitations on what their funds may be used for and others do not. Limitations might include using funding for collections and programs only or for special areas of the library such as children's materials and programming. Some Friends Groups sponsor the library newsletter or special programs, or an annual lecture series. However the Friends support the library it is important that the rationale behind the decision is understood and agreed to by the Friends, the library director and the Board of Trustees.

LIBRARY FOUNDATIONS

Library foundations have a similar purpose to Friends Groups in that their sole role is to obtain funds for the library. Where they differ is in their emphasis. Whereas the Friends serve to assist the library on a short-term basis through support of programs and special events, the Foundation is more long term in nature. It works to establish an endowment and manage that endowment to provide funds for projects that are more major in nature, such as building projects, or major purchases such as outreach vehicles or long-term support of collection areas or programs. There will also be the need for expertise in financial management on the Foundation Board.

A library foundation is set up similar to the Friends Group. It needs incorporation papers, bylaws, and must file with the IRS for 501-C3 status. Without the 501-C3 designation, donors to the foundation will not be able to claim their donations as tax-deductible on their income tax returns. In addition, the foundation will need to adopt an investment policy.

Before beginning a foundation in a small library the following questions need to be asked:

- Is there a need for a foundation or can the Friends Group be expanded to serve this role as well?
- Are there long-term library needs that would benefit from the formation of a foundation?
- Are there community resources that can be tapped to provide funding for a foundation, i.e., wealthy individuals or community businesses with donation possibility?
- Is there a sufficient source of capable board members for the foundation and a commitment on these individual's behalf to serve?
- Is there support from the library director and Board of Trustees for the establishment of the foundation?

Once these questions are answered the formation of the Foundation can proceed. The bylaws will be similar in nature to the Friends Group. Many library foundations are closed groups with the membership being the Board of the Foundation. In some libraries, the Board of Trustees of the library selects board members. In any case, the library director and president of the Board of Trustees should be ex-officio members of the foundation board.

Sometimes library foundations are set up as the result of a large donation through a bequest to the library. This is fine, but the above questions need to be answered before the foundation is established. There may be other ways of accepting a large bequest.

The foundation, unlike the Friends Group, needs to have plans in place for increasing its funding base. This means working with local attorneys, banks, insurance agents, and certified public accountants to make their clients aware of the foundation's availability as a recipient to receive resources for continued community growth and enhancement.

CARE AND FEEDING OF FRIENDS GROUPS AND FOUNDATIONS

Both Friends Groups and library foundations can wither on the vine. Like grapes they need constant care and tending to produce successful results for the library and its users.

Factors in the care and feeding of these groups include:

- Make sure that there is constant communication between the library and both Friends and Foundation. Have joint meetings of all bodies on a regular basis to share programs and ideas.
- Provide both groups with fundable projects and programs so that they will continue to feel needed and a part of the library effort.
- Head off early any attempt to deviate from their established purpose of assisting the library.
- Have a commitment by the library director to be an active participant in the processes and work programs of both groups.

Another unstated role of the library director and Board of Trustees is working with local funding agencies to make certain that these bodies understand that funds from these sources are not to be considered a part of the library's normal revenue stream, that is, that a Friends or Foundation dollar does not allow the funding agencies to drop their contributions to the library by that amount. This can be difficult but is essential if the Friends Group and/or foundation is to be successful in its role and mission in support of the library.

CONCLUSION

Friends Groups and library Foundations can be a vital component of the services that the small library provides to its community. Through being a source of additional funding beyond that available through governmental or parent body appropriations they enable the library to increase and enrich the programs and services offered to library users. They may also make it possible to have new or expanded facilities years earlier than otherwise possible.

For a library director, either group can be a godsend. However, do not underestimate the time and commitment that either group will take of a director's time if they are to be successful. A library director will need additional skills as well as time because Friends groups and Foundations are made up of individuals with egos and agendas of their own and for the group to work as a harmonious whole diplomacy and tact will be needed on a regular basis. Do not hesitate to use praise and recognition (sometimes even more than actually warranted) for this is the only payment these individuals will receive.

Does a small library need both groups? Not necessarily. Know your own community and know who has the time and willingness to volunteer their services to the library. In many instances, the Friends Group may be expanded to include the functions served by a Library Foundation.

This chapter is combining the "Further Reading" and "References" section as the material listed is core material useful in working with both Friends and Foundations. Also, the development of the chapter comes from the author's over 30 years of experience with Friends Groups and Foundations in four states. Chapter 14, "Development," goes into further detail on how libraries may raise additional funds to provide programs and services.

REFERENCES/FURTHER READING

Friends of the Library U.S.A. *www.folusa.org.*
Herring, Mark Y. 2004. *Raising funds with friends groups: A how-to-do-it manual for librarians.* New York: Neal-Schuman.
Reed, Sally et al. 2004. *101+ great ideas for libraries and friends.* New York: Neal-Schuman.
Swan, James. 2002. *Fundraising for libraries: 25 proven ways to get more money for your library.* New York: Neal-Schuman.
Taft Group. 2005. *The big book of library grant money 2006.* Chicago: American Library Association.

13 COMMUNITY PARTNERSHIP

Janet Crowther and Barry Trott

DEFINITION

Partnerships are formal, collaborative efforts between two or more community organizations that support the mission and goals of each of the participants.

OVERVIEW

This chapter covers:

- Partnerships for libraries using the Williamsburg Regional Library model
- Issues, challenges, and opportunities that collaborative efforts afford libraries
- Realities of partnering for small libraries

INTRODUCTION

The phrase "library partnerships" generates hundreds of thousands of hits in a search on the Internet. Libraries of all sizes say that they are partnering to achieve their goals. However, when libraries describe their partnering efforts, there does not seem to be any consistent definition of what the word partnership means. Since developing a formal partnering program involves a commitment of staff and resources, it is especially important for small and medium-size libraries to have a clear definition of what partnering means before they set out to establish collaborative ventures.

Partnerships and partnering have become important to libraries of all sizes for a variety of reasons. Businesses, non-profits, and government agencies are all looking to establish collaborative efforts. It is useful to understand what drives these different sectors to look for partnerships. In many cases, these sectors will seek out partnerships for financial reasons. As budgets are cut at the local, state, and national levels, non-profits and government agencies may seek out partnering opportunities to supplement declining revenues or to bolster decreased budgets. For all three of these sectors, partnerships offer the opportunity to increase visibility in the community and to establish leadership in the community on specific issues. At the same time, partnerships can also be a way for organizations to maintain a positive community image. Increasingly, grant funding organizations either require or reward collaboration, making partnering essential to organizations that operate with grant-based funding. All of these groups, businesses in particular, may look at partnering as a way to gain access to new customers and to expand the markets for their services.

For these reasons, and more, partnering is a strategic direction that can provide opportunities for libraries. Partnerships offer libraries a new way to engage their communities. Rather than working at the grassroots level, trying to reach individuals one at a time, partnering works through gatekeepers in the community. The library establishes a relationship with these gatekeeper organizations, and works through them to expand its reach into the community.

Libraries have every reason to be wary of faddish management trends, having seen the rise and fall of everything from TQM (total quality management) to team management. Is partnering just another in this line? We would argue not. Rather than being an internally focused process (as most management trends are), partnering is external, focused on the community and the library's role therein. Since the mission of any library, public, academic, or special is directed at serving its community and demands engagement with that community, partnership development will continue to be an important mechanism that libraries can use to fulfill their missions.

WHAT IS A PARTNERSHIP?

Partnering is a strategic tool used to achieve the library's goals. It is one of many tools that libraries can use as they seek to fulfill their missions. Many libraries would define partnering broadly, as simply working with another institution to develop a program or service. However, a true partnership between organizations is one that involves shared goals, visions, and responsibilities, and that involves a long-term commitment by both partners.

The Williamsburg Regional Library (WRL), a medium-size public library in southeastern Virginia, has developed a partnership program that balances the needs of the library and its partners. In order to capture the variety of possible collaborative relationships with all parts of the community, the Williamsburg Regional Library developed a tiered approach to partnering that includes those onetime events with another organization as well as the more involved and expansive relationships that are true partnerships.

The Williamsburg Regional Library partnering model establishes four levels of partnership (Fig. 13-1) that take place between the library and a community entity: glances, dates, engagements, and marriages:

Figure 13-1   Four Levels of Partnership

- **Glances** are any form of contact between the library and an outside organization. A glance can range from a phone conversation or e-mail from an outside group to a visit or participation in a meeting. A glance is the most basic level of contact between two organizations.

- **Dates** are any onetime or short-term collaboration between the library and an outside organization. Most library outreach efforts would usually fit into this category. A date usually involves a specific event or program that the library puts on with some collaboration from a community partner.

- **Engagements** are more formal arrangements between the library and a community partner to pursue some longer-term goals. Engagements by their very nature usually either evolve into marriages or dissolve. The engagement is a way for the partners to try out a relationship without making an extensive long-term commitment. Grant-funded collaborations, supported by soft money, can be an example of an engagement between the library and a partner.

- **Marriages** are long-term collaborative agreements. They should include a formal, written agreement between the library and the community partner in which the partners agree to common goals, develop initiatives, and share in both the risks and rewards of the relationship. Marriages are established where there is an opportunity for each of the partners to bring resources of similar value to the relationship, and commit to an ongoing alliance.

Regardless of how your library decides to define partnering, it is essential that there be agreement within the institution about what a partnership is. This definition will be useful both internally and externally. Within the library, a clear understanding of partnering makes it easier for staff to see how partnership development fits within the mission of the library. Externally, a clear definition of what a partnership is means that possible partners will be better able to understand what the library needs to get out of a collaboration.

There are many tools that libraries can use to achieve their goals. Marketing the library's resources and services can bring new users into the library. Library outreach programs take the resources and services of the institution out into the community, reaching users who may not be able to physically access the library resources. Working with funding bodies and library boards to build the library's assets by adding additional internal resources is an essential ingredient to remain viable. All of these tools are important ways that libraries can advance their missions and best serve their users. Community partnership development is simply another mechanism that libraries can use to achieve their vision. These tools are by no means mutually exclusive, and libraries should explore all of them as they plan for the future.

THE WILLIAMSBURG REGIONAL LIBRARY PARTNERING MODEL

The partnering model developed by the Williamsburg Regional Library is based on several principles.

- Partnering needs to be done strategically, and flows from the organization's strategic plan.
- In order to develop partnerships, a library must assess what it can offer to potential partners. By developing this list of assets and strengths, it will be better able to see what it is that the institution can bring to a collaborative effort.
- All segments of the community are considered potential partners.
- Few other institutions in a community reach as broad a population as does the public library. This is one of the strengths that the library brings to any potential partnership.

- Partnering is a library-wide effort. To be successful, library partnering efforts need to be embraced by everyone in the organization, from the library board through administration to library staff.
- Partnering is a formal process, and involves establishing structures.
- To succeed at community partnering, establish clear communication channels both within the library and between the library and its partners.
- The developing and managing of partnerships needs to follow directions established by the library.
- Periodically evaluate both individual partnerships and partnering as a tool.

PARTNERING IS SCALEABLE

It is important for libraries to understand that developing a community partnering program will require staff time and resources. This can be a particular concern for smaller libraries that may not be rich in either of these areas. It is important for smaller institutions to remember that it is possible to scale partnering programs to the needs and size of almost any library. In fact, partnering offers some particular advantages to smaller libraries that can make the time spent on developing a partnering program even more worthwhile. Choosing the right partner can actually save the library time by: (1) allowing small libraries to bundle initiatives together, and (2) by developing collaborative relationships, the library can reach out into the community in a more focused fashion. For instance, rather than working with each of the individual schools in one's community, the library can partner with the school system, and combine all of its school-related projects under a single relationship.

Figure 13-2   Williamsburg/James City County Schools Partnership

---

For many years, the Williamsburg Regional Library (WRL) provided a variety of programs and services to the Williamsburg/James City County Public Schools (WJCC). These included class-room reading visits, library tours, author programs, and database training for media specialists and students. As the library began to explore the value of collaborative relationships, it became clear that the existing relationship with the schools provided the foundation for a more formal partnership to be developed. The partnership between the library and the schools is based on four principles:

1. The mission statements, core values, and goals of WRL and WJCC reflect common purposes to support the educational goals of students and their families; and to work collaboratively through the community to achieve excellence.
2. Historically, the library has been an active participant in enriching area schools' access to children's programming, library collections, student study space, and meeting room space for adult education. Formalizing this relationship acknowledges the value of the library's support. It also creates a strengthened framework that will enable the relationship to grow through systemwide planning and coordination.
3. While the partnership draws on the unique strengths of the two institutions it also benefits from serving the same city-county population.
4. The community is best served by the library and school system working together toward common goals.

   The goal of the relationship is to (a) "bring a love of reading and books to area students; (b) teach students to access and analyze information in all formats; and (c) support individuals in their goals for lifelong learning."

   This partnership has brought all of the services and programs that the library offers to the schools together under a single umbrella. In this fashion, we have been able to make better use of library resources and staff time, and avoid duplication of effort between library depart-ments. At the same time, the library has also been able to offer these services and programs to schools in a more consistent way. Rather than simply reacting to an individual principal or teacher coming to ask for a program, we can now work through the communication mecha-nisms established by the partnership to offer programs more directly to all the schools, so that no school feels left out. In addition, this partnership has expanded the opportunities for the library to reach both students and teachers. The library now hosts a luncheon for new teachers prior to the start of school to introduce them to the resources and services that the library offers. Working with the media specialists, the library has also been able to expand the promotion of its database collection to students and teachers. The library has seen signifi-cant increases in database use in the past few years, attributable in part to the relationship with the schools. The partnership with the schools has also allowed us to tap into student and

(continued)

Figure 13-2 Williamsburg/James City County Schools Partnership (*Continued*)

---

faculty interests as we plan for the future. As part of a project to improve services to teens, the library worked through the schools' partnership to survey middle and high school students about their needs and interests. During a recent round of strategic planning, the schools helped us to set up student focus groups to gain insight into what directions teens thought would be best for the library. An additional benefit that the library has gained from formalizing its relationship with the schools is the recognition that the library does a great deal to support the school system. Bringing all of the library's work with the schools under the partnership reinforces the two-way nature of the relationship between the schools and the library. Each institution has roles and responsibilities that they must take on for the partnership to be successful. Formalizing the collaboration ensures that neither partner is bearing all of the responsibilities, and that each partner is gaining what it needs to be successful.

- By working through organizations that are community gatekeepers, the library can reach a broader audience than it could on its own.

How does the library scale its partnering efforts? It is essential to ensure that whatever partnering efforts take place are closely tied to the library's mission and vision. Partnering must be strategic, that is, tied to where the library is trying to go. Partnership development should not be adopted simply because it is a trendy topic. There have to be clear goals that the library is trying to achieve and that can be addressed through collaborative efforts. So, a clear vision and mission are crucial first steps to successful partnership development.

Once your library has an understanding of where it wants to go, then you can begin to look at what you want your potential partnerships to accomplish. The Williamsburg Regional Library has developed six "reasons for partnering" that guide staff in considering partnerships and guide administrators in prioritizing partnering possibilities. Partnerships established at WRL must successfully achieve at least one of the following goals. Some partnerships may achieve more. If a relationship does not meet at least one of these requirements, a partnership should not be established.

Figure 13-3   Reasons for a Library to Partner

- Reach new library users
- Reach current library users in a new way
- Tap into unique community assets and strengths
- Gain support for library resources and/or programs
- Gain valuable community feedback
- Create new resources

Figure 13-4   Williamsburg Community Health Foundation Partnership

The Williamsburg Community Health Foundation (WCHF) is a local non-profit organization that supports health-related community programs in the Williamsburg area community through a community grant fund. The WCHF approached the library to discuss establishing a resources center at the library based on the library's award-winning Phillip West Memorial Cancer Resource Center. A partnership was established in 2000 to set up the Funding Research Center, with $15,000 from the WCHF. The center contains print and electronic resources for local residents and non-profit agencies to use in seeking grant opportunities and in developing and administering funding programs. These resources are provided in the library and through the Funding Research Center Web site, hosted by the library.

In addition to providing funding for building a collection of materials related to fundraising and grantsmanship, the partnership involves the development of programs for non-profits in the community covering such topics as legal issues and technology issues for non-profits. In 2005, an e-mail listserv, hosted by the library, was established under the auspices of the partnership to improve communication between local non-profits.

By working through a community gatekeeper, this partnership has enabled the library to enhance its collections, improve services, and to build a lasting relationship with an important community organization. Through the partnership, the library has been able to reach a new user group, area non-profits, and to increase the importance of the library within the community.

In a smaller library, one way to keep partnering efforts manageable is to choose fewer reasons for partnering. Instead of six reasons, perhaps look at one or two. Look at what is currently important to your institution, and build your reasons around a particular need. It may be that the current priority for your library is to reach new library users. If this is the case, then your partnering efforts should focus primarily on looking for relationships that will help you to meet this need. Remember, partnering needs to bring some specific benefit to the library. Too often, libraries are willing to give without expecting any return, but a true partnership must have some reward for the library. Each year it will be important to look at the current reason or reasons for partnering to determine whether this reason is still valid or whether there is a more pressing need to address.

ISSUES, CHALLENGES, AND OPPORTUNITIES

Developing a partnering program is a challenge for all libraries. It requires that library staff and administration be willing to take on a new way of thinking about the institution and its mission, which can create a level of discomfort in the initial stages. As smaller libraries embark on building partnerships, they will find that they face some challenges that are particular to their size.

The most common challenge that small libraries will encounter is realistically assessing what they have to offer to a potential partner. The size of your library will place some limits on the assets that are available. There are several areas where these limits may have an effect on partnering efforts.

- **Staff limits**
  Typically, a smaller library may have only one or two professional librarians. Although partnership development is by no means limited to those who have an MLS degree, the library may find it harder to find staff with a library-wide view or project management expertise to become involved in partnering.
- **Facility limits**
  Many potential partners will be attracted to collaborative efforts with libraries to gain access to library facilities. In a smaller library, there may be limited meeting

room space available to use as a bargaining chip in partnership negotiations.

- **Financial limits**
  Although partnerships do not always come with a direct price tag, there can be costs involved in partnerships that may be difficult for smaller libraries to absorb. These could include developing promotional materials and extra staff time.

- **Time limits**
  Small institutions will find that becoming active in partnering means that decisions have to be made about the allocation of staff time. Partnering initiatives may cause conflicts with other programs and services that the library is trying to offer.

- **Administrative limits**
  It is not uncommon for smaller institutions to have boards of governance that take a more active role in the day-to-day affairs of the institution. This offers both opportunities and challenges to smaller libraries. The governing boards often are well-connected in the community, and can open doors to potential partnerships. At the same time, there is always the potential that a board member will see partnering as a way to promote pet projects. The library needs to be careful that favoritism does not set aside library priorities for partnership development.

In all of these cases, the limits are by no means insurmountable. They will require careful analysis and work on the part of the library staff and administration to address. One question to ask when you are considering partnership development as a strategic tool should be, "Is community partnership development a priority for the library?" and another, "Why is it important?"

In addition to these internal challenges, libraries that serve smaller communities (be they public, academic, or special libraries) will find that the smaller size of their community presents challenges as well. A smaller and/or rural community will, by its nature, present fewer potential partners. This is particularly the case when looking at partnering with government agencies. Consolidation of services such as motor vehicle departments, post offices, and hospitals into regional centers means that small-town libraries may find it harder to locate strong local partners.

In smaller or more rural communities, obstacles to partnering may arise that are less common in larger settings. The past relationship of community members to the library may play a bigger role in smaller communities than it does elsewhere. Political issues between members of the community may also have a larger impact on small libraries, which may find themselves caught in the middle of disputes.

Despite all of these concerns, partnership development does offer small libraries the same opportunities that it offers to larger institutions. Partnering can be an important tool to make the library relevant in the community. Successful partnerships build support for the library that can be drawn on during funding periods or when difficulties arise. Establishing a formal partnership can result in increased recognition for existing work that the library is already doing. Finally, partnerships make the library valuable to community institutions not just to individuals. Again, this kind of support can prove invaluable to the library as an institution. Basic promotion of the library and a stronger connection to the community may be the best reasons for smaller libraries to consider partnering.

THE REALITIES OF PARTNERING

There are some realities to keep in mind as you explore the opportunities afforded by developing community partnerships.

- **The library must have something to offer:** Assess your library's assets and strengths to understand what it is that the library can bring to the table in a partnership. It may be physical space, staff skills, collections, unique role in the community, the library name, or other items. But you must have something to offer. Partnering is a shared relationship.
- **Partnering is not a substitute for sound funding:** While some partnerships have a financial component, particularly grant-funded collaborations, do not count on getting funds to supplement your current budget through partnerships. It is particularly crucial that your funding agencies understand this, and that they do not penalize the library for developing successful partnerships. Also, it is important that the library recognize that grants that require evidence of collaborative efforts should only be sought if there is a strong need, not simply because they offer a partnering opportunity.
- **Partnering is not going to solve existing problems:** If there are staffing problems or communication issues in your in-

stitution, do not look to partnering to put them right. In fact, it is most likely that these sorts of issues will be exacerbated by the time and effort needed to establish a partnering program. Things do not have to be perfect (where are things ever perfect?) but you do need to have strong internal communication and a staff that is willing to work interdepartmentally in order to partner successfully.

CONCLUSION

Having considered the advantages and disadvantages of establishing a partnering program, and concluded that it is something that your institution wants to implement, what are the next steps?

1. Know where your institution wants to go. Have a clear plan in mind, and use the library's mission and vision to guide your partnering efforts.
2. Carefully and honestly assess what your library has to offer to a potential partner.
3. Do not be afraid to ask potential partners what they have to offer you. Remember that partnering is a shared relationship.
4. Think about your community in a broad fashion. Don't limit yourself when considering potential partners. Non-profits, government agencies, businesses, and other libraries all offer possibilities for collaborative endeavors.
5. Look at what you are already doing collaboratively as a starting point for partnership development. What organizations in the community are you currently working with? Are these relationships meeting the library's priorities? And which of these relationships would benefit from formalization?
6. Know why you are entering into a particular partnership. Be clear about the reasons for each relationship you develop.
7. Remember that partnership development is only a tool, not an end to itself. It should serve the library not the other way around.

REFERENCES

Austin, James E. 2000. *The collaborative challenge: How non-profits and businesses succeed through strategic alliances.* San Francisco: Jossey-Bass.

Crowther, Janet L., and Barry Trott. 2004. *Partnering with purpose: A guide to strategic partnership development for libraries and other organizations.* Westport, CT: Libraries Unlimited.

Holt, Glen. "Public library partnerships: Mission-driven tools for 21st century success." www.public-libraries.net/html/x_media/pdf/holt6en.pdf (accessed November 29, 2005).

Sagawa, Shirley, and Eli Segal. 2000. *Common interest, common good: Creating value through business and social sector partnerships.* Boston: Harvard Business School Press.

14 DEVELOPMENT

Jean A. Major

DEFINITION

Development is the name for raising money for the library from sources outside the entities that provide ongoing funding to the institution. Expertise in library development—fundraising—is an essential skill for today's library managers. It provides the financing to fill in gaps left by the uncertainties of public funding, and it can be available to serve the needs of the library's clientele *as they develop*. A full-scale library fundraising program, therefore, provides for several distinct kinds of special funding to address distinct needs.

OVERVIEW

This chapter covers:

- Major fundraising techniques and the structure through which they can be combined to form a full-scale program
- Annual supplementary funding supplied through an annual fundraising campaign, Friends of the Library annual memberships, memorial and honorary gifts, and annual fundraising events
- Special project or special purpose funding secured through major gifts from individuals, grants, and corporate gifts
- Building an endowment through funds raised in a capital campaign or by fostering planned giving

ANNUAL SUPPLEMENTARY FUNDING

Annual Fund. An annual fundraising campaign is carried out to maintain a cash reserve that can be used to fund an unusual opportunity or an unexpected expense. Its participants form the broad base of library supporters, many of whom make relatively small gifts. Often, people become library supporters initially through participation in the annual fund campaign and then develop as donors of larger gifts over time. Prospects for gifts to the library's annual fund campaign include registered borrowers, members of the library's governing board (or the board of the parent organization), guest card holders, library volunteers, attendees at library events, members of groups that meet regularly in the library, and individuals identified by fundraising campaign volunteers.

Annual fund campaigns most often are carried out through mail solicitation—that is, a well-written letter addressed personally to an individual, asking him/her to consider making a gift to the library's campaign. When the individual is already a library supporter, he/she should be asked to consider increasing the donation to the next higher level (name the desired figure in the letter). The best letters are personal and warm. Often they are written by prominent volunteers in the campaign, not by the library's administrative leadership. Of course, an addressed return envelope for donations is enclosed in each letter.

A phonathon—a telephone solicitation—sometimes is used in place of mail solicitation or for follow-up to people who have not responded to the initial mailing. Campaign volunteers may contact those on their phone lists individually at their own convenience, but much is gained in focus and efficiency by arranging for all volunteers to do phone solicitation at the same time. Borrow an office with multiple phone lines and separate workspaces, and recruit several volunteers to spend an evening telephoning. Supply a coordinator who can answer questions and solve problems if they arise. Confirm phone commitments with mail follow-ups.

Friends of the Library Memberships. A formal Friends of the Library organization has the potential to make a variety of contributions to the library, and the subject is treated more fully elsewhere in this volume. The annual membership dues, however, can be viewed as a variation on the annual fund campaign. Potential members can be recruited from the same groups, and mail solicitation is often used to recruit new or renewing members. Renewing members can and should be asked to renew at a higher membership level.

Memorial and Honorary Gifts. Giving opportunities for memorials or to honor living people is a graceful component of the library's annual giving program. Publicizing the program can take several forms: a separate brochure displayed throughout the library, an invitation in the library's newsletter or the Friends' newsletter, or a separate check-off or enclosure in the Friends' membership materials. Memorial and honorary gifts and the individuals honored must be acknowledged separately when the library publishes its list of supporters.

Annual Fundraising Events. Library fundraisers have several functions in addition to raising money for library purposes—visibility, cohesion for the library's volunteers, attraction of new library supporters, and, of course, fun. Sustaining and expanding the same event each year makes the event increasingly recognizable as a library benefit and enhances the library's image if the occasion is well chosen with image in mind. The FOLUSA newsletter (Friends of Libraries USA) contains news items of other libraries' experiences with fundraising events and is an especially good source of ideas. In order to raise significant funds, the annual fundraiser must be fun, and wide publicity is essential to draw new attendees. Some of these newcomers will/must become library friends and supporters.

SPECIAL PROJECT OR SPECIAL PURPOSE FUNDING

Major Gifts. Sometimes a large purchase is desired—an existing collection of materials, a technology upgrade, specialized staff training, facilities renovation or addition, for example. The price tag exceeds funds available through the annual fund or would bankrupt that account. Prospective major donors should be approached for support. This kind of fundraising requires a donor cultivation *process*. A single contact will not suffice, and the cultivation must take place face-to-face.

Relationships with prospective major gift donors are best developed over time by the library's administrative leadership. Accepted techniques include personally guided visits to the library, small group or individual social events (lunches, for example), personal notes or phone calls with news and updates, visits to the prospect's home—all measures intended to acquaint the prospective donor with the library's programs and establish the credibility of the library director before developing the prospective donor's interest in the current project. After cultivating a relationship with the prospective donor for a time, it is appropriate to ask specifically, "Are you ready to review a proposal?"

A handsome packet of information about the library's programs must be presented along with the library's gift proposal. In addition to the proposal itself, contents of the "cultivation packet" could include, for example, a fact sheet describing the library, a single-page history of the library, copies of the annual "Highlights" publication for the past several years, and a description of the ways that the library recognizes donors.

Grants. For smaller libraries, local or in-state foundations are possible grant sources if the library's project has significant potential impact for the local area. A statewide directory of foundations, if available, is very useful to identify those whose interests and parameters fit the library's funding need. Occasional news items about grants awarded and information appearing on Web sites of individual foundations provide additional information. To avoid working at cross-purposes with the parent organization, libraries must seek clearance from them before contacting any foundations. Telephone contact to foundation personnel can be used to verify that the library project fits the foundation's mission as well as to verify deadlines, required formats, and the like for the submission of a written proposal. As a proposal is developed, multiple contacts with the grant officer can foster an effective shared partnership.

Corporate Philanthropy. Libraries may approach local corporations for cash support, in-kind contributions, and event sponsorships that can contribute to the funding of a major project. The initial step is to research potential donor companies to verify that your library's project matches the company's area of gift support. Once common interest has been verified, contact the company to ascertain its structure for selecting projects to support, the schedule for considering proposals, and guidelines for submitting a proposal. At that time, identify someone in the company to be your principal contact, and cultivate him/her like any other donor. If a member of the company serves on the Friends board or is otherwise involved with your library in a leadership position, that person may be asked for advice, an introduction, or to serve as an internal advocate for the library's project.

Good friends of the library—board members and current donors, for example—can be very helpful by providing introductions, contacts, and entrée in other forms to prospective major donors, foundation board members, or corporate executives. Each of these types of development work is facilitated through contacts, and the library's influential or well-placed friends should be asked to make initial contacts for the purposes of these gift solicitations.

ENDOWMENTS

Capital Campaign. Although a library may use a capital campaign to finance construction of a building, the technique very often is used to fund an endowment—a large sum that is invested and thereby earns interest to be used annually by the library. A capital campaign closely resembles fundraising for major gifts. The financial target is considerably larger, and a number of large, medium, and small donors will be needed to reach it. The cultivation process for major donors is the same, though.

Capital campaigns often use a special donor recognition technique, the naming opportunity. At the start of the campaign, discrete parts of a library building or a service are made available for naming in honor of donors of significant gifts. For example, a large, well-appointed conference room might be named for the donor of a gift of $100,000 or the library's lecture series could be named to honor the donor of a $50,000 gift.

Donors to a capital campaign typically make generous gifts, and the library's recognition program must be designed so that major givers are thanked appropriately. They must be thanked with personal letters and listed in published lists of campaign donors. A wall plaque usually marks an area financed with a "naming opportunity." Sometimes, a larger wall plaque or display lists the names of all major donors. A public celebration or recognition may be considered appropriate. In summary, donors to capital campaigns must be thanked in multiple ways and recognized publicly.

Planned Giving. Estate gifts make a major contribution to a library's endowment and should be treated as a significant part of the development program. The time horizon may be long or short, and a bequest may be designated for a single component of the library's program, or it may be designated for the library as a whole.

Although some estate gifts result from thorough cultivation of the eventual donor, a library's entry into this kind of fundraising also can be done by publicizing planned giving as a gift option.

Newsletter articles about planned giving should include information about the various instruments typically employed, and a "response mechanism" should be included—that is, something to fill out and return to request additional information. Planned giving can be presented as an option on the library's Web site, too. Include information about different instruments and donor testimonials, as well as a way to request more information. A more ambitious technique is to organize a "philanthropy" seminar or workshop for potential donors in which gifts to "the charity of your choice" are discussed. This technique has the added benefit of identifying firm prospects and assuring that they have appropriate information about the necessary steps.

When the library's planned giving option is established and in operation, consideration should be given to creating a "legacy society," that is a special category of donors who have designated the library as a beneficiary in their formal estate plan. The society is named with a title that suggests selectivity, and periodic events are held for its members exclusively.

The seriousness of purpose involving an estate gift is marked by a more stringent infrastructure requirement than is usually connected with other development techniques. The library or its parent institution must have an established written policy for administering endowment funds. It must specify the treatment of principal held in the endowment and the use of interest, and the policy must state the application procedures for use of endowment funds. This policy statement is required to establish the trust necessary between the donor and the library for this especially important gift.

FOUNDATIONS FOR LIBRARY DEVELOPMENT

Creating a library development program is a long-term process that rests on fundamental elements of the library's service program. These elements must be maintained in order to move the development program forward.

Good Customer Service is fundamental. Briefly, treat all your staff with consideration and respect. Train them specifically in appropriate customer service techniques. Finally, empower them to resolve problems themselves, on the front lines.

Several Public Relations Approaches should be employed. A library newsletter is a vehicle to celebrate large and small victories, as well as to communicate information about new services, policy changes, and introduction of new staff members. Although the newsletter can be mailed, e-mail dissemination is an effective alternative. A library Web site is almost essential now; it can be used to communicate library hours and policies, for example, to highlight volunteer programs, and to publicize giving opportunities. It also can provide links to other relevant sites. The library's annual report can be used to summarize the year's highlights and *must* publish the library's donor list for the year. Finally, opportunities should be sought out for library personnel to make presentations to groups about the library's services, its volunteer programs, and development opportunities.

The Volunteer Program plays an important role in a library's development program. Prospective donors must have or must develop a personal investment in the library, and serving as a volunteer is an effective way to initiate that investment process.

Visibility of Library Leaders is necessary because they must be known and respected in order to draw in prospective supporters. Administrators must seek opportunities to meet potential supporters through participation in or presentations to local organizations. When the library's leadership becomes involved in community organizations, their standing as real members of the community is raised. Viewed from the perspective of the library's leadership, visibility outside the library's sphere leads to an ever-wider circle of contacts—people who can be approached as acquaintances and brought into the circle of the library's valued friends.

Development has grown in scope to become a major responsibility of library leaders today. Understanding the multiple approaches and the results they can be expected to achieve is essential to the program's effectiveness. A full development program represents a significant investment of effort, but it is essential to compensate for the uncertainties of traditional funding processes. And maintaining an ever-increasing group of supporters who appreciate your work enough to invest time and resources in programs you believe in is very rewarding.

CONCLUSION

In today's library world a solid development program is an essential part of any library's operation. No library will be able to provide all the services that it desires, or its user's demand, with funding from the parent organization or local government funding. It is essential that even the smallest library take steps to secure additional resources through some of the activities and organizations discussed in this chapter.

REFERENCES

Bauer, David G. 2003. *The "how to" grants manual: Successful grantseeking techniques for obtaining public and private grants.* Westport, CT: Praeger.

Corson-Finnerty, Adam, and Laura Blanchard. 1998. *Fundraising and friend-raising on the web.* Chicago: American Library Association.

Dewey, Barbara I., ed. 1991. *Raising money for academic and research libraries.* New York: Neal-Schuman.

Friends of Libraries U.S.A. *www.folusa.org.*

Gerding, Stephanie K., and Pamela H. MacKellar. 2006. *Grants for libraries: A how-to-do-it manual.* New York: Neal-Schuman.

Herring, Mark Y. 2004. *Raising funds with friends groups: A how-to-do-it manual for libraries.* New York: Neal-Schuman.

Kuniholm, Roland. 1995. *The complete book of model fund-raising letters.* Paramus, NJ: Prentice Hall.

Reed, Sally Gardner, and Beth Nawalinski. 2005. *Getting grants in your community.* Philadelphia: FOLUSA.

Sheldon, K. Scott. 2000. *Successful corporate fund raising: Effective strategies for today's nonprofits.* New York: Wiley.

Smith, Amy Sherman, and Matthew D. Lehrer. 2000. *Legacies for libraries: A practical guide to planned giving.* Chicago: American Library Association.

Swan, James. 2002. *Fundraising for libraries: 25 proven ways to get more money for your library.* New York: Neal-Schuman.

Women's Philanthropy Institute. www.women-philanthropy.org.

FURTHER READING

Butler, Meredith A., ed. 2001. *Successful fundraising: Case studies of academic libraries.* Washington, D.C.: Association of Research Libraries.

Shaw, Sondra C., and Martha A. Taylor. 1995. *Reinventing fundraising: Realizing the potential of women's philanthropy.* San Francisco: Jossey-Bass.

Steele, Victoria, and Stephen D. Elder. 2000. *Becoming a fundraiser: The principles and practice of library development,* 2nd ed. Chicago: American Library Association.

Part III

Public Services in the Small Library

15 ADULT SERVICES

Alicia Willson-Metzger

DEFINITION

Adult Services involves all the help provided library users on a daily basis. An adult services library professional deals primarily with the over-18 crowd, providing services such as circulation and reference services.

OVERVIEW

This chapter covers:

- Reference work
- Programming
- Readers' advisory
- Displays
- Outreach

REFERENCE WORK

In the first class meeting of a reference class somewhere in the Midwest, a professor smiled and said, "I can tell you essentially all you need to know about reference work in one sentence: 'The patron is always wrong.'"

Shock, horror! Ray didn't mean that patrons are as a rule either uninformed or not too bright. He meant that (a) people often have a difficult time verbalizing precisely what it is that they need and (b) it can be a long trip from what they say they need to what they actually do need. Since the librarian is their tour guide on that trip, it is up to them to point out what would best serve their needs, and it is done through conducting what's popularly known as the "reference interview."

What is the "reference interview?" The phrase makes the whole process sound decidedly more formal than it needs to be. It is simply the give-and-take discussion between the reference staff member and the patron seeking information. Part of what is needed to determine in the opening moments of a discussion with a patron is what sort of response is required, including the breadth and depth of the answer. Doing this involves knowing the types of questions likely to be asked. There are different terms used for a variety of question types, but, generally, questions can be broken down into two categories: directional and informational.

Directional questions are what they sound like: "Where's the bathroom?" or "Where are the study rooms?" While responses to these questions are generally no-brainers, do keep in mind that you work in your library every day, and the patron probably doesn't. If you tend to give awkward directions, and if it is at all possible, walk the patron over to whatever area he/she is trying to find.

Informational questions will require some effort to answer. These sorts of questions can range from "How do I use your online catalog?" to "I need five book reviews of an extremely obscure work only my professor has heard of." These are the sorts of questions the reference interview will help you to answer.

THE REFERENCE INTERVIEW

- The reference interview essentially begins before either you or the patron begins to speak. Make eye contact with people who seem to be about to request assistance; look pleasant and attentive. This does not mean that you have to greet someone as though he is your long-lost relative. If you are naturally somewhat reserved, a pleasant "how can I help you?" will get the interview ball rolling.
- Let the patron tell you what he/she needs in his/her own words without your interrupting. Once this has been done, rephrase what was said to ensure that you understand what has been said. ("Do I understand correctly that you need to find out something about the history of men's Olympic figure skating?") Although rephrasing the question can sound somewhat stilted, the natural exchange of information between you and the patron should obviate this problem to some degree.

- Use open-ended questions to glean more information from the patron regarding the specific information needed. Open-ended questions involve a response other than "yes" or "no," and are invaluable in discovering what the patron actually requires. Although a whole generation of reference librarians seems to have been trained never to ask the one most obvious question, that is, some variation of "Why do you need this information?" Properly phrased, the question can elicit a response guaranteed to help you answer the patron's inquiry. For instance, given the sample inquiry above, in which your patron has requested something about the history of men's Olympic figure skating, you as reference professional have absolutely no idea if the patron needs a list of male figure-skating medalists, a comprehensive history of Olympic figure skating in the United States, or an autobiography of Scott Hamilton. Knowing that the inquiry relates to the assignment you have already helped five other people with will help to focus your response immediately and give the patron the level of information needed.
- Find out where the patron has looked previously for information, or if he/she is at the beginning of his/her search. Doing this can achieve two goals: (1) Obviously, you'll find out where to begin in helping the person and (2) if the patron is missing the mark in his/her choice of reference tools, you will be able to guide him/her to the right one(s). Frequently, patrons stick to the tried-and-true in their approaches to locating answers. "Oh, well, I looked in Proquest and didn't see anything helpful." If the tool they know doesn't have what they need, they often give up. You're there to show them how, and particularly where, to search for information.
- Now it's time to find out WHY Proquest wasn't helpful, unless of course the patron's initial description of his/her information need was a clear-cut case of "wrong information source for the question." Patron missteps seem to fall into two broad categories: (1) Some aspect of the mechanics of using the reference source, be it a database or print resource, is unclear to the patron. In all fairness, this is often a matter of the reference source not being intuitively designed for a novice user. For instance, until recently, the JSTOR database required that a patron check off boxes indicating the broad subject areas he/she wished to search before actually performing the search. Of course, the check boxes were beneath the search term box, and

seemingly were always ignored by patrons unused to the database. Tell the patron about the major quirks of the reference source he/she is using—ultimately, it will save both of you a good deal of searching time; (2) the patron has developed the tunnel vision of the novice library user. Often, your user will envision one—and only one—way to describe and define a topic. Frequently, which is even more frustrating for the user, it is an entirely viable description; it isn't, however, how that topic is indexed by the Library of Congress or your user's favorite reference database. Help the user find synonyms for his topic; for instance, doing a keyword online catalog search on "Civil War" would certainly give the patron some items on the American Civil War, but so would searching "War of the Rebellion," "War of Northern Aggression," "Ulysses S. Grant." Be a human thesaurus for your patron, and even more importantly, teach him/her how to use "see" and "see also" links, as well as subject heading links in online catalogs to find other information on a chosen topic.

- Finally, and this is a really, REALLY important rule in the book of reference "do's," do TEACH the patron how to perform the search for himself/herself. Although it is extremely tempting to simply do it for him/her, particularly if there's a long line of patrons waiting, you will only make more work for both of you in the long run. You will hear any number of reasons why the patron can't do it for himself/herself—"I'm late for class," "You're so much better at this than I am," "I'm just no good at computers." Don't fall for any of it, because you will see the same person with the same question back at the reference desk over and over again. Be both patient and persistent. A big smile with an accompanying "Let me show you how to do this yourself," or "Remember yesterday when I showed you how to search for a title in WorldCat?" can begin to wean the patron from excessive librarian intervention. The reference interview is ultimately one more teaching tool afforded to librarians. Don't waste the opportunity.

- As the transaction comes to a close, ask the patron if you have answered his/her question and, even more importantly, mention that if it turns out that he/she hasn't found what was needed, to please come back for more help.

HOW TO BLOW THE REFERENCE INTERVIEW, OR PROBLEM PATRONS IN OUR MIDST

Everybody's different—it's a terribly banal observation, but wholly relevant to reference work. Cultural misunderstandings and sheer human nature can disrupt the reference interview, and it is incumbent upon you, the person doing the helping, to avoid these misunderstandings as much as possible. Remember, one reference librarian's "difficult" patron is another's "quirky" or "interesting" patron. However the patron appears to you, you still have to learn to deal with him or her effectively. What follows is some simple advice for some of the more common distractions in reference work.

Language Barriers: Any reference librarian, if he/she hasn't already, has to develop an "ear" for accents other than his/her own. And this doesn't necessarily mean the accents of international students, either. A former supervisor once remarked that a student she referred to as "the Hickory Hick," (the student was from Hickory, North Carolina) had stopped by to chat with her. The condescending attitude that dripped from her remark was shocking. Because someone has an accent, or because she uses non-standard English for whatever reason, does not indicate a lack of knowledge or intelligence on her part. It does, though, tell you that you may have to work a little harder to get to what she needs. Don't be shy about repeating what you think a patron has said, just to make sure you've got it, and if you have to ask the patron to reiterate what was said, do it. While you may feel understandably awkward asking that the patron do this, that awkwardness is nothing compared to how you will feel if you send the person in the utterly wrong direction. Your positive attitude will go a long way toward making a success out of what otherwise could be a tricky transaction.

The "I'm having a bad day" patron: These are the patrons who come to the reference desk with an air of anger and frustration before either of you say a word. The questions asked might indeed be laced with an undertone of combativeness, that is, "Well, you probably wouldn't know this . . . " or "I never can find anything in this place anyway, so I don't know why I'm asking . . . " To the best of your ability (this is nearly impossible for me, but I know it's good advice), ignore the extra added snarkiness and proceed straight to the question that's hidden under the layers of anger. Stay calm—for one, the anger in all likelihood is not directed at you personally, and, even more importantly, being combative in return gives credence to the person's inappropriate behavior. Getting a rise out of you might make the patron feel better, but it's not going to help you at all, and it will certainly make a bad situation even worse. If the patron's attitude becomes too combative to handle, either (a) politely excuse yourself so you can find someone else to help the person—sometimes a change of face can help; or (b) put the onus of the patron's behavior squarely on his or her shoulders: "What specifically is it that you would like me to do to assist you?" Most people will not be able to answer that question, and it will make them realize that they are being quite difficult, and at that point you can move the dialogue to a higher level.

The homeless and/or mentally ill patron: The homeless and/or mentally ill patron has long been viewed as a problem within public libraries, although such patrons appear in every type of library; they are from every walk of life. They are grouped together here because many homeless patrons are mentally ill, and vice versa. Here are some basic tips for effectively dealing with them:

- Take their information requests seriously and answer them to the best of your ability. For instance, the patron who consistently requests tomorrow's newspaper or the one who needs rocket fuel for his rocket double-parked in front of the library (each honest-to-goodness questions from public library land) has a genuine concern. Taking the time to simply and seriously respond to the request is often all these patrons really want. No, you can provide neither tomorrow's newspaper nor rocket fuel for an imaginary rocket, but you can be respectful in communicating those facts.

- Although not all homeless and mentally ill patrons have issues with personal cleanliness and hygiene, many do. A trick (learned at the reference desk of a public library within a block of a homeless shelter) is to keep Vicks Vapor Rub in your desk, and before leaving for reference desk duty, put a very small amount in your nostrils. This is an unobtrusive and inoffensive way to deal with a very real problem that many people feel uncomfortable discussing.

- Compose a security/library behavior policy and have it approved by your library's board, or if you are in a small academic or special library, your administration. Clearly delineate those things you will and will not tolerate, and stick to it. Have your institution's lawyer vet the document to ensure its legality, and then post the policy in prominent places throughout your library. Refer to it when indicating to a patron's noncompliance. Have a good working relationship with your building's security guard (if you have one), and always keep emergency (police, fire, ambulance) numbers close at hand. Don't assume that these patrons will be difficult to the point of requiring a police presence, but don't be naive, either. Have all the resources at hand to deal with a sticky situation, and simply hope you never have to use them.

The "Clingy" Patron: This patron believes that you, and only you, can provide the reference assistance that he or she has come to count on. Invariably, this patron shows up when you're not scheduled at the reference desk, when you're eating lunch at your desk, when you're on your way to an important meeting. The reason this situation is a catch–22 is that, invariably, the patron likes and trusts you because you've provided excellent service in the past and knows you will continue to do so. You've also probably always listened, as we're all trained to do, to his reference queries and (possibly endless) stories with great patience. Although each of these falls under the category of "good service," you have to learn to draw the line somewhere. If the patron calls the desk and won't let you go, say you have a patron waiting for help (whether you do or not). Enlist the help of coworkers—don't refuse to help the patron; after all, chances are he's a decent person with interesting questions. But there are other fish in the sea (or librarians in the office) who can assist him/her every bit as well as you can. Introduce the patron to one or more of them; make him/her feel special; tell the patron these other librarians will assist him/her with the greatest attention. In short, broaden his/her narrow viewpoint a bit. Don't offend; just show the patron other people who can help.

Multiple Patrons, One You: It's lunchtime and every patron in the library has descended upon the reference desk. What do you do?

- Always acknowledge the person or persons waiting in line. A pleasant smile, accompanied by "I'll be with you in just a moment," establishes a relationship with the patron and shows that you recognize his/her presence and the importance of his/her question.
- If you know immediately that the person you're helping has an extremely involved question—say one that's going to take more than five minutes to answer properly—ask if you might quickly respond to any directional inquiries from people waiting in line. That way, they'll go away happy, and you'll be able to focus your full attention on the involved question.
- Develop pathfinders for those common research questions

you receive day in and day out. Pathfinders are simple bibliographies, often with brief annotations, of resources readily available in your library. While not every reference resource lends itself to being placed on a library's Web page, pathfinders certainly do, providing another means of accessing this information for your patrons.

- The phone rings. and rings. and rings. and you've still got that pesky patron with the involved question. Every library employee has a different take on this topic, but I personally like to handle the real live person in front of me first, politely asking the phone patron if he would be willing to hold for a few moments. If the phone patron doesn't want to hold, get his name and number and call back when your line of patrons is gone. You might also consider voice mail as an option to immediately answering questions, with a message indicating that you are with another patron and will return the person's call as soon as possible. Doing this could prove a little tricky, as your public may think that you don't care to answer the phone, but it can offer an "out" for you during your busiest moments at the reference desk.
- Offer a service through which you can provide in-depth reference assistance by appointment, away from the reference desk. In my library, we call this a "research assistance" form, and ask the patron to fill out a one-page form with such basic questions as "Where have you looked for information so far?" and "Specifically describe your information need." Once the patron has completed the form, you can make an appointment to meet with him/her, allowing enough time for you to do some preliminary research on the topic. Use this time to identify search terms and synonyms for the topic at hand; make a special effort to point out sources of information that the patron may not have considered; that is, perhaps use Project Muse in addition to Proquest in his/her search.
- Have a "ready reference" shelf within reach of the reference desk. This shelf should include a basic encyclopedia set, a statistical abstract, a general dictionary, a world almanac, and whatever other items you most frequently use to answer reference questions. Keeping a selection of reference books close at hand gives you the opportunity to answer phone inquiries much more efficiently—you don't have to actually go to the reference stacks to answer the question—and also speeds up in-person transactions at the reference desk.

Virtual Reference: Virtual reference is, in essence, a patron's communicating a question or questions to you electronically and your responding to these questions. Although many companies have created products that allow real-time discussions between librarian and patron (for instance, OCLC and Library of Congress' QuestionPoint), an e-mail address dedicated solely to reference inquiries can be a relatively low-tech, inexpensive way to provide virtual reference service. Consult with your systems administrator or with the person responsible for maintaining your server for the best way to go about this. It is essential to have a set time (or times) for accessing this e-mail so you can tell patrons that their requests will be answered within a particular amount of time (to be determined by you.) You do lose every non-verbal clue in the reference interview by using such an approach, but the trade-off is having one more way to juggle reference questions with a limited reference staff. If you feel that you wouldn't receive enough information from a patron through a free-text e-mail, post an online information request form much like the "paper trace" form mentioned earlier to elicit as much information as possible. Clearly indicate that the patron must provide another form of contact information (phone number, alternate e-mail address) in case you have questions for him. Virtual reference services do not supplant traditional reference interviews, but do provide a viable alternative for the manager of a small library searching for additional ways to serve patrons well.

PRINT VS. ONLINE REFERENCE RESOURCES

Great—now you've done the reference interview, but how do you find the answer to the question? A combination of online and print reference resources, plus e-mail capability and a telephone, can carry you through most reference inquiries. Having access, whether print or electronic, to the following basic reference resources is a must:

An unabridged dictionary: Especially in the public library, word spelling and definition questions are legion. *Webster's* and *American Heritage* are still among the best resources in this category. Online dictionaries, too, are equally helpful; check out Merriam-Webster Online at *www.m-w.com*; Dictionary.com at *www.dictionary.com*; and a comprehensive online reference source, Bartleby.com, at *www.bartleby.com*. Bartleby includes access to many standard reference sources (for free!), including the *Columbia Encyclopedia*, 6th edition; the *American Heritage Dictionary*, 4th edition; *Roget's II: The New Thesaurus*; the *American Heritage Book of English Usage*; the *Columbia World of Quotations*; *Simpson's Contemporary Quotations*; *Bartlett's Familiar Quota-*

tions; *Gray's Anatomy*; the *World Factbook*; and the *Columbia Gazetteer*.

A general encyclopedia: If you are financially strapped, use the online encyclopedia Wikipedia at *www.wikipedia.com*. It is quite comprehensive for a free online resource; the only catch is that readers can edit the information in it. Other outstanding general print (and often available online) encyclopedias include *Encyclopaedia Britannica, The World Book Encyclopedia,* and *Encyclopedia Americana.* Each is available by subscription.

A world almanac: Again, whether it's online or hard-copy, a world almanac provides access to statistics, addresses, esoteric facts, and weather-related information. Popular almanacs include *The World Almanac and Book of Facts* and *The Farmer's Almanac* and are but a few of the almanacs currently available on the market.

A world and/or road atlas: Geographical questions are always popular in almost every library. Make sure you have a current world atlas (countries' names and borders change more frequently than we often think) and a detailed atlas for the United States. Such atlases include *The Times Atlas of the World* and the deservedly popular *Rand-McNally Road Atlas.* Several free online services provide maps to and from worldwide locations. Among the best are Mapquest at *www.mapquest.com* and Yahoo Maps, available at *www.yahoo.com*.

A local phonebook: This is probably the most-used reference resource in any library. Visit your local phone company to obtain a book. There are also several excellent free phone number/address resources on the Internet, such as AnyWho, at *www.anywho.com* and the 411.com database (rather obviously) at *www.411.com*. Each of these sites provides name, address, and mapping capabilities, as well as a "reverse lookup" feature that will allow you to discover what name and address are associated with a particular phone number. (Cell phone and unlisted numbers are not available in these resources.)

Subject resources: The specific resources you choose in this area will depend upon the focus and scope of your reference work. Subject encyclopedias and dictionaries are available in every discipline; decide which are most important for you and purchase them.

Periodical indices: Increasingly, these resources are being published in an electronic format and are unfortunately increasingly expensive as a result. Any items published by the Wilson Company are excellent in depth and breadth (for instance, *Readers' Guide to Periodical Literature*, the granddaddy of all periodical indexes). There are, however, also very good free periodical indexes online, including Google's "Google Scholar" database at *www.google.com*. (Click on the link to Google Scholar.) Another good free resource is the Web site *www.findarticles.com*. Each of these databases indicates whether full-text access to the listed articles is free or not. (If there is a charge listed, try ordering the item through your interlibrary loan service, or send the patron to the local public library for interlibrary loan. Frequently, there is no charge incurred for interlibrary loan services.)

PRINT OR ONLINE?

Part of the decision regarding whether to have print, online, or mixed reference resources is your and your staff's preference regarding the availability and accessibility of computers on which to access reference resources. The vast majority of reference works, no matter what the format, are expensive. If you do want to develop a basic print reference collection and cannot afford new titles, keep an eye out for large public library book sales, in which entire reference sets, often only one year out of date, are offered to the public for sale at drastically reduced prices. Also investigate consortial agreements with area libraries—the aggregated resources of several small libraries can result in online access to reference databases for far less money than an individual subscription. Always consider your telephone, e-mail, and Internet access extensions of your reference collection, and keep a list of area libraries and librarians who have been helpful in answering reference questions. State libraries, in particular, provide excellent reference assistance for other, smaller libraries, and have virtual reference service, as well. Take advantage of every opportunity for networking.

READERS' ADVISORY

Readers' advisory is a service both formally and informally provided to patrons of all types of libraries; essentially, it involves the library employee giving patrons advice about books he or she might enjoy reading, particularly given prior reading selections. This service is most often utilized in public libraries, and you as library employee can do many things to assist patrons in making appropriate and enjoyable reading choices.

- Read, read, read. While this may seem like an obvious suggestion, many librarians have said that they "don't have time" to read. Make time, especially if there is a likelihood that you will be doing readers' advisory work. You can't advise if you don't DO.

- Monitor the major bestseller lists: *New York Times*, *Publishers Weekly*, etc. Notice that these journals have both fiction and non-fiction bestsellers lists, as well as specialty lists such as "Religion Bestsellers" and "Young Adult Bestsellers." Knowing the titles and authors of popular books will give you a start in recommending good reads for your patrons.

- Listen to what books your co-workers, friends, and acquaintances are discussing, anywhere, any time. Your best friend might have picked up a good beach read to take on vacation; your minister might have just read something by St. Augustine. Stop, look, and listen for reading suggestions everywhere.

- National Public Radio (NPR) has some of the best in-depth book discussions available. Frequently, Terry Gross' NPR staple "Fresh Air" offers hour-long interviews with popular-but-not-always-wildly-well-known authors; a current example was an interview with author Augustin Burroughs, author of *Running with Scissors*. A wide variety of authors guarantees you'll find someone whom you might not normally have taken the time to read. My local NPR station offers a weekly five-minute book review called "Lisa's List" during Friday afternoon rush hour. It's a perfect way to spend a couple of minutes in the car, listening to "book talk." To find information about books at NPR, go to *www.npr.org*; also link to your local NPR station's Web page from the national Web site.

- Any number of books and commercial databases provide readers' advisory in general, as well as genre-oriented, information. Some of the best are:
  - *Book Lust: Recommended Reading for Every Mood, Moment, and Reason*, by Nancy Pearl (the action-figure librarian). Pearl's book is an esoteric, delightful summary of suggested books (fiction and nonfiction) in such categories as "Techno-Thrillers," "Chick-Lit," and "Bicycling." A sequel, *More Book Lust*, was published in 2005.
  - *What Do I Read Next?* A Gale-Thomson database, *What Do I Read Next* provides access to reading lists by author, title/series, genre, award winners and librarians' top picks, who/what/where/when, and a particularly useful category, "Help Me Find a Book," in which

the reader enters the genre, time period, authors, etc., that she likes, and the system provides a list of "read-alike" titles. Readers may limit searches to fiction, non-fiction, adult, or children's titles, or may search all of these categories at once.

- *Genreflecting: A Guide to Reading Interests in Genre Fiction*, by Diana Tixier Herald. Now in its fifth edition (2000), this work spawned an entire series of *Genreflecting* titles for the overworked and underappreciated readers' advisory librarian. Chapters devoted to such genres as crime, the western, romance, and adventure are subdivided into types; for instance, the "Adventure" chapter includes survival, military and naval adventure, and political intrigue and terrorism, with titles and main characters listed. Additional titles in this series include *Teen Genreflecting, Make Mine a Mystery: A Reader's Guide to Mystery and Detective Fiction*, and *Jewish-American Literature: A Guide to Reading Interests*.

- *The Reading List: Contemporary Fiction: A Critical Guide to the Complete Works of 125 Authors*, by David Rubel. Rubel provides complete bibliographies of listed authors' works, as well as a synopsis of critical and public opinion of the titles.

- *The Reader's Choice: 200 Book Club Favorites*, by Victoria Golden McMains. McMains, a book review columnist, includes titles based upon the recommendations of book clubs in New York, Oregon, California, and Colorado. Titles are both fiction and non-fiction works from a variety of genres. McMains also provides instructions for starting a book club in her introduction.

- *A Year of Reading: A Month-By-Month Guide to Classics and Crowd-Pleasers for You and Your Book Group*, by Elizabeth Ellington and Jane Freimiller. Five titles in each of the following categories are listed for each month of the year: crowd pleasers, classics, challenges, memoirs, or potluck options. Includes bibliographies of related readings and discussion questions, with brief annotations of each work listed.

DISPLAYS, EXHIBITS, AND PROGRAMS

LIBRARY DISPLAYS AND EXHIBITS

The main goals of any library display or exhibit are to (a) catch the attention of the patron and (b) interest him/her in some aspect of your library, campus, or institution. The ideal library display will result in some benefit for the patron—increased knowledge by reading books associated with a certain topic, learning about a community service, or finding a new hobby, for instance. The library benefits in several ways, as well. Well-designed library displays can potentially increase the library's circulation by showcasing certain authors, topics, or collections. The library can become a more integral part of the parent institution by highlighting various activities or topics that are not specifically library-related. In addition, a well-designed display will make the library seem more inviting and less institutional, thereby contributing to patron enjoyment of the facilities.

A current library display policy is a must, and should be completed and approved by your governing board or administration before you mount any displays. Particularly important issues that should be addressed include whether or not community groups may use the library's display areas and if controversial issues may or will be addressed (for instance, a hotly contested community bond issue; gay rights in your community, and so on). Having a well-written, comprehensive policy will save you and your library's administration a great deal of trouble.

The initial stages of designing a display are perhaps the most difficult, beginning with the task of identifying a catchy focus. Use all the resources at your disposal to find a topic, and go beyond the tried-and-true. A resource such as the annual *Chase's Calendar of Events* lists both popular and obscure holidays and celebrations, and provides ample starting points for an interesting display. Local celebrations, such as a fall carnival or the community choir concert season, can also be the impetus for a prominent display. If you have enough people on your library staff, form a small committee to discuss possible displays and to rotate responsibility for designing them.

Basic materials for constructing a display need not be expensive. Purchase a few lengths of cloth, even remnants, to use as an attractive backdrop in a display case. Use small boxes or Princeton files as pedestals (to be covered up by that inexpensive cloth you just purchased). Small clear plastic book stands serve well to display books. Above all, resist the urge to clutter up the space—the

KISS rule (Keep it simple, stupid) works very well in this venue. Clearly label items that require explanation, but otherwise, let the display tell its story through its items. Use library books and videos, CDs, and the like, but also use coworkers as a resource for unique display items. For instance, last year on the 60th anniversary of D-Day, our library entered a History Channel library display contest. The only rule was that posters provided by the History Channel had to be included in the display. Our staff came together to mount this display, and it ended up being a very meaningful experience for all of us. One staff member donated letters her father, a high-ranking officer in World War II, had written to his wife about the experiences and privations of war; another staff member donated a picture of the crew of her father's destroyer. Keeping up with world and local events can be a great way to generate ideas for a display.

A final note: Rotate your displays on a regular basis. There is nothing worse than seeing the same display in the same display case for months on end. If you've run out of ideas, talk to coworkers and patrons, peruse the newspaper, think about authors you would like to know more about—and start displaying!

LIBRARY PROGRAMMING

Library programs can run the gamut from book talks to musical performances. Think about the following when planning a program for your library:

- What is your institution all about? Are you running a rural public library or a small branch library of a research university? What topics would be interesting to or informative for your patrons? Remember that a library program can be a performance, a lecture, a discussion group, a town hall meeting . . . you name it, it can happen in your library. If you're at a loss for ideas, sit down and brainstorm ten general subjects for a library program. Don't censor yourself; just let the ink flow. Just as with a reader's advisory service, each part of your life and community is a potential resource for a terrific library program. Don't think "can't."
- After you brainstorm your program list, consider the resources that you would need to offer the session. The first and most obvious of these is money. Remember that, even if you are the person doing the program, you will require some form of advertising in order to boost attendance. Advertising can be as simple as putting an announcement on your library's or institution's Web site, or placing flyers around your institution. Informally publicizing the ses-

sion among colleagues is always useful. Find out advertising rates among your local newspapers, and consider that free community-based newspapers have an audience that's probably ready-made for your program. Public radio stations are dedicated to serving the community; if your city has a local NPR affiliate, call them and ask about their advertising rates. Think carefully about the populations that would enjoy the program, and target those audiences in your advertising. Also remember that you will need refreshments for the program, which can be as simple as punch and cookies; in addition, it is good form to offer the speaker a small honorarium or gift for presenting his or her program.

- Start small—if you have never done programming in your library, or it's been a while since you have, plan a few well-designed, interesting programs to see how they go. If you're reading this book, chances are your staff is small, so do only what you can comfortably do.

- Where to find speakers? If you're in an academic library, or in a small public library in a college town, look to the educational institutions in your area for speakers. Every professor has an academic specialty; most, if not all, enjoy sharing their knowledge and would be naturals at leading a book discussion. Local authors love sharing their material; host a creative writing seminar led by an author and/or discuss one of the author's works. Local clubs are rich resources for presentations—ask the president of the club to give a talk or to suggest a speaker from the club's ranks. Use everyone you know as a resource for a presentation—you may not know everybody in your town or city, but invariably, somebody knows somebody else who would be a fascinating speaker.

- Do construct an evaluation form for the session, and leave a few minutes at the end of the program for attendees to complete it. (You have a much better chance of getting feedback at the event rather than doing a Web evaluation or snail-mailing after the fact). The form doesn't have to be fancy—go for basic information such as what the attendee enjoyed most/least about the program, suggestions for improvement, suggestions for future programming, etc. Always leave a space for comments. The purpose of this evaluation is two-fold: (1) to see what works and what doesn't, and (2) if the evaluations are positive, to use them as ammunition when asking your administration for financial support for your next program.

OUTREACH

Outreach is another way to interact with the user community. It involves traveling to another location to deliver, or highlight, the services and collections available in the library. Whether it is done by special services such as a bookmobile or other mobile vehicle, or through individual staff visits to offsite locations, the library is interacting with users in a non-library setting.

Each type of library should seek to find opportunities to reach outside of the library. They can vary from providing awareness of the library's collections and service to an off-site location for the corporation that the special library serves, to a full-blown bookmobile service that brings 3,000 or more items on a regular basis to stops throughout the community that the library serves. Many community groups are constantly looking for new speakers to help them learn something out of the ordinary. This, too, is outreach and should be pursued.

In the public library setting, Boy and Girl Scout troops are good targets for your expertise. Show them books on activities that could help them earn merit badges, or find out what their "theme of the month" is and focus on that. The more creative you can be in developing ideas, the better your program will be. Although you work in a small library, and may be the only—or one of the few—employees, outreach activities can inspire goodwill among different populations for your library and your institution.

As with any other kind of service, start small, have the audience evaluate it (as discussed in the programming section above), and find out what works and what doesn't. Outreach services are important in even the smallest library and can be a gold mine of good publicity for the library.

CONCLUSION

If there is a theme for this chapter, it would probably be "Network, network, network." In addition to good service orientation and reference knowledge, know colleagues, the community, and area libraries. That knowledge will go far in making the library the best that it can be. While it is sometimes daunting being the only adult services employee—or perhaps the only employee, period—of a library, think of it as a positive. There is a unique opportunity to serve a number of different populations through outreach, programming, and the simple good service given every day will make the library the best it can possibly be.

REFERENCES/FURTHER READING

Arant, Wendi, and Pixey Anne Mosley, eds. 2000. *Library outreach, partnerships, and distance education: Reference librarians at the gateway.* New York: Haworth Information Press.

Chase's Calendar of Events. (1994-). Chicago: Contemporary Books.

Ellington, Elizabeth, and Jane Freimiller. 2002. *A year of reading: A month-by-month guide to classics and crowd-pleasers for you and your book group.* Naperville, IL: Sourcebooks.

Herald, Diana Tixier. 2000. *Genreflecting: A guide to reading interests in genre fiction, 5th ed.* Englewood, CO: Libraries Unlimited.

Katz, William A. 2002. *Introduction to reference work.* Boston: McGraw-Hill.

McMains, Victoria Golden. 2000. *The reader's choice: 200 book club favorites.* New York: Quill.

Pearl, Nancy. 2003. *Book lust: Recommended reading for every mood, moment, and reason.* Seattle, WA: Sasquatch Books.

Rubel, David. 1998. *The reading list: Contemporary fiction/A critical guide to the complete works of 110 authors.* New York: H. Holt.

Schaeffer, Mark. 1991. *Library displays handbook.* New York: H. W. Wilson.

Shearer, Kenneth D., and Robert Burgin, eds. 2001. *The reader's advisor's companion.* Englewood, CO: Libraries Unlimited.

What Do I Read Next? Available from Thomson-Gale, www.galegroup.com.

16 YOUTH SERVICES

Noreen Bernstein

DEFINITION

Youth Services involves all the help provided to library users on a daily basis. A Youth Services staff member deals primarily with the under-18 age crowd, through providing circulation and reference services.

OVERVIEW

This chapter covers:

- Triangular model of children's services
- History of children's services in public libraries
- Services offered by children's services staff
- Importance of collection development
- Library programming, including author visits

There is an old Siberian proverb that says, "If as a child you don't learn the trees, as an adult you may get lost in the forest. And if, as a child, you don't learn the stories, as an adult you may get lost in life." In essence, children's librarianship is about making sure that children do learn the stories, both fact and fiction, that will keep them from getting lost in life.

TRIANGULAR MODEL

Using a triangular model to delineate children's library services may make it easier to determine how to divide time and resources. Basically, there are three broad categories: reference and reader's advisory; collection development and maintenance; and programming. Combined they are the basis of comprehensive library services for children, their parents and/or caregivers, and teachers. All three parts of the triangle are equally important and integrated.

Triangular Model

Historically, public libraries were not established for children, and the development of children's departments and libraries was literally due to demands of children themselves. As children flooded into public libraries about 100 years ago, it became clear to librarians that the comfort of adult users was at risk. As the children would not be denied, it seemed prudent to provide a separate area to keep them from disrupting the more serious work of adults. Research on the importance of early language experiences was basically nonexistent; illiteracy rates did not overly concern the public in general. And illiteracy rates were far lower since early language experiences for children were largely accomplished through communication with stay-at-home mothers. Single-parent families and children relegated to daycare were an anomaly. Our economy and growth as a nation were predicated on agrarian and product productivity. Jobs for people with limited literacy skills were more prevalent. In essence, almost no one was concerned.

Nineteenth-century literature for children was largely comprised of cautionary tales that helped to teach children appropriate models of behavior, morality, and Judeo-Christian values. Reading the original versions of Grimm, Andersen, and Perrault, one finds a body of literature filled with morality tales that are dark and a far cry from the modern versions such as Disney adaptations that fill library shelves today. Today's students of children's literature may find humor in the tales of Hilaire Belloc such as *Melinda Who Told Lies and Was Burned to Death*, but whose original purpose was to teach and mold behavior. Story times were socialization experiences promoting good behavior by contemporary standards.

For information about the importance of fairy tales see *The Uses of Enchantment* by Bruno Bettleheim.

Moving forward, Betty Smith's *A Tree Grows in Brooklyn* provides an interesting snapshot of children's library services as we moved into the twentieth century.

> The library was a little old shabby place. Francie thought it was beautiful . . . She stood at the desk a long time before the librarian deigned to attend to her . . . "Could you recommend a good book for a girl?" "How old?" "She is eleven." Each week Francie made the same request and each week the librarian asked the same question. A name on a card meant nothing to her and since she never looked up into the child's face, she never did get to know the little girl who took a book out every day and two on Sunday. A smile would have meant a lot to Francie and a friendly comment would have made her so happy. She loved the library and was anxious to worship the lady in charge.

Children's librarianship has come a long way. Children's librarians have a unique opportunity to enrich the lives of children through providing information and books for pleasure reading, and by fostering a love of reading and literature. They also now have current research that provides a scientific basis for confirming that role.

CHILDREN'S STAFF

The base of the triangle is the children's staff. The best collections in the world are useless unless they are appropriately put into the hands of children. Reader's Advisory services can help to promote emergent literacy and to shape a child's future love of reading by providing the most appropriate and best books. Books that rhyme, that teach concepts, and that provide a rich experience literarily and visually are crucial to reading readiness. Therefore, it is critical that a children's librarian knows the collection and understands how to connect a child, a parent, and/or a caregiver with the book that best meets a current need.

While most children's librarians bring a certain level of knowledge of children's literature to the job, this can be somewhat cursory, focusing on fiction, mostly the "classics" and award winners. The ability to mine the depth of a collection takes on-the-job work. One way to start is by perusing all new books as they are added to the collection and reading as much new fiction as possible. Browsing non-fiction shelves is also a must, and browsing fiction shelves with standard sources such as *What Do Children Read Next* or *Best Books for Children* makes the task easier. You will find new picture books for story times, and new recommendations for older readers. Reading older fiction also gives you advance knowledge of any potential problems a book might present. In some cases, the maturity of content or the language may suggest re-cataloging the book to a teen collection.

With non-fiction, checking tables of contents and scanning the books will provide a quick snapshot of the information included. Even the most sophisticated cataloging system cannot substitute for personal knowledge of the contents of your collection.

While learning a collection, another tool to help with reader's advisory is *A to Zoo*, a subject guide to picture books, in addition to the aforementioned *What Do Children Read Next* and *Best Books for Children,* which help with older readers.

The other essential tool for both reference and reader's advisory is an appropriate, effective reference interview. Most people using a library do not clearly articulate their need. A good children's librarian knows how to probe gently to determine what the patron really wants or needs. With reader's advisory, a librarian generally needs to know the age and general reading ability of the child, subjects of interest, and other books that he/she has enjoyed. With reference, the need to isolate just what information is required and what types of sources are usable for the assignment, if it is a school assignment, are foremost. Many new librarians tend to start off with search engines and other electronic sources. However, children need to learn that research is more than typing Google.com. They need to gain analytical skills to determine which sources are the best. Books, although they can contain errors, do have some accountability. They have an author and publisher who have presumably done their jobs. Many Internet sources do not. Starting with printed material helps children to gain these skills.

COLLECTION DEVELOPMENT

Learning the collection is a start, but library collections are living things that must be both developed and maintained. Collection Development includes adding newly published items as well as finding collection areas in need of expansion or updating. Weeding outdated items, books in poor condition, or shelf sitters, is a must on a regular basis. In this twenty-first century it is embarrassing to find books on the shelves that speculate about potential space travel! How and what to weed is often obvious, but the industry standard is usually *Crew Method: Expanded Guidelines for Collection Evaluation and Weeding for Small and Medium-Sized Libraries*.

> Many publishers offer series on presidents, countries, and other curriculum-related topics. Oddly, these series are usually updated at approximately the same time. This is one time when previewing is extremely helpful. Try to arrange sales representative visits to examine new series and decide which are most suited for your users.

The basis of collection development is a Materials Selection Policy. This policy needs to be broad enough to allow the inclusion of a wide range of materials that meet the different sensibilities and needs of a community, but, at the same time, is specific enough to provide a rationale for any items that might be challenged. While developing and maintaining a collection, a librarian needs to keep the scope of the materials selection policy in mind. *Children's Catalog* is a standard source that lists a basic collection for small and medium-size libraries. It is invaluable when building a collection.

Libraries manage collection development in several ways. Some libraries have centralized acquisitions with specific staff responsible for selecting new materials for all collections. While this can be efficient, often this staff has little interaction with the public, which can result in their overlooking items that may appeal to specific populations. Children's librarians working in this structure need to take action to keep their collections as strong as possible. First, they need to stay aware of what is being published by staying current with selection tools such as *School Library Journal* and *Booklist*. Second, they need to work with selectors to fill gaps and to request those items that are appropriate for their particular population.

In other libraries, particularly smaller systems, front-line librarians make their own selection using tools such as *School Library Journal*, *Booklist*, and *Kirkus Review*. Each review journal is structured differently. *Kirkus* uses paid reviewers and publishes reviews both good and bad. *Booklist* also uses paid reviewers, but primarily only publishes reviews of books it recommends for inclusion in medium and large libraries. Any caveats for inclusion in the collection are included in the reviews. *School Library Journal* uses the skills of front-line librarians who volunteer to review books. They attempt to review everything published by mainstream publishers. The reviews vary with the sensibility of the reviewers. The *Horn Book* is a trusted review source, but it reviews far fewer books than other journals and its publication schedule often makes them the last reviews to become available.

> While not always timely, *The Horn Book* is an excellent tool for making sure that excellent titles have not been missed. Use it as a clean-up tool for collection development.

The Voice of Youth Advocates (VOYA) is also useful for those dealing with teen collections. The reviews include ratings for excellence of content and writing plus a second rating for teen appeal. By balancing the two ratings, a librarian can find excellent choices for a teen fiction collection.

Generally, using the sources together results in making intelligent choices for your collection. However, access to information about materials from non-mainstream publishers and Christian presses is much harder to find. Librarians can contact them directly, using *Literary Market Place* to find addresses and request catalogs. If a library serves a large number of home-schooled children from the community, staff can check on the periodic Home School Book Fairs that are held. Attending them provides an opportunity to observe personally many of the materials that are not found in reviews.

Previewing is another selection tool with pluses and minuses. Staff actually get to look at items before purchasing, which is a plus. Previewing can be done through plans from publishers that send periodic boxes of new books from which staff can return those that are not desirable for the collection. Salespeople from publishers will happily visit and preview new titles. Previewing provides the advantage of actually seeing what is being purchased, but it is time intensive and will not provide access to everything available.

Subscriptions can be purchased for series items and periodicals. These make sense for basic sets necessary about countries, states, presidents, and various other topics. It saves time and ensures ultimately getting the entire set. It is necessary to examine the sets from various publishers and decide which ones best meet local needs. Popular paperback series can also be done through subscriptions, which will save time.

However, in selecting and purchasing a collection, librarians must be vigilant about including items that express multiple viewpoints on sensitive topics such as gun control, animals rights, and a multitude of others. Collections need to include materials that satisfy the needs of all users. This is equally true of fiction. One way to avoid many book challenges is to have a wide variety of choices for readers. There are numerous Christian presses that produce children's fiction, which fits the sensibilities of many parents. Offering these choices allows staff to comfortably give parents a wide selection of materials from which to choose those that they find most appropriate for their children.

Collections need to reflect the needs of users. More and more materials are becoming available in multiple languages. As populations change, decisions about multiple-language collections need to be made not only for children's materials, but also for the entire collection. These decisions will be based on local and administrative dictates, space, and budgetary decisions. However, children's librarians do have to be aware of a special collection responsibility. We now know that in order to attain language and future reading skills, all babies need early language experiences. Those experiences are primarily provided by parents or child care providers. Unless materials are available in the languages spoken by parents and child care providers, those early experiences will not happen. Therefore, small collections of board books and picture books in whatever languages are prevalent in your community are important. These collections are an investment in the future.

Collection development is also controlled by what is made available by the publishing industry. Librarians need to be aware that changes in children's publishing will have an increasingly powerful impact on collections. The number of children's publishers is diminishing, and most of the publishing houses are now part of large conglomerates. This has led to significant changes in what is published and what remains in print. Marketing and licensing are often driving the bus. For example, the *Curious George* books have been part of children's collections for years. And Curious George is still with us, but in a different way. Just log on to Amazon.com and look at the Curious George sheets, pajamas, lunch boxes, cereal bowls, blankets, stuffed toys, and whatever. A child today can eat, sleep, and play with Curious George without ever reading or even knowing that books exist. Children's publishing is a multimillion dollar industry, but most of that money comes from the licensing and marketing of realia rather than books. The popularity of the American Girl stores in New York and Chicago are another example. The books are a minuscule piece of what is sold and bought. School book fairs contain at least as many non-book items as they do books. For more information on this publishing trend you can read articles by Daniel

Hade, "Storytelling: Are Publishers Changing the Way Children Read?" (Horn Book 2002) and "Reading May Be Harmful to Your Kids," by Tom Engelhardt (Harper's 1991).

> Children's librarians need to know that one of the major forces determining what is published today is not library sales or even chain bookstore sales, but materials that can be easily marketed by giants like Wal-Mart, Kmart, and Target.

And just look at the series of books inspired by Blue's Clues, Care Bears, and Barbie. Inclusion of these in a collection is a personal choice dictated by the Materials Selection Policy, space, and budget. If one believes it is important that early language experiences include excellence in language and demand the best that is available, consider passing on books that are created solely to merchandise or capitalize on other items. If one believes in always providing customers with what they want, and space and budget are not a problem, selection should include these series that are good sellers in bookstores. But it is important to be aware that if this publishing trend, supported by licensing and marketing potential, continues, what will be available for collections may ultimately lack the depth of diversity and richness that can be found today.

CHALLENGES TO ITEMS IN THE COLLECTION

> A good children's library acts in two ways to ensure a minimum of book challenges: The library's selection policy contains a statement that parents are the final arbiters on what is appropriate for their child to read; and, there is a timely process in place for reviewing challenged items.

The final piece of collection maintenance is handling any book challenges that might arise. Every library needs a procedure for handling these challenges. Librarians need to know this procedure and need to be prepared to handle these challenges quickly and carefully. Philosophically, the parents that challenge a book are those parents who are doing exactly what librarians ask parents to do. They are paying attention to what their children are reading. The librarian's job is to acknowledge that, to listen carefully to their concerns, and to help them to understand that he/she respects and applauds their interest in what their children read. The hard part is helping them to understand that they can and should be making these decisions for their child, but not necessarily for *all* children. Many challenges can end with an honest and tactful discussion, those that do not need to be handled quickly, tactfully, and according to library procedure. It is important to keep in mind that with older fiction and some non-fiction, a book that is equally appropriate in a teen collection can be re-cataloged and moved, which can often solve the problem. While the library culture certainly includes a strong intellectual freedom component, it is sometimes more beneficial to retain a title without a public quarrel.

PROGRAMMING

The third leg of our triangle is library programming. This is the area of library service to children that provides the widest latitude for creativity and imagination. It is also the part of children's library services that is changing as more and more information about emergent literacy and reading development becomes available. The basic and most traditional piece of library programming is story time. Originally story times were primarily aimed at pre-school children, ages three and up. Children, with or without their parents, gathered together to enjoy stories shared by enthusiastic librarians. Children's librarians felt secure in the knowledge that they were building future reading skills as they shared the treasures from their collections with young children. As more and more research about emergent literacy became available, children's librarians adapted by creating and offering age and developmentally appropriate story times. Lap-sits for babies, Time for Twos, and Toddler Times were added to library schedules in the 1980s. In the late 1990s, things changed again. First, as families became busier and busier, the trend was to come to whatever story time was convenient with whatever age children one had. The solution here is to offer specific story times, but to allow whoever is present to participate. It is appropriate to advertise the story time for whatever age group it is intended, but no child will be hurt by attending a story time developed for younger children.

A note on advertising your story times. In communities with varied cultural and religious groups, it helps to advertise that holiday stories at Christmas, Halloween, Valentine's Day and Easter may be included. While in many ways these holidays have become very secular, there are still families who may prefer not to expose their children to holidays with a religious content that they do not share. Be inclusive; include Hanukkah, Passover,

Kawanza, and any other holidays celebrated in your area. Be sure to advertise this also. Just a general statement that holiday stories may be used during a particular month allows parents for whom this might be a concern to inquire about a specific story time and then make a personal decision to attend or not.

> A librarian concerned with providing a good modeling experience for parents will include comments during the story time such as, "I chose this book because of the rhyming language, or I chose these books so the children could count the items on each page."

In the last five years scientific research on how emergent literacy develops and how children become ready to read has exploded. It is now believed that the literacy value of a group story time is relatively small, although the socialization value of being part of a group is significant. And research shows that one early language experience a week is not sufficient. Children's librarians need to shift their focus slightly, but not necessarily change what they do, except in minor ways. The real value of library story times is modeling how to use books with young children for parents and care givers who spend much more time with a child than a librarian can. The first step is opening up all story times to the adults accompanying the children. Many librarians prefer not to do this for many reasons, including space and the fact that adults can be disruptive with talking during the story time. However providing the modeling of how to use books is vital and, in our litigious society, it just makes sense for librarians to include adults in all programs for young children. The second step is a simple amplification of any story time. As a story is finished, one or two questions for the adults will help them to see what the particular book is accomplishing. For example, explaining that this book was chosen because it uses rhyme and repetitive language which help a child's brain to develop the synaptic connections needed for reading readiness is a valuable clue for parents when selecting books to use at home.

Research also tells us that movement and music provide the cross-lateral brain action needed for reading readiness. Finger plays and musical ditties with movement should be a part of every story time. It does not matter if a librarian cannot sing! Get that CD player out and go from there. The inclusion of crafts is another issue. Current research says that including the kinds of crafts most libraries use with very young children is actually counterproductive to artistic development. Using precut pieces and coloring sheets that result in a presentable product actually retards artistic development, particularly in very young children. The dilemma here is that parents love these crafts! Ironically, just as a once-a-week literacy experience is not sufficient, a once-a week craft experience is not detrimental. However, if librarians are modeling for parents, they should not model behavior that will be repeated but will not be productive. Rather than a carefully prepared craft, give children a large piece of paper and a crayon or marker and let them draw!

> If you choose to do a family literacy program, choose one based on the cost of training and materials, whether or not every staff member must be trained, and the cost of supporting materials. It's also important to consider when you offer the program. Evenings work for many families, but you usually need to provide both dinner and child care. Maybe a Saturday morning or Sunday afternoon is a better choice.

Currently, more and more libraries are offering or participating in Family Literacy programs. These include MotherRead, the Mother Goose Programs offered by the Vermont Center for the Book, Prime Time, Family Place Libraries, and Every Child Ready to Read@Your Library offered by the Public Library Association, among others. Each library needs to assess its needs and resources when deciding to purchase and/or train staff in a particular program. The costs vary widely; some are proprietary, others are not. Prepackaged programs can save time, and they often include scripts that can be used which are helpful to librarians for whom this is a new direction. When choosing a program, be sure it is research-based. This will afford better opportunities to seek and receive grant funding.

Successful Family Literacy programs are usually done in collaboration or partnership with schools, Head Start, Human Service Departments, or other agencies that work with children. Before starting, find out what is already available in your community and make connections with the people and agencies involved. Many of them may have funding or other resources available that will help a library get started and continue the program. And many of them may not have considered the library as a potential resource and partner.

The second, sacred part of library programming is Summer Reading. Traditionally Summer Reading was almost a contest with children competing with each other or with themselves to see how many books they could read. Small prizes were given for achievement; a certificate of completion was awarded at the end of the program. Special programs such as Puppet Shows and other entertainment were offered to attract children to the library. In recent history, state libraries and other local consortiums have banded together to produce Summer Reading themes and materials. This certainly made it easier for children's librarians and resulted in better graphics, which are often done by children's illustrators. In the 1990s, the philosophy behind Summer Reading started changing. Rewarding consistency in both reading and library visits was considered more important than quantity. Libraries refashioned programs stressing weekly library visits and daily reading.

Programs for teens often have a different theme and incentives. Using teen volunteers during the summer cannot only help you by providing extra laborers, but also can help to promote their participation in the program.

Since modeling for young children is an important part of emergent literacy, having a reading program for adults makes sense. Children seeing parents reading and enjoying it can be a powerful literacy tool.

Summer Reading programs may be undergoing more changes in the near future. The Johns Hopkins Institute for Summer Learning is doing research on the efficacy of Summer Reading programs, summer school, and other summer activities. The results of that research may shape Summer Reading in the future. In 2005, the states of Georgia and Virginia piloted a Summer Reading program that is predicated on family literacy activities rather than individual reading. This may be the wave of the future. The exciting aspect of these changes is that there is research being done and published that can substantiate the value of Summer Reading. This is important information to use with administrators, funders, and the public when seeking money for summer programs. Since this research looks at the broad picture of summer learning, this may also be an excellent opportunity for schools and libraries to collaborate on summer programs.

Library programming throughout the year serves multiple purposes. It attracts new people to the library, it highlights collections, people, and organizations in your community, and it affords additional opportunities to promote emergent literacy. Programming includes paid performers such as puppeteers, storytellers, musical groups, and children's theater groups. These performers come in all price ranges and quality levels. And, this is one time where libraries do not necessarily get what they pay for. There are many groups, storytellers, and entertainers who are just getting started who provide charming programs at reasonable prices. Librarians need to check with other libraries and schools to ferret them out. The best way to decide if a performer meets a library's needs is to preview a performance at another library or a performers' showcase. If that is not possible, then ask for and check references. When hiring a performer or group be sure to check space and technical needs.

> Almost every community has people willing to share their expertise or hobbies. Chess clubs, gardening groups, dancing schools, college professors, and local businesses may be excellent sources of programs. Ask around and be creative.

Local museums can be an excellent source of programs. Many have educational departments that create and offer programs to the community. Local colleges and universities often have faculty that are happy to do programs in their areas of expertise. Local police and fire departments are usually happy to provide programs. And don't forget the business community. Many small businesses and professional offices are happy to collaborate with the public library. A series of story times featuring community helpers is always popular. So check with local veterinarians, bakeries dancing schools, karate instructors, newspaper writers, weather forecasters, construction workers (ask them to bring trucks), artists, and musicians. The librarian's job is to find an appropriate story for them or a staff member to read, and then have them talk about a typical day in their life.

> Authors are available through publishers. Most large publishing companies have staff, which arranges such visits. Visitingauthors.com has a good selection of authors and illustrators. They have excellent guidelines on doing a first author visit and will provide books for purchase at a discount if you want to include a book sale to offset costs.

Author visits are another wonderful programming event. However, these are a lot of work and often very expensive. Author honoraria range from a few hundred to several thousand dollars a day. And all authors are not created equal when it comes to speaking with children. Some of the best include Claudia Mills, Mary Downing Hahn, Katharine Patterson, Steven Kellogg, Eric Kimmel, Tedd Arnold, George Ella Lyon, Amy Hest, Diane Stanley, Judith Caseley, Megan McDonald, Peter Catalanotto, Bernard Most, R. L. Stine, Phyllis Haislip, Marc Brown, and Vicki Cobb. One of the best places to get information about author visits is: *www.visitingauthors.com*. Whether or not one of the authors they represent appeals, the mechanics of the visit are the same. Author visits can also be arranged through publishers. And keep in mind that local authors may well have as good a program as the more well known. When hosting an author be sure to understand all of your responsibilities. Libraries will be paying not only an honorarium but also expenses. Many authors require a hotel rather than staying in someone's home. Some have dietary requirements. Others will or won't autograph books. These are all reasonable questions to ask up front. Most authors do three presentations a day for their basic honorarium. Programs can be offered to schools or shared with schools and/or other closely located libraries helping to defray costs.

Sharing programs leads to the last piece of complete children's services—outreach. Librarians have long known that many of the children who need library services the most do not have easy access to library buildings or bookmobiles. Busier schedules, more children in daycare, and increased Internet access at home have changed the face of who comes to the library. Simultaneously, increased school accountability has left less time for inclusion of literature in the classroom.

Librarians need to find ways to go to where the children are or to arrange library visits by schools and daycare centers. This includes not only the school year but the summer as well. A carefully devised outreach program includes bringing story times to daycare centers and preschool programs such as Head Start. It includes finding ways to read to school-age children at before and after school programs as well as in the classroom. When planned collaboratively, these programs not only allow libraries to reach more children, but they also help to share the expertise in children's literature and how to effectively use it with children and with those educators and daycare providers who spend much more time with children than any librarian can. It is definitely a win-win situation. It also helps to make a library visible in all parts of the community.

CONCLUSION

In conclusion, a good children's librarian has an excellent working knowledge of the collection, which he/she maintains rigorously, provides opportunities to model the use of books with adults who have frequent access to young children, and offers a variety of programs, both in the library and on an outreach basis. A children's librarian does everything possible to be sure that the children who live in his/her community learn those stories that will keep them from becoming lost in life.

REFERENCES

Crew method: Expanded guidelines for collection evaluation and weeding for small and medium-size public libraries. Austin, TX: Texas State Library.

Gillespie, John T. 1998. *Best books for children.* R. R. Bowker.

Gillespie, John T., and Barr, Catherine. 2004. *Best books for middle school and junior high readers.* Englewood, CO: Libraries Unlimited.

Holley, Pam Spencer. 2002. *What do children and young adults read next.* Farmington Hills, MI: Thomson Gale Research.

Lima, Carolyn. 2001. *A to zoo.* Westport, CT: Bowker Greenwood.

Price, Anne, and Yaakov, Juliette editors. 2001. *Childrens catalog, 18th ed.* New York: H. W. Wilson.

FURTHER READING

Anderson, Sheila. 2005. *Extreme teens.* Englewood, CO: Libraries Unlimited.

Bettleheim, Bruno. 1976. *The Uses of Enchantment.* New York: Knopf.

Blanshard, Catherine, ed. 1997. *Children and young people*: Library association guidelines for public library services. New York: Neal-Schuman.

Chelton, Mary K. 2000. *Excellence in library services for young adults.* Chicago, IL: Young adult library services.

Feinberg, Sandra ed. 2006. *Family centered library handbook.* New York: Neal-Schuman.

Fiore, Carole D. 2005. *Fiore's summer library reading program handbook.* New York: Neal-Schuman.

Maddigan, Beth. 2005. *Big book of reading, rhymes and resources.* Englewood, CO: Libraries Unlimited.

Robb, Laura. 2003. *Literacy links.* New York: Heinemann.

Trotta, Marcia. 1993. *Managing library outreach programs.* New York: Neal-Schuman.

Part IV

Collection Development in the Small Library

17 SELECTION

Barbara Rice

DEFINITION

Selection is the decision process for adding new materials to the collection.

OVERVIEW

This chapter covers:

- Difference between selection and collection development
- Selection and collection development policies
- Sources for obtaining information on materials
- Ideas to stretch selection funds
- Need for and process of materials reconsideration

SELECTION AND COLLECTION DEVELOPMENT

Selection, as defined above, is the decision process for adding new materials to the collection. Collection development includes selection, however, it is a broader term that takes in the whole approach to the selection of materials. Figure 17-1 is selection policy from the Williamsburg Regional Library. It assigns who has the responsibility for the selection process and makes general comments about the collection as a whole. How that responsibility is carried out and how selection decisions are made in specific areas are not delineated.

Figure 17-1 Selection Policy

The Williamsburg Regional Library Board of Trustees delegates responsibility for selection of the library's collection to the Library Director. Staff members choose items for the collection based on the wide range of community tastes and interests. Therefore, items in the collection will not necessarily appeal to all community tastes and interests.

Materials chosen for the youth services section are selected to appeal to children of different ages and interests. Therefore, not everything in the youth services section will be appropriate for all children. Library staff members will help parents and children locate materials, but they cannot presume to make decisions for parents as to which library materials are appropriate for their children.

[Approved by WRL Board of Trustees September 13,1995. Approved as amended by WRL Board of Trustees January 23, 2002. Reaffirmed by WRL Board of Trustees March 10, 2004]. Used with permission.

A collection development policy, on the other hand is much more specific about the collection and how it is to be developed. See Figure 17-2 for an example developed by the Lilly and Wildman Libraries at Earlham College.

Figure 17-2 Collection Development Policy

Purpose: This statement is designed to be a set of guidelines to stimulate our thinking about the purposes for which the Libraries' collections are created and maintained. As guidelines, this statement should help empower individuals to make decisions about additions to the collection. The statement also outlines basic procedures and responsibilities. Through the creation and revision of the statement, it is hoped that we will have a collective sense of the goals of our collection development effort and the procedures for handling order requests. This statement is supplemented by a Collection Development Policy Statement prepared by the Joint Library Committee of Bethany Theological Seminary and the Earlham School of Religion.

Introduction: Selection of materials for the College's libraries is a community effort that involves faculty and other College staff, librarians, and other library staff, and students. The selection is done within the restrictions of a materials budget allocated to the library each year plus restricted gift and endowment income funds. The library director and the acquisitions supervisor manage the funds and the acquisition process.

Scope: The College's collections that are the responsibility of the library include: (1) monographs, serials and periodicals regardless of format, (2) audio recordings, (3) CD-ROMs and (4) online databases. (Media Services has responsibility for video formats and Computing Services is responsible for the selection of multimedia used in classroom and lab instruction. Because there is no campus policy about who is responsible for multimedia of general reference value there is a need for open communication among the three units about the areas of overlap, especially as new formats of material appear.)

These collections are developed primarily to support the academic program of the College. This includes support of students' course related research projects and faculty course preparation. Support is also provided for independent studies, faculty/student collaborative research activities such as the Ford/Knight Projects, student initiated courses, and any other academic activities in which students are involved. Items are also added to the collection to provide a basic coverage of disciplines and subjects outside the curriculum. The collections, in a limited fashion, also support the general interests of the community. Collection development in support of faculty's personal research is a lesser priority. The library borrows material from other libraries to support faculty research, and the College provides support for professional development activities through the Professional Development Fund.

Criteria: In the selection process, individuals make decisions within the context of these guidelines. To make a selection, each individual applies the scope and criteria statements outlined in this document to the items being considered for purchase. The criteria can be grouped in five categories (1) the quality of the material, (2) importance of the material within its respective discipline and scholarship in general, (3) relevance to the academic program, (4) usefulness to the academic program and (5) intellectual accessibility.

(1) Quality. The quality of an item is based upon its accuracy, its currency, and its physical characteristics (e.g., printing, paper and binding quality). In accessing quality, book reviews are helpful along with reputational information about the author and/or publisher.

(continued)

Figure 17-2   Collection Development Policy (*Continued*)

(2)   Importance of the material within its respective field of study and scholarship in general. The "importance" characteristic of an item calls for a high level of discernment that takes into account a number of factors. Some of the factors include the reputation of the author and/or publisher, the uniqueness of its contribution to the field, and its reputation within the field, and the impact of the material's content on the development of the field.

(3)   Relevance to the academic program. Relevance refers to the degree of connection between an item's content and the content of the Earlham academic program.

(4)   Usefulness to the academic program. In simplest terms, the question is: How likely is the material to be used given the current and future curriculum? If there is a high probability students and faculty will use an item, then it should be a high priority.

(5)   Intellectual accessibility. The content of the work should be accessible to undergraduate students. Therefore material aimed exclusively or primarily at research specialists is of lower priority.

None of these five criteria has veto power over the other four. Instead the five criteria must be balanced against one another. An item may be important within its respective field of study but its subject is not part of our curriculum and therefore not immediately useful or relevant. However, because adequate coverage of all areas of scholarship at some basic level is important such a work should be acquired. On the other hand an item that will be, with a high degree of certainty, heavily used by students but is less important within a discipline would also be purchased. Other combinations of characteristics can also be imagined. These guidelines are not intended to provide specific rules for every set of circumstances. They are designed to articulate the characteristics that should be considered in making a decision to purchase.

Source: www.earlham.edu/~libr/library/coldev.htm

The collection development document discusses how the various principles are applied to specific areas of the collection, including monographs, periodicals, indexes, and other library resources.

As Figures 17-1 and 17-2 indicate, before materials can be properly selected for the collection, there must be a thorough understanding of where the responsibility for this selection rests and what criteria will be used in the selection process. Otherwise, time and money will be wasted and a collection developed that will likely not meet user needs or expectations.

An important part of any collection development policy is to make sure that the collection reflects the needs of all community residents. It is easy to let personal interest and bias creep into the selection process. The American Library Association's Library Bill of Rights directly addresses this basic expectation of library service. See Figure 17-3.

Figure 17-3   Library Bill of Rights

The American Library Association affirms that all libraries are forums for information and ideas, and that the following basic policies should guide their services.

1.   Books and other library resources should be provided for the interest, information, and enlightenment of all people of the community the library serves. Materials should not be excluded because of the origin, background, or views of those contributing to their creation.

2.   Libraries should provide materials and information presenting all points of view on current and historical issues. Materials should not be proscribed or removed because of partisan or doctrinal disapproval.

3.   Libraries should challenge censorship in the fulfillment of their responsibility to provide information and enlightenment.

4.   Libraries should cooperate with all persons and groups concerned with resisting abridgement of free expression and free access to ideas.

5.   A person's right to use a library should not be denied or abridged because of origin, age, background, or views.

6.   Libraries which make exhibit spaces and meeting rooms available to the public they serve should make such facilities available on an equitable basis, regardless of the beliefs or affiliations of individual or groups requesting their use.

Source: American Library Association. *Intellectual Freedom Manual 6th Edition.*, pp. 57–58

The first four parts of the Library Bill of Rights relate directly to the process of material selection for any library and should be a cornerstone of any procedure or policy document developed to assist in the process of acquiring new materials for the collection.

SOURCES

There are several ways to find information on new books and other materials. Traditional resources like *Choice, Kirkus Reviews, Library Journal, Publisher's Weekly,* and *School Library Journal* are mainstays. They can be expensive for the small library. However, through working with other libraries in the area the library can obtain access to these resources without having to purchase all of them. Ask area libraries if they would like to share subscriptions. The more institutions that participate the lower the cost to any one library. For example, three libraries decide to go in together for *Library Journal, Publishers Weekly,* and *Kirkus Reviews.* The total for all three subscriptions is divided three ways and each library gets one of the three periodicals mailed to them. After a week, each library sends their copy to the next library and in three weeks time, all three libraries have had a chance to look through the issues.

Another good source is book reviews found in newspapers and magazines. Ones that are read by library patrons can be especially useful. Try to look through the book review section before they do to get some information about the books before patrons ask about them. Good resources to which the library may already subscribe are any newspapers from major cities; many of these newspapers have a weekly book section with reviews or bestseller lists. For ones in the collection, use the Internet. Many newspapers have online versions, which will include their book review sections. Other resources such as *People Magazine* and *Southern Living* are very popular with the many library users and each issue contains a section with book reviews. Never underestimate reviews from these "non-traditional" sources. They may actually have reviews of books from some of the smaller publishing firms that may not get picked up by the professional journals. And keep in mind: If it's something patrons read about, there is a greater chance of that title being requested.

Make use of free online sources such as *Library Journal's* Prepub Alert for popular authors and topics. Amazon.com is another free source that should be used. Look at other libraries' online catalogs for items that are on order and find titles of interest for your community. It's free and easy to do.

> Word of mouth is an important part of the selection process.

Word of mouth is always a sure thing in small communities. If one person hears about a book and talks to a friend about it, chances are the library will soon be next in line to hear about this new "must have" for the collection. In some cases, when the title may not be a bestseller or may be something out of the mainstream, suggest the patron buy a copy of a book, read it, and then donate it to the library. The library benefits by getting a donated copy and the patron benefits by counting it on their taxes as a taxable donation. Another enticement is to ask them to write up what they thought about it as well. If the library has a newsletter or another type of informational flyer, consider adding a column of reader reviews. This is a surefire way to get more people interested in helping out. Buy a book, read it, and have their review put into the library newsletter. People love seeing their name in print and the library will likely have regular contributors in no time.

Ask patrons to donate their magazines after they have read them. One small county in East Tennessee had no funds for magazines but still had a wall full of magazines in their library. How was this possible? They created a successful program that involved their patrons promising to buy a magazine subscription, get it delivered to their homes where they had three days to read it then bring it into the library where it became part of the magazine collection. In addition, several local businesses donated subscriptions to magazines that were delivered directly to the library. Plaques or signs for each item bearing the name of the person or business donating it may also be made. Include a tag line letting others know that they can participate in this program as well.

Ask patrons to donate those gently read books. Tell them about the tax deduction they may receive for donations to the library. Get local businesses in on the deal, too. Talk to the local businesses and their employees. Create or purchase attractive bookplates to be placed in the books that get donated. Most individuals like to see their name in print. For those that don't mind the extra publicity, put their name in a column of the library newsletter that thanks those who donated that month. Even offer a contest to the individual and business that make the most donations in one year. The prize can be something as simple as a basket of fresh baked muffins to putting their picture in the lobby as "Patron of the Year." It's a very inexpensive way to get donations and patrons will get a tax deduction in the process.

MATERIALS RECONSIDERATION

When a user brings a request to remove an item from the collection it is important to have a good procedure in place. All staff must understand this procedure and know how to follow it. Three important elements are the library's materials selection policy/procedure; a request for reconsideration form, and procedures for handling such requests. The procedure needs to be well written describing how the process works and what considerations are used in selecting materials for the collection. The reconsideration form asks the individual to discuss in detail his/her objections to the material. See Figure 17-4 for a sample form and statement.

Figure 17-4   Materials Reconsideration Form

Tuscarawas County Public Library
New Philadelphia, OH
Citizen's Request for Reconsideration of Materials
Format (Book, Video, etc.) _____

Author (if applicable) _____

Title (or URL) _____

Publisher _____

Your Name _____

Address _____

Telephone _____

Group you represent (if any)

Did you examine the entire work? _____. If not, what parts?

What do you believe is the purpose of this material? _____

_____

Specifically, to what in the material do you object? _____

What harmful effect do you feel might be/was the effect of your using this material?

_____

Is there anything good or useful about this material?

What? _____

What prompted you to use this item?_____

For what age group would you recommend this item?_____

What would you recommend to replace this item?

_____

_____

Figure 17-5   Materials Reconsideration Statement

We are sorry if you have been offended by any material in our collection. The Tuscarawas County Public Library subscribes to the Library Bill of Rights as adopted by the American Library Association, June 27, 1967, and its subsequent amendments. This document reads, in part: "as a responsibility of library service, books and other library materials selected should be chosen for values of interest, information and enlightenment of all the people of the community." We realize that everyone's tastes are different, and that it is our responsibility to provide materials on a multitude of subjects and viewpoints, in many styles.

The Internet makes available a wide variety of material, most of it useful and worthwhile, but some Internet sites are unsuitable for children and offensive to many adults. Unfortunately, we cannot filter out such sites without also eliminating access to many good resources. We have no control over Internet information, and we caution parents and others that objectionable sites do exist, although they are not usually accessible except by deliberate choice on the part of the browser. Library policy prohibits the use of sites, which may reasonably be construed as obscene, and individuals who access such sites may lose their Internet privileges.

If you honestly feel that a book or other item in our collection does not belong in the library of a free society, we invite you to fill out the form on the reverse side of this sheet and leave it at the front desk. The desk clerk will see that it is given to the library director, who will be in touch with you regarding your complaint.

The Tuscarawas County Public Library believes in the rights of a free press guaranteed by the Constitution of the United States of America. We further believe that the parents of a child are the only people who should be allowed to monitor the reading, watching or listening activities of that child. Conversely, we believe that it is every parent's duty to monitor his or her child's activity, and that this is not the prerogative of the library.

Source: *winslo.state.oh.us/publib/material_tuscaw.html*

Both sample form and procedure presented may be modified to be used in any type of library.

The main point in any reconsideration request is to listen to the concerns of the individual, make sure that you understand them, and then quietly explain the library's material selection process and ask for suggestions as to materials that might be added to the collection to address their concern. Many reconsideration requests will end at this level, as many individuals simply desire that their complaint be registered and understood. However, if it goes further, make sure that the procedure for handling these requests is thorough and well thought out.

If the request proceeds beyond the initial filing make sure that it is brought to the attention of the local governing body. Prepare them for receipt of the request and remind them of what will be required of them and for the publicity that such a request will bring to them.

Smaller communities are often tight-knit so be sensitive to the patron's request while defending the material using the materials selection procedures. Make sure that all steps of the reconsideration process are documented.

The following is an example of how a decision was made on a controversial newsletter. The library was approached by an atheist organization and offered free subscriptions to their newsletter for all five branches of the system. After talking to the branch managers, who all felt uneasy about this item, a compromise was struck. The library agreed to receive only one subscription at the main library. The group agreed and the library started getting the quarterly newsletter. It was placed with the other newspapers and periodicals.

Close to two years after the library began receiving this newsletter, a complaint was received from a local church minister who wanted the item removed immediately. The library director thanked him for his concern and asked that he put his request in writing. The request was brought to the attention of the library Board of Trustees. The library director met with the branch managers and staff. The director asked if someone would volunteer to read a few issues of the newsletter and give her a fair unbiased review. Not one issue of the newsletter had ever been checked out, nor did anyone on staff ever recall seeing anyone reading it or remember ever re-shelving an issue. In fact, the minister himself admitted that he did not read the newsletter and had no desire to ever do so. He had heard from someone in his congregation that we had the newsletter on our magazine shelves.

The director read reviews of the newsletter, which were fairly neutral. One staff member made the comment that what better way to know how to understand a group you disagree with than to read their newsletter. Most said that while they had no interest in it and could see why some would take offense to having it in our system, it did have a place in our collection based on the fact that we had other material on religion including books that had sections on atheism. The item remained in the collection. However, about six months later, the director did an annual review of the periodical collection. Items with little or no use were usually discontinued and sometimes replaced with something similar. It was during this review that the controversial newsletter was still found not to have been read once, even after all the commotion from months earlier, so it was decided to discontinue it. The director contacted the person who was giving the library the subscription, thanked her for her generosity and explained that after more than two years, there was no interest in it. She understood and agreed to end our subscription. It should be noted that in that same review period, other changes were made to our periodical collection based on the same criteria used in this case.

CONCLUSION

Selection of materials for the library collection is one of the most enjoyable and challenging tasks facing any library employee. The joy comes in being able to use one's knowledge of the library and the community it serves to bring new resources to people hungry for knowledge, relaxation reading, or information to assist them in their daily lives. The challenge comes in making sure that all segments of the library's public are provided with resources to satisfy their needs for information. The information presented in this chapter and the additional resources listed below should assist librarians in all types of libraries to successfully complete the materials selection process.

REFERENCES

American Library Association. 2002. *Intellectual freedom manual 6th edition.* Chicago: American Library Association.

Cirino, Paul John. 1991. *The business of running a library: A handbook for public library directors.* Jefferson, NC: McFarland & Company.

Earlham College Library. 2005. *Collection development policy.* Richmond, IN: Earlham College.

Evans, G. Edward. 1979. *Developing library collections.* Westport, CT: Libraries Unlimited.

Turner, Anne M. 1993. *It comes with the territory: Handling problem situations in libraries.* Jefferson, NC: McFarland & Company.

Tuscarawas County Public Library. 2005. *Materials reconsideration policy.* New Philadelphia, OH: Tuscarawas County Public Library.

Williamsburg Regional Library. *Selection policy.* Williamsburg, VA: Williamsburg Regional Library.

FURTHER READING

Alabaster, Carol. 2002. *Developing an outstanding core collection: A guide for libraries.* Chicago: American Library Association.

Burgett, James et al. 2004. *Collaborative collection development: A practical guide for your library.* Chicago: American Library Association.

Curtis, Donnelyn, and Virginia M. Scheachy. 2005. *E-journals: A how-to-do-it manual for building, managing, and supporting electronic journal collections.* New York: Neal-Schuman.

Eaglen, Audrey. 2000. *Buying books: A how-to-do-it manual for librarians.* New York: Neal-Schuman.

Johnson, Peggy. 2003. *Fundamentals of collection development and management.* Chicago: American Library Association.

Lee, Stuart D. 2002. *Electronic collection development: A practical guide.* New York: Neal Schuman.

Nisinger, Thomas E. 2003. *Evaluation of library collections, access and electronic resources.* Westport, CT: Libraries Unlimited.

18 ORDERING

Barbara Rice

DEFINITION

Ordering is the process whereby desired items for addition to the library's collection are obtained from a supplier and brought to the library.

OVERVIEW

This chapter covers:

- Management tools available to aid the ordering process
- Options available for ordering materials
- Receipt of materials once they have arrived in the library

While this book separates ordering and selection, ordering is really an extension of the selection process and could as well be covered together with selection. A few of the items covered here could be considered as a part of the selection process as well but are covered in this chapter.

The first step in the ordering process is deciding whether the items to be ordered are appropriate for the collection. Do they fit into the mission of the library's collection, do they fill gaps, are they appropriate updates to older materials, is there evidence that they will be used by patrons (particularly in the public and school library setting)? How can this be determined? Most libraries have automated catalog systems. These systems can issue reports by subject or call number areas to indicate age of collection, dates of last use, give an indication of circulation frequency, and give number of holdings in specific classification areas. Make use of these reports.

Another good source for collection analysis is the *World Cat Collection Analysis* product developed by OCLC. If the library's holdings are in *World Cat* the publication becomes an invaluable tool through which the library's holdings may be compared with the holdings of other libraries in its peer group, and strengths and gaps in the collection can be quickly obtained. In addition, it would be a good tool for academic libraries for the creation of reports needed during the institutional re-accreditation process. While the cost of this product may be out of reach for many small libraries, it could be purchased by academic consortia or state library agencies and made available to small libraries at a reasonable cost.

Once it has been determined that an item is to be ordered a record is made of that item. This record needs to include author, title, publisher, who requested the item, cataloging information if it is available, relevant information to the order, that is, order number, place from which it was ordered, anticipated cost, which account to charge the item to, and then space to record the information relevant to the eventual receipt of the item. The form on which this record is made will need to have sufficient sheets so that copies may be sent to the supplier, and be available for attaching to financial records and to the item once it is received in the library.

Many libraries now have an acquisitions system as part of their automated systems. With these systems this information is generated automatically and the need for paper copies is limited or totally eliminated.

> Collect only the information necessary for the acquisitions process.

Materials acquisition is as much an art as a science. The individual(s) responsible for the purchasing of materials need to have a good familiarity with the variety of sources for materials. These include:

- Wholesalers
- Publishers
- Publishers overstock/remainder houses
- Local book and music stores
- Online sources
- Out-of-print dealers
- Specialty dealers

Wholesalers are one of the best sources for library materials. These are companies that carry many titles from a variety of publishers in large quantities. Examples of wholesalers include Baker and Taylor, Ingram, and Midwest Library Service. Due to their large volume of business they can offer discounts off the list price of items. If the library orders from wholesalers, it usually has access to computerized listings of their holdings and the number of volumes of each title available. Titles can be ordered online. The advantages of using wholesalers include cost savings, knowledge of immediate availability of titles, and the ability to consolidate ordering through one source.

A publishing company is the entity that produces the title. While many publishers' titles are also sold through wholesalers, wholesalers may be selective in what they handle and the publisher may not be represented in their inventory. Sometimes the only source for a title is the publisher. An advantage of using the publisher is that it can be the fastest way of acquiring the title and also may be the only source for the title. Disadvantages include the lower discount usually given by publishers and the additional paperwork necessary to complete the transaction.

Firms that deal in publishers' overstock are sometimes also referred to as remainder houses. These firms specialize in purchasing the remaining stock of publishers when the publisher no longer desires to carry a title. Many publishers keep titles in stock for only a short time so the only way to acquire items is through this source. Examples of remainder houses include Main Book Shop, Daedalus Books and Music, and American Book Company. Location information is listed in the Reference section at the end of the chapter.

Local book and music stores are other sources for collection materials. The advantage to using these sources is the immediacy of acquisition. If you need something today and they have it in stock, it is in the library today. Advantages of this source include the immediacy of availability and the fact that the library is supporting local business. Disadvantages include minimal discount and the extra work that is involved in processing books acquired in this manner.

Online sources are an increasing factor in materials acquisition. Firms such as Amazon and Alibris provide additional sources for the items that a library needs. The advantages of this source include discounts, rapid availability of titles, and the additional information that is available on titles including readers' reviews. They may be located at www.amazon.com and www.alibris.com.

Out-of-print dealers specialize in obtaining titles that are no longer available through the publisher. As indicated above, the in-print life of a title may be short as publishers need to move stock to keep profit margins at a satisfactory level. Thus, poor selling titles will be quickly disposed of to overstock or remainder firms. Sometimes even popular titles will no longer be available as the initial run is sold out and it is not in the publisher's interest to reprint. There may be out-of-print dealers in your area that would delight in working with the library. A good Internet source to find out-of-print books is *www.abebooks.com*.

Specialty dealers are companies that deal with specific subject areas or genres. Because their scope is narrower than jobbers' and they have a thorough knowledge of the areas in which they specialize, these dealers are of great assistance in locating hard to find items.

A good source for locating specialty dealers would be the American Booksellers Association's web site at: *www.bookweb.org*. They can also be located through the *www.abebooks.com* site listed above.

The above sources are good for the location and purchase of most types of library materials. For magazines there are two basic purchase options: going direct to the publisher or purchasing through a supplier that specializes in this type of material. Even in the smallest library there will likely be 50 to 100 magazines being purchased. Ordering each title directly from the publisher is a time-consuming and costly task.

The best solution is to use the services of a vendor who specializes in this area. These vendors, similar to the wholesalers described above, have access to large numbers of publications. They can provide needed magazines often at a discount and can coordinate subscription terms to meet budget requirements of the small library. Examples of these vendors include EBSCO, DEMCO, and W.T. Cox. Location information can be found in the Reference section at the end of the chapter.

Newspapers are usually purchased directly from the publisher. Sometimes they can be purchased through a distributor in the library's area that handles more than one newspaper. Sometimes a periodical vendor can also be a source of newspapers, particularly those with national interest.

Another source to look at in the purchase of materials is cooperative purchasing agreements. These may be with an academic library consortium, regional or state school district purchasing agreements, or any type of public library consortium. An example of this arrangement is the SWING consortium in Virginia. This consortium of libraries primarily in the western part of the state, is open to all Virginia libraries. Through the combined materials budgets of the participating libraries they are able to negotiate substantial discounts with major book wholesalers.

> Types of Binding
> - Library binding
> - Trade
> - Paperback
> - Plastic bound paperback

When ordering materials be sure to specify the type of binding desired. Most libraries will prefer to have library binding wherever possible, as it is more durable. This is particularly important where items will receive heavy use. Particularly in the public library setting, paperback binding should be used sparingly as it has a short shelf life before wearing out.

Another aspect of the ordering process is the decision on processing. Before a book is ready for the shelves, in addition to it being cataloged (subject of the next chapter) it must receive a book jacket and have a spine label indicating the call number of the item. This can be done in-house or can be done by the book vendor as a part of the ordering process.

In deciding whether to process materials in-house or have processing done by the wholesaler the following needs to be considered:

- Number of items purchased each year from sources that do not offer processing, i.e., publishers, out-of-print companies, overstock/remainder houses
- Staffing level of the library
- Availability of volunteers to perform processing tasks
- Space available for processing of materials

The answers to these questions will vary from library to library and type of library to type of library. Some libraries, such as special libraries, may order most of their materials from sources other than wholesalers and will of necessity do processing in-house. However, having processing accomplished as a part of the ordering process can be cost effective and a way to get material quickly available to the library's patrons upon receipt.

Upon receipt of an item by the library the following needs to be done:

- Make sure that the invoice number matches the number on the packing slip, mailing label, and any other paperwork that comes with the order. Never start processing any item until the invoice is in hand.
- Examine each item against the original order and against the packing slip enclosed with the order.

- Examine each item to make sure it is in proper condition to be accepted by the library. Look at binding and quickly rifle through the book to make sure that signatures are in correct order.
- Place item in its proper place for next step in getting ready for use.
- Indicate in your record system the receipt of item, date received, and cost.
- Indicate in your record system any item that is no longer available from the ordering source. This item then becomes a candidate for sending to another source for acquisition.
- Approve invoice for payment and forward it to proper individual for payment.

For a magazine or newspaper a similar check-in process is used. Some libraries will have a serials check-in system as a part of their automation system. In this case it is a simple matter to enter the receipt of each issue into the system. The system can also flag when an expected issue has not been received so that a claim for the issue can be made with the supplier. If the library does not have an automated serials check-in system then a simple spreadsheet, or card, system can be used to check in materials.

CONCLUSION

The process of ordering materials for the library is one of the most enjoyable and challenging to be found within the library. Being involved in the process that brings new materials into the library and seeing patrons delight upon their receipt is one of the pleasures of librarianship. The challenge comes in finding sources for collection needs and in dealing with the wide variety of sources needed to bring materials to the library's public. It is a task that requires tact, patience, accuracy, and a good knowledge of the community the library serves.

RESOURCES

Alibris. *www.alibris.com.*
Amazon. *www.amazon.com.*

American Book Company. *www.americanbookcompany.com.*
Baker and Taylor. *www.btol.com.*
Daedalus Books and Music. *www.daedalusbooks.com.*
DEMCO. *www.demco.com.*
EBSCO. *www.ebsco.com.*
Ingram. *www.ingramlibrary.com.*
Main Bookshop. *www.mainbookshop.com.*
Midwest Library Services. *www.midwestls.com.*
SWING. *www.swing-lib.org.*
W.T. Cox. *www.wtcox.com.*
World Cat Collection Analysis. *www.oclc.org.*

FURTHER READING

Chapman, Liz. 2004. *Managing acquisitions in library and information services 3rd ed.* New York: Neal-Schuman.

Eaglin, Audrey. 2000. *Buying books: A how-to-do-it manual for librarians, 2nd ed.* New York: Neal-Schuman.

Lukenbill, W. Bernard. 2002. *Collection management for a new century in the school library media center.* Westport, CT: Libraries Unlimited.

Nisonger, Thomas E. 1998. *Management of serials in libraries.* Westport, CT.: Libraries Unlimited.

Stein, Barbara L., and Risa W. Brown. 2002. *Running a school library media center: A how-to-do-it manual 2nd ed.* New York: Neal-Schuman.

Wilkinson, Frances C., and Linda K. Lewis. 2003. *The complete guide to acquisitions management.* Westport, CT: Libraries Unlimited.

19 CATALOGING

John A. Moorman

DEFINITION

Cataloging is the process whereby an item is assigned a classification number and subject headings and entered into the library's catalog.

OVERVIEW

This chapter covers:

- Two major classification systems used in libraries
- Two major subject-heading systems used in libraries
- Authority control
- Options for cataloging available to libraries

Cataloging is one of librarianship's most interesting and frustrating topics. Without cataloging, material becomes difficult for the library user to locate. However, librarians by the nature of their profession, seek to be accurate in the information they provide to their public. With catalogers sometimes that nature can be exaggerated to the point that cataloging becomes a seeking after a perfection that cannot be accomplished.

One of the challenges of cataloging is to realize when enough is enough and that the item has been described and classified as best as it can be. Of course, there will always be a difference of opinion here between the cataloger and the library administrator.

Cataloging is not perfection. It exists so that the user can easily find desired material.

There are three main aspects to cataloging:

- Assigning a classification number
- Assigning subject heading(s)
- Authority control

CLASSIFICATION SYSTEMS

The classification number enables like material to be found in proximity to similar materials on the same subject or topic. There are two major classification systems in use in libraries in the United States: the Dewey Decimal System and the Library of Congress System.

The Dewey Decimal System is found mostly in public and school libraries. Melvil Dewey began the Dewey Decimal System in 1876. It is now owned by OCLC and is into its 22nd edition. The system is numerically based and assigns a number to each item based upon where it fits within the classification. The Dewey Decimal System (Fig. 19-1) classifies all knowledge into ten numerical categories.

Figure 19-1 Dewey Decimal System
100 – Generalities 200 – Philosophy and Psychology 300 – Social Sciences 400 – Language 500 – Natural Sciences and Mathematics 600 – Technology (Applied Sciences) 700 – The Arts 800 – Literature and Rhetoric 900 – Geography and History
Each subclass can be subdivided into ten subclasses such as: 300 – Social Sciences 310 – General Statistics 320 – Political Sciences 330 – Economics 340 – Law 350 – Public Administration 360 – Social Services, Association 370 – Economics 380 – Commerce 390 – Customs, Etiquette, Folklore

The classification system is further extended by ten to give the final classification number to a book. An example would be the book *Free To Choose* by Milton Friedman dealing with economics. Its classification number would be 330.122 FRI. The FRI is a cutter system that the Dewey Decimal System uses to identify either the author or title if there is no author. This further helps to find the material in areas where there are many books on the same subject.

The Dewey Decimal Classification classes fiction materials using a variety of letter headings. These include F, SF, M, and SS, depending upon the genre. The REF designation is for books that do not leave the collection. The letters J and E may be placed above the numerical designation to indicate a book in the children's collection.

The complete Dewey Decimal Classification System is available from OCLC at www.oclc.org/dewey.

The Library of Congress Classification System was developed in the late nineteenth and early twentieth century by the Library of Congress to arrange its book collection. It uses 21 basic classes denoted by letters. It is further subdivided into more specific subclasses identified by two- and three-letter combinations. See Figure 19-2 for the basic classes.

> ### Figure 19-2 Library of Congress Classification System
>
> A – General Works
> B – Philosophy, Psychology, Religion
> C – Auxiliary Sciences of History
> D – History (General) and History of Europe
> E – History: America
> F – History: America
> G – Geography, Anthropology, Recreation
> H – Social Sciences
> J – Political Science
> K – Law
> L – Education
> M – Music and Books on Music
> N – Fine Arts
> P – Language and Literature
> Q – Science
> R – Medicine
> S – Agriculture
> T – Technology
> U – Military Science
> V – Naval Science
> Z – Bibliography, Library Science, Information Resources (General)
>
> The Milton Friedman book listed above would have a classification of HB.501.F72 in the Library of Congress Classification System. The Library of Congress Classification System is available at http://classificationweb.net.

Most public and school libraries use the Dewey Decimal System. It is the older system and for the small public library does a good job of placing like material close to like material in a manner that makes location of it easier for the user. Where it runs into problems are in larger collections where specificity would require a long string of numbers after the decimal point to place items exactly in the collection. The Dewey Decimal System also suffers the limitation of a 10-based hierarchical system that has difficulty in finding space for topics that were not known in 1876, as well as a world that was much more European-American–centered than it is today.

The Library of Congress Classification is employed primarily in academic library collections. It has the advantage of being easily expandable and can more easily accommodate advances in knowledge and geo-political changes.

SUBJECT HEADINGS

In order for a user to locate an item in the collection if the author and title are not known but the area of interest is, subject headings are needed. Subject headings are also needed so the user can find all materials that the library has on his/her area of interest. There are two primary subject-heading systems used in the United States. These are Sears Subject Headings and the Library of Congress Subject Headings.

The Sears Subject Headings were first begun as *A List of Subject Headings for Small Libraries* by Minnie Earl Sears in 1923. She was employed by H. W. Wilson Company and compiled the list to aid librarians in small and medium-size libraries in assigning subject headings to collection materials. She followed the form of the Library of Congress Subject Headings. The initial work is now in its 18th Edition and has taken her last name as its formal title. It may be purchased through H. W. Wilson at www.hwwilson. com.

The Library of Congress Subject Headings was developed by the Library of Congress. It is more detailed than the *Sears List of Subject Headings*. It may be obtained at http://classificationweb. net.

A major difference between the two lists is that Sears uses the direct form of entry instead of the inverted form. The Milton Friedman book used as an example earlier would have Library of Congress Subject headings of Capitalism, Welfare State, and Industrial Policy.

AUTHORITY CONTROL

Authority control is an essential aspect of a good classification system. Authority control is defined as: "The consistent use of and maintenance of the forms of names, subjects, uniform titles, etc., used as headings in a catalog. Since this process creates a

link between bibliographic records and the authority file, authority control provides the underlying structure of the catalog."
[Source: University of Buffalo Libraries]

An authority file is defined as: "A set of authority records listing the chosen form of a heading and its appropriate cross-references. Types of authority files include name authority files, serials authority files, and subject authority files."
[Source: University of Buffalo Libraries]

With the wide variation of names used by authors, the differences in how titles may be rendered, and how subjects are presented, any library catalog must employ authority control to enable users to have quick access to what they are looking for. The user may have a term or variation of an author's name in mind that will not be the one employed in the catalog. A familiar example is Samuel Clemens. Is he listed as Samuel Clemens, his birth name, or by his assumed name of Mark Twain? Authority control makes sure that regardless of how he might be listed there is one preferred form and cross-references are made so that no matter how an individual searches for his works or works about him they can be located, despite the fact that sometimes the term they have in mind may not be the one that is used in the subject heading. Authority control lists may be obtained through the Library of Congress for Library of Congress Subject Headings or H. W. Wilson Company for Sears Subject Heading lists.

Authority control can be done in-house or through sending files of holdings to companies who perform this service for a fee.

CONCLUSION

This chapter has discussed the basics of cataloging for the small library. There are many methods for the library to obtain cataloging for materials in the collection. The small library may do it all on its own when the material is received in-house. However, in this day and age of computerized systems, local in-house cataloging of all materials is fast becoming obsolete.

Many vendors supply material already cataloged and ready for the shelf. They will also supply OCLC cataloging for the library to download into the online catalog and have sent to OCLC for addition to their records. If the library is not yet online catalog cards can be acquired when material is purchased.

Cataloging, particularly in the small library, should have as its goal enabling the user to easily locate needed material. Material on similar topics should be located together and the cataloging system used should not throw roadblocks in the way of easy access.

While using a vendor for cataloging may appear to be the most expensive option, consider what the staff costs would be if the items were processed in-house. Having the vendor perform this task may be the quickest and easiest way to go. Check with the vendor about different processing options. There is usually a set fee per item for processing based on what they do. Items can be sent fully processed and ready to go out on the shelf. Sometimes vendors will partially process the items by printing spine and pocket labels, preparing barcode labels, and putting covers on the book jackets. All that needs to be done when the books arrive is place the labels on the books and they are ready for circulation. Weigh your options carefully.

While in-house cataloging may seem to be a cheaper option, when staff costs are factored in, the per item price may actually be higher than if the cataloging had been prepared by the vendor. And if the library has a small staff, the extra workload will have an impact on the rest of the duties assigned to the staff.

A regional cooperative is another cataloging option. Some states have regional centers that act as a consortium for the local libraries. In Tennessee, as well as in other states, they are supported and staffed by the State Library. If this option is available in your state, check to see how it would assist the library. Orders can be sent to the regional center where they are placed, processed, and delivered to the library ready to go on the shelves. And because the centers are ordering for several libraries, they can get a price break on the costs of the items.

If the state does not offer a regional center, consider working with neighboring counties and cities. This may require talking to local governing officials as well, but the library director should be on a first-name basis with these folks already. Cooperative agreements may be needed to allow the library to place orders within other jurisdictions.

In any case, remember that cataloging, in spite of what some catalogers would claim, is not rocket science, it is the assigning of a number and appropriate subject headings to a work and clarifying its authorship so that users can easily locate it. Each of the commonly used classification systems has detailed instructions on where material should be placed. In addition, most books have Library of Congress Cataloging-in-Publication data on the back of their title pages.

REFERENCES

http://classificationweb.net.
http://ublib.buffalo.edu/libraries/units/cts/ac/def.html.
www.hwwilson.com.
www.oclc.org/dewey.

FURTHER READING

Bowman, J. H. 2002. *Essential cataloging.* New York: Neal-Schuman.

Broughton, Vanda. 2004. *Essential classification.* New York: Neal-Schuman.

Fritz, Deborah A., and Richard J. Fritz. 2002. *MARC21 for everyone: A practical guide.* Chicago: American Library Association.

Gorman, Michael, preparer. 2004. *The concise AACRC 4ᵗʰ ed.* Chicago: American Library Association.

Maxwell, Robert. 2002. *Maxwell's guide to authority work.* Chicago: American Library Association.

Mitchell, Anne M., and Brian E. Surratt. 2005. *Cataloging and organizing digital information: A how-to-do-it manual for librarians.* New York: Neal-Schuman.

Taylor, Arlene G. 2000. *Wyan's introduction to cataloging and classification.* Westport, CT: Libraries Unlimited.

Weber, Mary Beth. 2002. *Cataloging nonprint and Internet resources: A how-to-do-it manual for librarians.* New York: Neal-Schuman.

20 CIRCULATION

John A. Moorman

DEFINITION

Circulation is the process by which items in the collection are taken out of the library by a user and returned to the library.

OVERVIEW

This chapter covers:

- Main factors in developing circulation policies and procedures
- The problem of late return of materials
- How materials are returned to the library

While the circulation of materials is a straightforward operation, there are several factors that must be considered in developing policies and procedures for this operation. Each of these factors will vary according to individual libraries and the communities in which they operate. The main factors are:

- To whom does the library circulate materials?
- For what time periods does the library circulate materials?
- How does the library handle materials when they become overdue?
- How does the library get materials back on the shelves?

The question of to whom does the library circulate materials is more nuanced that it might appear at first glance. *School library* questions include: Does the library allow circulation of materials beyond the faculty and staff of the school in which the library is housed? Does the library allow faculty and students from other schools in the district to check out materials from its library? Does the library allow the public to have access to the collection? Is the collection available through interlibrary loan? Each of these questions will have a different answer depending upon the local setting and the relationships that the library has with other libraries in the community.

Special library questions include: Does the library allow circulation of materials beyond the facility in which the library is housed? To whom within the agency are materials permitted to be accessed and used? Some businesses will have categories of users depending upon security clearances and other factors. What level of access, if any, does the general public have to the collections, either in person or through interlibrary loan? Unlike other types of libraries, special libraries have wide variations in their organizational support from entities that are totally governmentally funded, such as libraries within federal and state agencies, to entities that are non-profit, such as historical and museum libraries, to entities that are a part of a for-profit company. Each of these operational situations will bring different answers to the questions mentioned above.

Academic library questions include: Does the library circulate only to students, faculty, and staff? Does the library treat staff differently from faculty? Does the library allow individuals from the community access to its collections? If so, is their use of the collection limited to in-house use or may they use materials away from the library? What level of access does the library allow through interlibrary loan?

Public library questions include: Does the library permit individuals from outside the local jurisdiction to obtain materials from the collection? If so, is it free access, or does the library charge a fee for this use? What evidence of residence does the library require before the individual can obtain a library card? What information does the library keep on each library user and how is that material shared with other entities? Most states have privacy laws, which restrict access to patron records. Does the library require the presentation of a user card when circulating materials or can library staff look up their card number? What requirements does outside funding such as state aid bring to the question of library access? If the library is in a community with a large tourist presence, how does the library accommodate tourists' desire to use the facilities while in the community?

All of these questions are essential to the process of determining how the collection will be accessed and used. Much thought needs to be given to the answers as the process of determining the answers will involve not only library staff but also administrative and corporate personnel as well as members of the institution's governing body. In this process no answer should ever be considered final as changes and circumstances can dictate a new look at operating procedures.

For what time period does the library circulate materials? This question can have as many right answers as there are libraries. Circulation of library materials should be driven by the needs of the users, rather than the needs of the institution. This is a concept that sometimes is hard to get across to staff and governing officials. The library exists to serve the needs of its clientele for information necessary for education, leisure, and work. While some libraries, particularly special libraries, may have security requirements that effect use, most libraries should place the needs and desires of their users foremost in the setting of time limits for collection use.

Academic library loan periods are driven by the educational function of the institution. Loan periods for students may vary according to time periods of semesters or quarters as well as the number of students needing the material. Graduate students may get more extended loan periods than undergraduate students. Faculty and staff may get loans varying from semester to indefinite in length. A question to consider when determining loan periods is the ability to recall an item when another user requests it. Does the recall ability depend upon the status of the individual making the request and what recourse does the library have in getting material back from users when a request has been made? With faculty members this can be a difficult and touchy proposition.

Public library loan periods are always a point of controversy. No matter what loan periods are set up for materials there will always be a vocal minority of users who are displeased with them. One of the goals of the loan period policy will be to keep these users to a minority and a small minority at that. Does the library have different loan periods for different formats of materials? Does the library give new and popular materials a shorter loan period than other materials? If it is a new book but over a certain length, does the library still charge it out for a shorter period? In making these decisions look at what other public libraries in the area are doing with their loan periods, particularly those with whom the library has a close user interaction. Examine how loan periods might affect staff workload. If the building is crowded from a shelving standpoint a longer loan period might ease problems in this area.

OVERDUES

The problem of overdue material is one of the banes of library existence. Librarians are dealing with human beings not robots, and human beings besides having good characteristics are forgetful and irresponsible. This leads to the inevitable confrontation between library staff member and user in which the user claims that he/she did in fact return the material in question and the library has lost it somewhere. How libraries deal with that situation will be discussed later.

One of the first questions to be considered when developing policies and procedures for the collection of overdue materials is fines. Does the library charge or not charge individuals when they return library materials past the due date? Most libraries have some sort of monetary charge in this event, which is based upon the presumption that for extra time and the inconvenience that it causes staff and other users the person should pay a fee. Also, if there is no fee attached to late return of materials there is little penalty for non-return other than no further use of the library, or a blemish on one's credit rating. A few libraries charge no fines and have had a good experience with this. In any case, libraries should realize that fine money seldom pays for the expense of staff time in preparing notices, the cost of mailing notices, and the other responsibilities associated with this process.

Other factors in the overdue process include what procedures the library has in place for checking shelves and reading shelves to see that materials are in proper order. How well has staff responsible for checking in and shelving materials been trained? How well are they performing their tasks? No staff is perfect and mistakes will be made. Patrons will also put material back on the shelves to get around late fees.

How long do you wait until the library sends out a first overdue notice? How many notices does the library send out before it sends a bill? Does the library use a collection agency for overdue material and uncollected fines? When does the library send items to the agency? Does the library have a good working arrangement with the city or county attorney's office where they are willing to assist in the return of late material? These are all factors to consider as the library develops procedures in this area. Again, talk to other libraries in the area to see what their procedures are. Know the community. What works best in one community might be a disaster in another community.

How does the library handle that mad user who swears up and down that he/she has returned the material in question? The library staff has checked all possible locations and not come up with the material. What next? Always try to keep the situation calm and out of the public view, although this is hard in the small library. Questions to ask here are: Is this individual a chronic abuser of library materials? What is the situation in this instance? Who the individual is and his/her position in the community should not play a role in the final decision but will affect how staff handle the situation. At this stage, staff can buy time by requesting that a more thorough search be made of their home, car, work space, and belongings before a final determination is made. However, if it is beyond that stage there are really only two choices, waive the fine and count the material as lost, or be firm and let the individual know that he/she will be held accountable for the material in question. This is not one of the enjoyable tasks of librarianship but is necessary if policies and procedures are to be effective in the long run. If the material does turn up later, a heartfelt apology should be issued. However, very seldom, if never, will it if the proper steps are followed by library staff.

RETURNING OF MATERIALS

How does the library get materials back on the shelves? The simple answer is to shelve them. However, it is more complicated than that. Are materials brought back to the desk from which they are checked out? Does the library have inside materials return drops that go either to a central room or to a cart under the circulation desk? Does the library have outside materials return drops that are either walk-up or drive-through? Does the library have remote site materials return locations either inside or outside of a building? Any type of library can use each of these possibilities. However, most special, academic, and school libraries do not have return facilities outside of their buildings.

In any consideration of remote site materials several issues need to be examined. How secure is the site and how open to vandalism is it? Many good remote return sites are in stores such as grocery stores or malls where security is high. The second question is the availability of staff or volunteers to check the sites on a regular basis. Such locations tend to be popular and will fill up with materials more rapidly than anticipated. In some areas it is necessary to have seven-day-a-week pickup.

One factor to consider when developing an outside materials return drop or any interior drop that empties into a room is the need for extra fire suppression for this space. Material drops are places where flammable material may be inserted and libraries have been destroyed through such actions.

The second aspect of materials return is the checking in of the materials and the returning of them to the shelves. Generally, shelvers perform this task although in small libraries this can also be one of the duties of anyone from the library director to the custodian. This part of the process is one of the most important in the whole library operation. If materials are improperly checked in or not checked in at all, the library will have a problem with the last person of record who will be justly irritated at the lack of competence of library staff. If the materials are not properly shelved, they are for all intents and purposes unavailable to the public. Take your time to do it right the first time.

One concept to aid the small library with the reshelving issue is to have a section of shelving where returned books may be placed in the public area before being returned to the stacks. Users will appreciate this, as they like to see what is of interest to others. The library staff will appreciate it, too, as there will be fewer books to shelve as others take them to be checked out again.

CONCLUSION

Circulation is the most visible library function and the function in which there is the most direct patron contact. It is important to have good policies and procedures developed for this area. Also it is vital that all staff working in this area have a thorough understanding of these policies and procedures. It also helps if staff possess tact and common sense, for that is also a necessary ingredient for successful public service.

FURTHER READING

Evans, G. Edward et al. 1999. *Introduction to library public services, 6ᵗʰ ed.* Westport, CT: Libraries Unlimited.

Martin, Murray S., and Betsy Park. 1998. *Charging and collecting fees and fines: A handbook for libraries.* New York: Neal-Schuman.

21 WEEDING

John A. Moorman

DEFINITION

Weeding is the removal of items from the collection.

OVERVIEW

This chapter covers:

- Need for weeding
- Procedures to follow during weeding
- Things to avoid when weeding

INTRODUCTION

Any library that does not have a good weeding schedule for its total collection is not doing its job. Most materials over time become obsolete and/or worn out. Another reason for weeding is lack of space. A good source for use in weeding a collection is *The CREW Method: Expanded Guidelines for Collection Evaluation and Weeding for Small and Medium-Sized Public Libraries*. This work was revised and updated by Belinda Boon in 1995 and is available from the Texas State Library. Ordering information for this manual is found on their Web site: www.tsl.state.tx.us. *The Crew Method* takes the librarian through the steps in the weeding process including setting up criteria for weeding, determining what to weed, providing a checklist of what to consider in the weeding process, and giving general guidelines on types of materials that should remain in the collection. A good summary of the process is found in "The CREW Method in Ten Steps" on pages 13–19 of the manual.

There are CREW Guidelines by Dewey Class. The guidelines include formulas for the various Dewey Classes. As the book indicates: "The formulas given here for the various Dewey Classes are rules of thumb based on professional opinions in the literature and practical experience." The formula in each case consists of three parts:

1. The first figure refers to the years since the book's latest copyright date (age of material in the book);
2. The second figure refers to the maximum permissible time without usage (in terms of years since its last recorded circulation);
3. The third refers to the presence of various negative factors, called MUSTIE factors."

The following is an example from the manual:

510 (Mathematics)—5/3/MUSTIE—Replace older materials on algebra, geometry, trigonometry, and calculus with revised editions. Discard most titles covering slide rules and the "new math" of the 1960's.
[page 37. Used with permission of the Texas State Library]

PROCEDURES

When weeding, different standards will be used depending upon the type of library. Academic libraries will need to keep certain materials longer for use by classes and research. Public libraries will depend more upon circulation information and condition of materials. It is important to create a retention schedule for materials in the collection. Depending upon areas of the collection, or emphasis of the library, materials may have different retention schedules. In an academic library certain materials will have longer retention schedules than in a public library, where as an example fiction books that have not circulated in the last three years are prime candidates for removal from the collection.

> Develop a retention schedule for all library materials.

Set up a schedule for weeding and stick to it. It is often easy to find other things to do, but regular weeding is an important part of collection development. A collection full of outdated, worn, and unused material is not one that will be used. Good material can be hidden among the worn and outdated and patrons will give up before locating it.

Library staff can be assigned to sections or be permitted to choose sections to weed. The more staff involved enables not only a greater institutional commitment to weeding but makes the task easier on all. However, remember this is a commitment that is as important as other library duties and must be done on a regular and continuing basis. Weeding, like material selection, is never completed and is an ongoing part of library activities.

In some communities, patrons may be very sensitive to having items removed from the collection and not understand the need for the process. Here it may be good to refer to the process by terms such as "Collection Review" or "Collection Evaluation."

When discarding materials make sure that the item is prominently marked as discarded. Otherwise it may appear back in the collection. Make sure that any bookplate or statement identifying the material as donated by, or given in memory of, or other similar phrase is removed from the book. Nothing can cause negative publicity and long-term problems as much as someone seeing a book with a memorial plate in it indicating that it was given in memory of Aunt Sarah appearing in a book sale or having fallen off of a waste truck on the way to the dump.

> Never leave gifting information in an item removed from the collection.

CONCLUSION

While this chapter is one of the shorter chapters in the book, it is one of the most important. Weeding is an essential part of the provision of good library service to a community. Its value to the library cannot be emphasized enough. Without continual weeding a collection becomes one that contains out-of-date information, materials that are in poor condition, and materials that are no longer in use or in demand. In other words, a collection that is of no interest to most library users.

REFERENCES

Boon, Belinda. 1995. *The Crew Method: Expanded guidelines for collection evaluation and weeding for small and medium-size libraries.* Rev. and updated by Belinda Boon, Library Development Staff. Austin, TX: Texas State Library.

FURTHER READING

American Library Association. 2004. *Library fact sheet #15—Weeding library collections: A selected annotated bibliography for library collection evaluation.* Chicago: American Library Association.

Clayton, Peter, and G.E. Gorman. 2001. *Managing information resources in libraries and information services: Principles and procedures.* New York: Neal-Schuman.

Part V

Computers and Automation
in the Small Library

22 PERSONAL COMPUTERS AND IN-HOUSE NETWORKS

Kendra Morgan

DEFINITION

A computer is an electronic device that stores, retrieves, and processes data, and can be programmed with instructions. A computer is comprised of hardware and software and can exist in a variety of sizes and configurations. (Source: www.nces.ed.gov/pubs98/tech/glossary.asp) A computer network is a system for communication among two or more computers.

OVERVIEW

Computers have become an integral part of libraries of all sizes for staff and patrons alike. Library staff depend on computers to help manage their collection of materials and to facilitate job tasks. Patrons have become accustomed to the availability of computers that connect them to the Internet and provide access to entertainment or productivity software. This chapter covers:

- Issues associated with purchasing new equipment
- Issues related to protecting the library's resources
- Planning for the future of technology in the library

PURCHASING NEW EQUIPMENT

Deciding what equipment to purchase is a daunting task and may seem overwhelming, but help is available from many sources. One option is to read reviews and recommendations from magazines such as *Consumer Reports, PC Magazine, and PC World.* The reviews can provide excellent background information and a good starting point for purchasing new computers.

Another valuable resource to consider when investigating new hardware are colleagues in libraries and in the information technology field. If the library is interested in a particular product or vendor, ask for recommendations. When gathering these recommendations, remember that the point is not to find a 100 percent consensus on a brand name or specific product, but to obtain feedback that may point out any glaring issues with a vendor or particular product.

In addition to asking around locally or within the library community, consider using an online forum such as the one provided through WebJunction (www.webjunction.org). WebJunction was designed to connect libraries by providing a place to ask questions, share experiences, and support the library community. Questions about technology needs on WebJunction are common and the people who participate in the forums are sensitive to the concerns facing libraries.

Much of the planning and decision making about computers in libraries is affected by the fact that libraries are in a unique position of needing computers for the public and their staff. Patron machines are commonly referred to as public access computers and should have different rules and settings than staff computers. This could be as simple as prohibiting patrons from using a color printer, or as in-depth as preventing anything from being saved on the computer's hard drive. In general, restrictions on public access computers are designed to prevent settings established by the library from being changed. This helps the library to maintain a consistent standard on the public access computers and to limit the amount of time spent by staff on maintenance and troubleshooting.

Libraries are often approached by seemingly well meaning patrons about accepting a used computer donation. These computers can come with a host of problems and concerns that could easily outweigh the benefits of the donation. If the library does choose to allow donations, a policy should be established that outlines requirements for the equipment, such as age or operating systems. The policy should also allow for the possibility that the library could sell the computer and use the proceeds towards the purchase of new equipment.

PROTECTING THE INVESTMENT

As the library prepares to purchase new computers or assess the status of existing machines, it is necessary to consider some issues and protection measures.

A. WARRANTY AND TECHNICAL SUPPORT

Most new computers come with some form of warranty on parts and servicing. The length and conditions of a warranty and technical support are important considerations. For most libraries, four years is a reasonable time to expect hardware to last before replacement. The technical support and parts replacement details provided through vendors are especially important to those libraries that don't have dedicated information technology staff. Be careful to read the fine print of the agreement and understand what services and parts will be covered in the event that the equipment stops working. Keep all information relating to the computer, including software and warranty details, together so that it can be easily found if needed.

B. SURGE PROTECTORS

Computers can be damaged by spikes in electricity caused by lightning or other electrical problems. This type of damage can often be prevented by plugging the computer into a surge protector. A surge protector should not be confused with a simple power strip which allows multiple devices to use an electrical outlet. A surge protector can accommodate multiple devices, but it is also designed to protect against electrical damage. All of the computers in the library should be attached to a surge protector.

Computers that function as servers should use an additional form of protection called an Uninterrupted Power Supply (UPS). In the event of a power outage, the UPS will take over by providing battery power to run the server. This allows library staff to safely shut down the server without losing any data. The UPS can also be purchased with software that can successfully shut down the server by itself if the power is not restored.

C. ANTI-VIRUS SOFTWARE

Virus protection is an important form of software to have installed on all library computers. Viruses often infect computers through e-mail attachments or by opening files on disks or from other storage devices that contain a virus. A virus can cripple an individual computer or the library's network and be expensive to remove. As new viruses are found, the anti-virus vendors create updates called patches to protect against those viruses. If the computer doesn't have the latest patches, then it becomes vulnerable. If it is possible, set the anti-virus software to automatically obtain the updates. Updates can also be installed manually.

D. OPERATING SYSTEM UPDATES

Microsoft routinely releases security patches for their operating systems when they discover issues that can be exploited. Like the anti-virus software, the computer may be capable of automatically obtaining updates or they can be done manually.

E. ADWARE AND SPYWARE SOFTWARE

Adware and spyware are programs that can stop a computer from working efficiently and can also be used to collect information about computer users without their knowledge. The programs are often bundled together and downloaded from the Web as part of a package that includes something that a user is interested in, such as a free game or a music-sharing program. The effects of spyware or adware can include the constant appearance of pop-up ads even when the Web browser isn't open and the appearance of new toolbars in the Web browser.

To prevent problems with adware and spyware, staff should be educated about the importance of not downloading programs to their computers. Any software that is downloaded should be from trusted and reputable sources.

Several companies provide free versions of software that can help to remove spyware or adware. The software will scan the computer to search for programs that have been identified as spyware and adware and will try to remove the programs from the computer.

- Ad-Aware
  www.lavasoft.com
- Microsoft Anti-Spyware Beta
  www.microsoft.com/athome/security/spyware/software/default.mspx
- SpyBot Search and Destroy
  www.spybot.info

F. BACKUP

Backup is the term used to describe making a copy of information that is stored on computers and it is a crucial task in the library. A backup will probably not be necessary for the public access computers since they do not create files that are important to library operations. The concern will be primarily with staff computers and any files that are needed by the integrated library system. Consider what information needs to be saved and routinely backed up in the library and create a disaster recovery plan for data. If the building was damaged or destroyed, what information that is stored on computers would be critical? Budgets and financial records, human resources data, policies, and procedures would be among the areas of concern.

If the staff computers are not set up so that each user stores their files on a shared server, it may be necessary to back up data from several individual machines. A server is a computer that can function in many different ways, including as a common place that employees use for saving their work files. Consolidating files in this manner helps to ensure that the library can quickly identify what to back up. No matter what the setup, take some time to determine which machines in the library have important information on them and develop a plan for creating a backup.

Several methods can be used to create a backup, including using a CD or DVD recordable device, a magnetic tape drive, or having duplicate hard drives on a server. The method will be dependent on the amount of information being backed up, the availability of resources, and possibly the skill of the staff. Whatever the method, many organizations routinely create backups of their data but fail to ever check the data for reliability. If the backup is not actually doing what is expected, then when it is needed it may be of little use.

Another concern that should be addressed is where the backup data is stored. What often happens is that the backup is stored right next to the computer that was used to create the backup. The problem here is that backups are created not only to protect against hardware failure, but also to be used in the event that equipment in the building is damaged or destroyed. Backups left in the same building as the original data may be damaged or destroyed along with the physical structure. A backup should be stored in an off-site location once a month and a regular schedule should be created and followed to test the quality and integrity of the data.

PUBLIC ACCESS COMPUTERS

In addition to managing any staff computers, libraries must be aware and address the unique concerns that surround providing public access computers. Most libraries have encountered growing pains and service issues with regard to public access computing. With increasing numbers of patrons depending on libraries as a source of connecting to the Internet and digital resources, libraries must find a balance between providing service to patrons and protecting the library's resources. In addition to following the general principals of "Purchasing New Equipment" and "Protecting the Investment," as discussed earlier, there are some other particular concerns that libraries should address for the public access computers.

A. COMPUTER USE POLICY

The library should have a policy in place that helps patrons and staff to understand what computer resources and services are available from the library and any rules that govern the use of the computers, including accessing the Internet. The American Library Association makes the following recommendations regarding Internet Use Policies and these policies can also be extended to general computer use:

- Ensure that policies speak to access for all.
- Involve your library staff, board and Friends group in the policy writing process.
- Keep it simple. Avoid jargon. Making the policy too technical will confuse people.
- Make policies readily available and visible to the public.
- Provide an up-to-date code of conduct or etiquette guide for using the Internet at your library. Include specific suggestions for positive action. Also list prohibited behavior and the consequences of such behavior.
- Include a statement addressing patron privacy.
- Communicate clearly that users are responsible for what they access online; parents are responsible for their children's Internet use.

Staff should be familiar with the policy and be prepared to deal with violations or questions regarding the policy. The policy should be regularly reviewed and updated to reflect changes in technology or library rules.

B. MANAGEMENT SOFTWARE

Managing public access computers can be a job itself and while larger libraries generally have dedicated information technology staff, smaller libraries often depend on the skills and on-the-job training of staff in various departments. The protection that can be offered through management software can relieve staff of time-consuming and seemingly insurmountable daily computer problems. While management software is not always inexpensive, a cost analysis of the amount of staff time spent on computer issues or lost printing charges will probably demonstrate that the software is cost effective.

Some vendors have an entire line of products designed to work together to fulfill a wide range of public access computing needs while others specialize in specific services. The market for management software is fairly diverse, but these are the major areas that the products cover:

- Print management—require users to pay for printing before they can print or simply display a message that notifies the user of how many pages are going to print and what the cost of printing.
- Time management—limits the amount of time that a user can spend on the computer. These systems can also be used to allow patrons to make a reservation to use the computer at a future time or date.
- Filtering—blocks content or specific Web sites from being accessed on the Web. Filtering is required for libraries that participate in the federal E-rate program and receive funds for Internet access.
- PC management—of all the types of management software, PC management can definitely be the most beneficial. The software prevents unauthorized users from making any intentional or accidental changes to the configurations of the public access computers. Very inexpensive solutions are available for "locking down" computers and making it difficult for users to make unauthorized changes. Please see the section on further reading at the end of this chapter for a list of articles and publications that can help with the selection of PC management software.

CURRENT INVENTORY

If the library does not already have one, a thorough inventory of all computer and networking equipment should be taken so that a clear picture develops of what the library already owns. The inventory can include the following types of information:

- When the equipment/machine was purchased
- Brand (Dell, Gateway, Cisco, etc.)
- Where it is located in the building
- Name of the machine
- Processor speed
- Amount of RAM
- Hard drive size
- Additional drives (floppy, CD, DVD, etc.)
- Operating system
- Software licenses
- Length of warranty and when it expires

The inventory can take several different forms, and an example is provided at the end of this chapter. The inventory can help obtain an "at a glance" view of the library's technical status. If consultants or outside contractors are asked to provide recommendations for technology, a well maintained and prepared inventory can save time and money. The inventory should be updated as computers are purchased, upgraded, or removed from use.

Getting Organized. Many libraries have small stockpiles of used or broken computer equipment stored throughout the building. While it may be helpful to keep a few extra pieces to serve as replacement equipment, the reality is that boxes filled with old keyboards or computer mice are not likely to be of much use in the future and are usually taking up valuable space. Older computers may have useful spare parts, such as memory chips and hard drives and if the library is still using compatible equipment, these older computers may come in handy to help extend the life of another computer. Other used or broken equipment can be discarded or recycled. Recycling of old computer equipment is becoming increasingly popular and local city or county agencies may be able to help with information about recycling efforts.

NETWORK OPTIONS

A network refers to a group of computers that are able to share resources. These resources can include hardware such as printers, scanners, as well as applications and files. Networked computers are generally run in either a client-server or peer-to-peer relationship. In the peer-to-peer mode, any computer is capable of sharing data and resources, called serving, with other computers on the network. In client-server mode, a specific computer is dedicated to be a server to provide data and/or applications to the computers that are client workstations.

One example of a client-server relationship can be found with the software used to run an integrated library system (ILS). In most situations, a library will have a server running that provides client workstations with access to the ILS software and data. The server allows staff at the circulation desk using client workstations to check books out to patrons at the same time that other staff members are cataloging new materials to add to the collection. All of the ILS data is stored on the server and the client workstations are able to access it and with the proper authorization, make changes to the data as well.

The client-server relationship can also be used to establish centralized areas for the staff to save works files, which can facilitate both resource sharing and file backup. As discussed in the section on backups, this can be a time-saving and important step to ensuring that all of the files important to the operation of the library get backed up.

One technology gaining popularity for supporting public access computing in libraries is the thin client, a variation of the client-server. A thin client is little more than a monitor, mouse, keyboard, and a small device to bring the components together and then connect to the network. The hardware can vary greatly, but the simplest devices are about the size of a VHS tape. The thin clients rely on a server to provide all applications as well as any configuration settings. All changes, software updates, software additions are completed on the server and not on the individual clients.

Thin clients will not be a good solution for every library. Essentially all of the clients are dependent on the server and if the server is broken or loses a connection to the clients, the clients become useless. They can also require more expertise to maintain and install and can initially be more of an investment because of the cost to purchase the server needed for the system. However, in the long term, with centralized upgrades and reduced staff involvement, the system can pay for itself, and libraries are considering thin clients to help expand services.

WIRELESS TECHNOLOGY

Traditional computer networks are physically connected with wires or cables that send and receive information from one computer to another, or to a device such as a printer. Wireless networks allow libraries to do the same thing, but without the need for wires to connect the devices together. In order to provide wireless Internet access, the library must have an Internet connection and a wireless access point to send out the wireless signal. Any device, such as a computer, that wants to use the wireless service must be equipped to receive the signal that is sent from the access point. The piece of equipment that computers use to receive the signal is usually called a wireless adapter or a wireless network card.

The most common users of wireless services are patrons with their personal laptops equipped with a wireless network card. Wireless also has the flexibility to allow libraries to place computers where they can be best utilized by patrons and not just where the current layout of the building permits. This is of particular interest to libraries with limited options for adding new wired network connections in an old building. The library can add a wireless network card to an existing computer and move that machine to a better location without the need for a wired network connection.

Two options for providing wireless service:

1. Share the existing connection to the Internet. This option would take advantage of bandwidth already coming in to the library and attaching wireless components. Security will be of concern since the wireless network will be operating on the same network as the staff machines and possibly sensitive data. Setup will probably require the expertise of someone familiar with networking and who understands the risks associated with wireless.
2. Separate connection to the Internet. This option opens a separate connection to the Internet that in no way is tied in to the library's existing wired network. This may be a desirable option because there would be no impact on existing services. The downside would be paying for the use of a separate line dedicated to the wireless service.

PLANNING FOR WIRELESS

Security. Properly securing the wireless network should be a top concerns. This is an extremely relevant and important issue to address when choosing to implement wireless service in a library when the wireless network shares the wired network. Networks that have not been properly secured can be compromised when users unintentionally unleash viruses and by others with malicious intent. This is not a new concern, as the same issues exist with a traditional wired network. It may be necessary to bring in a consultant to ensure that the network is properly secured and that the wireless service does not impact the integrity of the network.

Bandwidth. Bandwidth refers to how much data the Internet connection can transfer. Can the library easily expand to additional users and not impact current services? If connection speeds are already slow, allowing additional users will have a negative impact on speed.

Placement and usage of access points. The access points should be placed out of reach to limit concerns with theft or tampering. Mounting the access point on a wall or high on a column places it out of reach and may also help to extend the distance and quality of the wireless signal.

Many libraries have expressed concern with having users sitting in their cars or outside the library using the wireless signal. The wireless signal is limited in how far it can travel, but open spaces and windows can allow that signal to go further than desired. This can be controlled to a limited extent by the placement of the access points in the building, but there should always be an expectation that the signal will be available outside of the building. If a library prefers not to allow people to use the wireless signal when the building is closed, the wireless service can be turned off when the library closes for the evening.

Electricity. It is becoming increasingly common for patrons to bring their laptops into the library to take advantage of wireless Internet access. This creates a need to provide patrons with access to electrical outlets to plug in the power cords for their laptops. If the outlets are not easily accessible, the power cords can create hazards for other people walking in the building.

Acceptable use policy. The library should consider what language, if any, needs to be added to existing policies for Internet usage.

Troubleshooting patron computers. Some of the issues that may arise include patrons having problems connecting to the wireless network and expecting library staff to be able to solve the issue. A policy should address the ability of library staff to assist with wireless issues.

Authenticating users. Vendors of integrated library system software are steadily introducing products that allow libraries to exercise more control over usage of the wireless network. These products can require patrons to authenticate with the integrated library system by entering their barcode before they can use their wireless laptop on the library's network. This requirement can allow the library staff to control more effectively usage and collect statistics for the wireless network.

TECHNOLOGY PLANNING

Technology planning is one of the best ways to help carve a path for the future of the library. A technology plan should support the library's mission or vision and exist as a means to an end, a tool to help the library determine what services can be enhanced through the use of technology. The plan can also serve as a reference point for staff, the library board, and funding bodies on the steps the library needs to take in order to provide quality services. A technology plan generally describes the technological goals of the library and what strategies will be used to ensure that the goals are met. Although some libraries develop technology plans voluntarily or in conjunction with their long-range planning, many libraries create technology plans as a requirement of participation in the federal E-rate program. The E-rate program provides discounts for schools and public libraries on telecommunications and Internet charges.

As with almost any planning process, just picking a place to start can be difficult. It isn't uncommon for one person to write the technology plan and then present the plan for feedback and approval, but a committee would be preferable. Begin by thinking of people who might be helpful during the planning process and that have something to contribute. This could include library staff, volunteers, board members, or outside contractors. There should be some technical expertise or a committee member willing to do research to help with decisions on what products or services can fit the needs of library, but it is also important to gather input from the end users and those who know firsthand the needs of the patrons and staff.

Figure 22-1 Components of a Technology Plan

Components that can be considered for inclusion in the technology plan are:

- mission and vision statements
- history of technology in the library
- current inventory of equipment
- staff training on new technologies and building on existing skills
- selection and promotion of online resources
- development of the library's Web site
- upgrades and maintenance of staff and public computers, which includes hardware and software
- upgrades and maintenance of servers, which includes hardware and software
- replacement or upgrades of local area network components (routers, hubs, wiring, etc.)
- evaluating the speed and quality of telecommunication lines that are used to connect to the Internet or between library branches
- introduction of new technologies to enhance services
- a budget that represents anticipated costs
- evaluation methods for the goals

One resource that can be particularly useful for technology planning is a free, online tool called TechAtlas (http://techatlas.web junction.org). Designed specifically to help libraries develop technology plans, TechAtlas goes step-by-step through the planning process, guiding the user to the creation of a functional technology plan. One of the most practical parts of TechAtlas is that it provides specific questions to ask during the planning process and even has online versions of forms that can be used to collect responses and information. It is a great tool for libraries of all sizes and it provides a practical approach to technology planning.

The writing and style of the technology plan can differ greatly between libraries. Plans can be two pages or 25 pages long; length will not be an indication of how well the plan is written or how effective it will be in helping the library to achieve the outlined goals. Figure 22-1 provided examples of information that can be included but each library may have additional needs not covered in the list. The overall goal when developing the technology plan should be to create a plan that is dynamic and relevant to the needs of the library, something that can be revisited and evaluated as changes occur in the library and progress is made on projects.

CONCLUSION

It is easy to become overwhelmed by the prospect of learning about new technologies. This is partly driven by the fact that products and services are constantly changing and the terminology surrounding technology is often confusing. Hopefully, the contents of this chapter will help to clarify some of the issues surrounding basic technology needs because, despite the challenges, it is important to take steps toward understanding how technology can be used to better serve the library and its patrons.

REFERENCES/FURTHER READING

PUBLIC ACCESS COMPUTERS

American Library Association. "Checklist for creating an Internet use policy." Chicago: American Library Association. www.ala.org/Template.cfm? Section=litoolkit&Template=/ContentManagement/ContentDisplay.cfm &ContentID=50647. (Accessed December 2003).

Barclay, Donald A. 2000. *Managing public-access computers: A-how-to-do-it manual for librarians*. New York: Neal Schuman.

Sauers, Michael P., and Louise E. Alcorn. 2003. *Directory of management software for public access computers*. New York: Neal Schuman.

Wayne, Richard. 2005. "Helping you buy: PC management software." *Computers in Libraries*, 25, 2 (February): 37–45.

Wayne, Richard. 2004. "An overview of public access computer software management." *Computers in Libraries*, 24, 6 (June): 25–30.

NETWORKS

Latham, Joyce M. 2001. "Everything old is thin again: Joyce M. Latham explains how thin clients—the current cousins of dumb terminals—might be a solution for a library's tech challenges." *School Library Journal,* 47, 11 (November): 20–22.

Pace, Andrew K. 2004. "The Atkins diet for library computing." *Computers in libraries,* 24, 6 (June): 38–40.

Patel, Heutel. 2005. "Thin client." New Jersey: Eastern New Jersey regional library cooperative. www.infolink.org/pdf_files/thinclient.ppt. (Accessed December).

TechSoup. "Computer networks" California: TechSoup. www.techsoup.org/howto/articles.cfm?topicid=3&topic=Networks. (Accessed December 2005).

WIRELESS

Breeding, Marshall. 2004. "Wireless networks connect libraries to a mobile society." *Computers in Libraries,* 24, 9 (October): 29–31.

Leland, Eric, and Russ King. "Wireless LANs: An introduction to wireless networking hardware." California: Tech Soup. www.techsoup.org/howto/articlepage.cfm?ArticleId=336&topicid=3. (Accessed May 2003).

TECHNOLOGY PLANNING

Cohn, John M., Ann L. Kelsey, and Keith Michael Fiels. 1999. *Writing and updating technology plans.* New York: Neal-Schuman.

Hale, Martha, Patti Butcher, and Cindi Hickey. "New pathways to planning." Kansas: Northeast Kansas Library System. http://skyways.lib.ks.us/pathway/index.html. (Accessed October 2003).

Mayo, Diane. 2005. *Technology for results: Developing service-based plans.* Chicago: American Library Association.

Mayo, Diane, and Sandra Nelson. 1998. *Wired for the future: Developing your library technology plan.* Chicago: American Library Association.

Matthews, Joseph R. 2004. *Technology planning: Preparing and updating a library technology plan.* Connecticut: Libraries Unlimited.

NPower. "TechAtlas" Washington: NPower. www.webjunction.techatlas.org. (Accessed December 2005).

INVENTORY SAMPLE

SMITH PUBLIC LIBRARY COMPUTER INVENTORY

Updated	*December 1, 2005*		
Computer Name	EGS_YS1	EGS_YS2	EGS_CIRC1
Brand	Gateway	Gateway	Hewlett Packard
Location	Children's Room	Children's Room	Circulation Desk
Processor	Pentium III 1.8 Ghz	Pentium II 350Mhz	Pentium III 550 Mhz
RAM	512 MB	256 MB	256 MB
Hard Drive Size	60 GB	40 GB	40 GB
Operating System	Windows XP	Windows 2000	Windows XP
Software	Office 2000 Professional, Encarta Encyclopedia 2003, Internet Explorer 6.0	Office 2000 Professional, various children's games, Internet Explorer 6.0	Office 2000 Professional, Internet Explorer 6.0
Antivirus Software	Norton, expires October 2006	Norton, expires May 2005	Norton, expires May 2005
Date Purchased	January 26, 2003	February 18, 2001	October 12, 2003
Warranty Expires	January 26, 2006	February 18, 2004–Expired	October 12, 2007
Technical Support	1–800–555–1234	Expired	1–800–555–7890
Serial Number	TAS–91299	GFL–11595	UKP–86753

23 INTEGRATED LIBRARY SYSTEMS

Kendra Morgan

DEFINITION

An integrated library system is a group of automated library subsystems working together and communicating within the same set or system of software to control such activities as circulation, cataloging, acquisitions, and serial control. (Source: www.odl.state.ok.us/servlibs/l-files/glossi.htm)

OVERVIEW

This chapter covers:

- Basic background information about the Integrated Library System
- Preparing to select a new Integrated Library System

INTRODUCTION

Using the card catalog is often one of the clearest memories that many people have about visiting a library. They can recall flipping through the index-size, paper cards to find books by their favorite author or on a particular subject. And, in fact, many smaller libraries still depend on a version of the classic card catalog. But today, most libraries have chosen to automate functions related to managing library materials. Automation has evolved to encompass what is now called the integrated library system or ILS. The ILS allows both staff and patrons to find resources available through the library and for staff to manage those resources. Through the combination of hardware and software, ILS products aid libraries in making the most of their collections.

BASIC FUNCTIONS

The components that can comprise an ILS are often referred to as modules, and the three most common modules are cataloging, circulation, and the online public access catalog (OPAC).

CATALOGING

Cataloging involves creating electronic records for the materials in the library's collection. These records are referred to as machine-readable cataloging, or MARC, records. Cataloged materials can include, but are not limited to, books, reference items, maps, journals, magazines, DVDs, books on tape/CD, and electronic resources. MARC records follow a format that was established by the Library of Congress and can include information such as:

- author
- title
- ISBN
- publisher
- publication date
- subject headings
- format (i.e., book, DVD, journal)
- cost of the item
- call number
- barcode number

MARC records can be created by the library, purchased from vendors and can even be electronically copied from other libraries that have the same item and then modified. Depending on the level of cataloging that the library prefers, the MARC records can be extremely detailed or very brief.

CIRCULATION

The circulation module is used by staff members to assist with checking materials in and out of the library. The circulation module is also used to create and manage patron records. Each patron will need to have a record in the system so that they can check out library materials. The patron record is usually connected to a library card that the patron presents when he/she wants to check out an item. Other features of circulation can include processing overdue and fine notices and creating inventory reports.

ONLINE PUBLIC ACCESS CATALOG (OPAC)

Through the use of the OPAC, patrons can find materials the library has available; this is essentially what has replaced the traditional card catalog for library users. The OPAC will generally allow patrons to search by title, keyword, or author name, and other more advanced search or limiting features may also be available.

The OPAC may need specific software in order to run on a computer, but most vendors also offer the option of accessing the catalog using a Web browser, such as Internet Explorer. The advantage to offering a Web-based OPAC is that the library can choose to allow patrons to search the library catalog from anywhere they have access to a computer and the Internet. Many libraries designate specific computers within the building that just access the OPAC to make sure that patrons who are only interested in finding library materials don't need to wait to use a public access terminal. Typically, the OPAC will also be available on computers that are used for other functions such as word processing or Internet use.

In addition to allowing patrons to search for materials, other basic OPAC features can include allowing the patron to review items that he/she currently has checked out or are overdue, the ability to renew items electronically, and to place holds on items that they wish to borrow.

At the simplest level, here is how the system would actually work:

1. The library purchases a new book called *Traveling through Europe,* for the collection.
2. Using the cataloging module, a staff member creates a new MARC record for this book and affixes a barcode to the book.
3. The book gets placed out on the shelf.
4. A patron comes into the library, uses the OPAC to look for travel books and finds that the library has a copy of *Traveling through Europe* and that the item is currently checked in. The patron then retrieves the book from the shelf.
5. The patron takes the book and his/her library card to

the circulation desk where a staff member checks the book out to the patron using the circulation module.

6. The patron returns the book to the library two weeks later and the item is checked back in and returned to the shelf.

Of course, the technical realities are much more complex and without actually performing the tasks, there is no way to get a true sense of the time and effort behind adding a new book to the collection and making it available to patrons. This also just begins to scratch the surface of what an ILS can do for a library. In addition to the basic functions, vendors also have other modules and features that libraries can select. Two popular choices are the serials and acquisitions modules. A serials module helps libraries manage magazine and journal subscriptions. The module is designed to track when issues should arrive at the library and generate notices to alert staff to follow up with the vendor when they don't. The acquisitions module allows the library to automate and consolidate the selection, ordering, and payment of new materials for the collection. The multitudes of options make selecting products very challenging and the next focus will be on navigating through that process.

SELECTING A NEW INTEGRATED LIBRARY SYSTEM

Although the general functions of an ILS are similar from one vendor to the next, the special features, modules, and interface designs that stand out are often factors for selecting one system over another. ILS vendors can generally customize a software and hardware package for each library and also offer additional modules or enhancements that can be purchased separately. Many vendors sell what are referred to as "vendor-neutral" products. These products can be used in conjunction with a library system purchased from other vendors. Each vendor packages and prices their product differently and what one considers a standard offering, may be considered an enhancement by another.

The effort that goes toward reviewing, selecting, purchasing, and deploying an integrated library system will present challenges for every library. The project is likely to take months and involve hours of staff time and eventually a considerable financial investment. It is a process that can be overwhelming and developing a clear plan of action can be difficult. It will be helpful to obtain a copy of one or both of these books, *Automating Media Centers and Small Libraries: A Microcomputer-Based Approach* (Bilal 2002) and *Planning for Integrated Systems and Technologies: A How-To-Do-It Manual for Librarians* (Cohn et al. 2001). These books were written specifically for libraries that are looking to automate for the first time or that need to migrate to a new system. Both books cover the entire spectrum of planning for automation, from the earliest needs assessment through the actual implementation.

Automating Media Centers and Small Libraries: A Microcomputer-Based Approach was written by Dania Bilal. The author provides detailed information about planning for automation, including helpful sheets that can be used when preparing a request for proposal from vendors, questions that the library should ask vendors about their products, and explanations of important issues such as network design.

Planning for Integrated Systems and Technologies: A How-To-Do-It Manual for Librarians was written by John M. Cohn, Ann L. Kelsey and Keith Michael Fiels. This book really gives the "How-To" approach to automation, including checklists, worksheets, suggestions on performing a needs assessment, writing a technology plan, and strategies for approaching the major issues that a library will face with a new automation system.

Assistance and information is also available from the ILS vendors, but while the vendors will be willing and eager to provide details and even demonstrations of their products, they have a vested interest in showing the best side of their companies and their products. It is important to also read written reviews about potential vendors and to ask for feedback from other libraries. There are libraries around the country and possibly in the next county over that can provide valuable help by relating their experiences with automation. Reach out to those libraries and ask for reactions to vendors and products, both the good and the bad, and help to better prepare the library for the decisions and changes ahead.

Libraries that are automating for the first time will find it particularly helpful to visit peer libraries to see firsthand how different ILS products work. A basic tour and demonstration of a product can be beneficial for understanding terminology and expressing needs to vendors. Some questions to ask during an informational visit:

- How long have they been automated?
- How long have they had the current system?

- What other vendors did they consider?
- What made them choose the current system over others?
- What challenges did they face during implementation?
- What would they have done differently during the implementation?
- What are their favorite features of the system?
- Can they demonstrate basic functions for how the staff and public use the system?
- What do they feel is missing from their current system?

The initial point of asking questions and seeing these demonstrations is not necessarily to eliminate vendors or particular products, but to better provide the library with an understanding of how the systems work. It is an information gathering process that can really be considered a form of brainstorming. Chances of finding a library that was 100 percent satisfied with every aspect of their selection is slim; they should have some suggestions and feedback. Every experience will be different and heeding any cautions or recommendations will help the library to prepare for the process as much as possible.

CONCLUSION

Perhaps even more than decisions about other forms of technology, the purchase of a new integrated library system can be intimidating and daunting. The best defense is to do research and allow time for hands-on demonstrations from different vendors and site visits with peer libraries. Careful planning and evaluation can give the library the best opportunity of selecting a system that fits current needs and that will also accommodate changes and developments in the future.

REFERENCES/FURTHER READING

Bilal, Dania. 2002. *Automating media centers and small libraries: A micro-computer-based approach, 2nd ed.* Englewood, CO: Libraries Unlimited.
Breeding, Marshall. 2004. "The trend toward outsourcing the ILS: Recognizing the benefits of shared systems." *Computers in Libraries*, 24, 5 (May): 36–39.

Breeding, Marshall. *Library technology guides.* Nashville: Tennessee www.librarytechnology.org. (Accessed December 2005).

Cibarelli, Pamela. 2003. "ILS marketplace. CIL's quarterly series on library automation markets: Your guide to vendor product facts and user ratings." *Computers in Libraries,* 23, 1 (January): 31–36.

Cibarelli, Pamela. 2004. *Directory of library automation software, systems and services, 2004–2005 Edition.* Medford, NJ: Information Today, Inc.

Cohn, John M., Ann L. Kelsey, and Keith Michael Fiels. 1997. *Planning for automation, 2nd ed.* New York: Neal-Schuman.

Cohn, John M., Ann L. Kelsey, and Keith Michael Fiels. 2001. *Planning for integrated systems and technologies: A how-to-do-it manual for librarians.* New York: Neal-Schuman.

Pace, Andrew K. 2005. "Helping you buy: Integrated library systems." *Computers in libraries,* 25, 8 (September): 25–32.

Running a Small Library
Sourcebook

SOURCE A: LIST OF STATE LIBRARY AGENCIES

Alabama Public Library Service, 6030 Monticello Drive, Montgomery 36130. Phone: 334–213–3900. Fax: 334–213–3993. Web page: www.apls.state.al.us

Alaska State Library, Archives and Museums, 333 Willoughby Avenue, State Office Building, 8th floor, Post Office Box 110571, Juneau 99811–0571. Phone: 907–465–2910. Fax: 907–465–2665. Web page: www.library.state.ak.us

Arizona State Library Department of Library, Archives and Public Records, 1700 West Washington, Suite 200, Phoenix, 85007. Phone: 602–542–4035 Fax: 602–542–4972. Web page: www.lib.az.us

Arkansas State Library, One Capitol Mall, Little Rock 72201–1085. Phone: 501–682–1527. Fax: 501–682–1529. Web page: www.asl.lib.ar.us

California State Library, 914 Capitol Mall, Stanley Mosk Library and Courts Building, Post Office Box 942837, Sacramento 94237–0001. Phone: 916–654–0183. Fax: 916–654–0064. Web page: www.library.ca.gov

Colorado State Library, Colorado Department of Education, 201 East Colfax Avenue, Room 309, Denver 80203–1799. Phone: 303–866–6900. Fax: 303–866–6940. Web page: www.cde.state.co.us/index_library.htm

Connecticut State Library, 231 Capitol Avenue, Hartford 06106. Phone: 860–757–6510. Fax: 860–757–6503. Web page: www.cslib.org

Delaware Division of Libraries—State Library, Department of State, 43 South Dupont Highway, Dover 19901. Phone 302–739–4748. Fax: 302–739–6787. Web page: www.lib.de.us

State Library of Florida, Division of Library and Information Services, R. A. Gray Building, 500 South Bronough Street, Tallahassee 32399–0250. Phone: 850–245–6600. Fax: 850–245–6651. Web page: www.dlis.dos.state.fl.us

Georgia Public Library Service, 1800 Century Place, Suite 150, Atlanta 30345–4304. Phone: 404–982–3560. Fax: 404–982–3563. Web page: www.georgialibraries.org

Hawaii State Public Library System, Office of the State Librarian, 465 South King Street, Room B–1, Honolulu 96813. Phone: 808–586–3704. Fax: 808–586–3715. Web page: www.librarieshawaii.org

Idaho State Library, 325 West State Street, Boise 83702–6072. Phone: 208–334–2150. Fax: 208–334–4016. Web page: www.lili.org

Illinois State Library, 300 South Second Street, Springfield 62701–1976. Phone: 217–782–7845. Fax: 217–782–6062. Web page: www.cyberdrive/illinois.com/departments/library/home.html

Indiana State Library, 140 North Senate Avenue, Indianapolis 46204–2296. Phone 317–232–3679. Fax: 317–232–0002. Web page: www.statelib.lib.in.us

State Library of Iowa, East 12th and Grand Avenue, Des Moines 50319. Phone 515–281–4015. Fax: 515–281–6191. Web page: www.silo.lib.ia.us

Kansas State Library, State Capitol Building, 300 S.W. Tenth St, Room 343N, Topeka 66612–1593. Phone: 785–296–3296. Fax: 785–296–6650. Web page: skyways.lib.ks.us

Kentucky Department for Libraries and Archives, 300 Coffee Tree Road, Frankfort 40602–0537. Phone 502–564–8300. Fax: 502–564–5773. Web page: www.kdla.ky.gov

State Library of Louisiana, 701 North Fourth Street, Post Office Box 131, Baton Rouge 70802–0131. Phone 225–342–4923. Fax: 225–219–4804. Web page: www.state.lib.la.us

Maine State Library, 64 State House Station, Augusta 0433–0064. Phone 207–287–5600. Fax: 207–287–5615. Web page: www.state.me.us./msl

Maryland State Department of Education, Division of Library Development and Services, 200 West Baltimore Street, Baltimore 21201–2595. Phone: 410–767–0444. Fax: 410–333–2507. Web page: www.marylandpublic schools.org/msde/divisions/library

Massachusetts Board of Library Commissioners, 648 Beacon Street, Boston 02215. Phone: 617–267–9400. Fax: 617–421–9833. Web page: www.mlin.lib.ma.us

Library of Michigan, 702 West Kalamazoo Street, Post Office Box 30007, Lansing 48909. Phone: 517–373–1580. Fax: 517–373–4480. Web page: www.michigan.gov/nal

Minnesota State Library Agency, Library Development and Services, 1500 Highway 36 West, Roseville 55113. Phone: 651–582–8791. Fax: 651–582–8752. Web page: education.state.mn.us/html/intro_lib_about.htm

Mississippi Library Commission, 1221 Ellis Avenue, Jackson 39209–7328. Phone 601–961–4111. Fax: 601–354–4181. Web page: www.jlc.lib.ms.us

Missouri State Library, 600 West Main, Post Office Box 387, Jefferson City 65102–0387. Phone: 573–751–3615. Fax: 573–751–3612. Web page: www.sos.mo.gov/library

Montana State Library, 1515 Sixth Avenue, Post Office Box 201800, Helena 59620–1800. Phone: 406–444–3115. Fax: 406–444–0766. Web page: www.msl.state.mt.us

Nebraska Library Commission, The Atrium, 1200 North Street, Suite 120, Lincoln 68508–2023. Phone: 402–471–2045. Fax: 402–471–2083. Web page: www.nlc.state.ne.us

Nevada State Library and Archives, 100 North Stewart Street, Carson City 89701–4285. Phone: 775–684–3360. Fax: 775–684–3330. Web page: dmla.clan.lib.nv.us

New Hampshire State Library, 20 Park Street, Concord 03301–6314. Phone: 603–271–2149. Fax: 603–271–6826. Web page: www.state.nh.us/nhs

New Jersey State Library, 185 West State Street, Post Office Box 520, Trenton 08625–0520. Phone: 609–292–6220. Fax: 609–984–7900. Web page: www.nj statelib.org

New Mexico State Library, 1209 Camino Carlos Rey, Santa Fe 87507. Phone: 505–476–9700. Fax: 505–476–9701. Web page: www.state.ib.state.nm.us

New York State Library, Cultural Education Center, Empire State Plaza, Albany 12230. Phone: 518–474–5355. Fax: 518–474–5786. Web page: www.nysed.gov

State Library of North Carolina, 109 East Jones Street, 4640 Mail Service Center, Raleigh 27699–4640. Phone 919–807–7400. Fax: 919–733–8748. Web page: www.statelibrary.dcr.state.nc.us/ncslhome.htm

North Dakota State Library, 604 East Boulevard Avenue, Department 250, Bismarck 58505–0800. Phone: 701–328–2492. Fax: 701–328–2040. Web page: ndsl.lib.state.nd.us

State Library of Ohio, 247 East First Street, Columbus 43201. Phone 614–644–7061. Fax: 614–466–3584. Web page: winslo.state.oh.us

Oklahoma Department of Libraries, 200 N.E. 18th Street, Oklahoma City 73105. Phone: 405–521–2502. Fax: 405–525–7804. Web page: www.odl.state.ok.us

Oregon State Library, 250 Winter Street N.E., Salem 97301–3950. Phone: 503–378–4243. Fax: 503–585–8059. Web page: Oregon.gov/OSL

State Library of Pennsylvania, Department of Education, Office of Commonwealth Libraries, Forum Building, Walnut Street and Commonwealth Avenue, 333 Market Street, Harrisburg 17126–1745. Phone: 717–783–5950. Fax: 717–783–2070. Web page: www.state library.state.pa.us

Office of Library and Information Services, OLIS Library Programs, One Capitol Hill, Providence, RI 02908. Phone: 401–222–2726. Fax: 401–222–4195. Web page: www.olis.state.ri.us

South Carolina State Library, Senate and Bull Streets, Post Office Box 11469, Columbia 29211. Phone: 803–734–8666. Fax: 803–734–8676. Web page: www.state.sc.us

South Dakota State Library, 800 Governors Drive, Pierre 57501–2294. Phone: 605–773–3131. Fax: 605–773–6962. Web page: www.sdstatelibrary.com

Tennessee State Library and Archives, 403 Seventh Avenue North, Nashville 37242–0312. Phone: 615–741–2764. Fax: 615–741–6471. Web page: www.state.tn/sos/statelib/tslahome.htm

Texas State Library and Archives Commission, 1201 Brazos, Post Office Box 12927, Austin 78711–2927. Phone: 512–463–5460. Fax: 512–463–5436. Web page: www.tsl.state.tx.us

Utah State Library Division, 250 North 1950 West, Suite A, Salt Lake City. Phone: 801–715–6777. Fax: 801–715–6767. Web page: www.library.utah.gov

State of Vermont Department of Libraries, 109 State Street, Montpelier 05609–0601. Phone: 802–828–3261. Fax: 802–828–2199. Web page: dol.state.vt.us

The Library of Virginia, 800 East Broad Street, Richmond 23219–8000. Phone: 804–692–3500. Fax: 804–692–3594. Web page: www.lva.lib.va.us

Washington State Library, Post Office Box 42460, Olympia 98504–2460. Phone: 360–753–5200. Fax: 360–586–7575. Web page: www.secstate.wa.gov/library

West Virginia Library Commission, Cultural Center, 1900 Kanawha Boulevard, Charleston 25305. Phone: 304–588–2041. Fax: 304–558–2044. Web page: www.library commission.lib.wv.us

Wisconsin Department of Public Instruction, Division for Libraries, Technology and Community Learning, 125 South Webster Street, Post Office Box 7841, Madison 53707–7841. Phone: 608–266–2205. Fax: 608–266–8770. Web page: www.dpi.state.wi.us/dpi/dltcl

Wyoming State Library, 2301 Capitol Avenue, Cheyenne 82002–0060. Phone: 307–777–6333. Fax: 307–777–6289. Web page: www-wsl.state.wy.us

SOURCE B: LIST OF BOOK AND PERIODICAL VENDORS

Amazon Books. www.amazon.com.

Ambassador Book Service, 42 Chasner Street, Hempsted, New York 11550. 800–431–8913. www.absbooks.com

B.H. Blackwell, Ltd., Beaver House, Hythe Bridge Street, Oxford, England OX12ET. 44 (0) 1865–792792.

Baker and Taylor Company, 2550 West Tyvola Road, Suite 300, Charlotte, N.C. 28217. 800–775–1800. www.btol.com

Barnes and Noble, 122 Fifth Avenue, 2nd Floor, New York, New York 10011. 800–422–7717. www.barnesandnoble.com

Bernan Associates, 4611-F. Assembly Drive, Lanham, Maryland 20706. 800–865–3450. www.bernan.com (Government publications)

Blackwell Publishers, 350 Main Street, Malden, Massachusetts 02148. 781–388–8200. www.blackwell.com

Book Depot, 1707 Ridge Road, Lewiston, New York 14092. 800–865–3450. www.bookdepot.com.

Book House, 208 West Chicago Street, Jonesville, Michigan 49250. 800–248–1146. www.thebookhouse.com

Bookmen, Inc. 525 North 3rd Street, Minneapolis, Minnesota 55401. 800–328–8411. www.bookmen.com.

Bound To Stay Bound, Inc. 1880 West Morton Road, Jacksonville, Illinois 62650. 800–637–6586. www.btsbbooks.com

Brodart Company 500 Arch Street, Williamsport, Pennsylvania 17705. 800–233–8467. www.brodart.com

Coutts Library Services, Inc., 1823 Maryland Avenue, Niagara Falls, New York 14302. 800–772–4304. www.coutts-ls.com

Eastern Book Company, 13 Middle Street, Post Office Box 4540 DTS, Portland, Maine 04112. 800–937–0331. www.ebc.com

EBSCO Industries, Inc., Periodical Sales Division, 5724 Highway 280 East, Birmingham, Alabama 35242–6818. 205–991–1369. www.ebsco.com

Econo-Clad Books, Post Office Box 1777, Topeka, Kansas 66601. 800–255–3502. www.sagebrush.com/books.econoclad.cfm

Emery-Pratt, 1966 West Main Street, Owosso, Michigan 48867. 800–248–3887. www.emerypratt.com

ERIC Document Reproduction Services, 7420 Fullerton Road, Suite 110, Springfield, Virginia 22153. 800–443–3742. www.edrs.com

EVA Subscription Services, 56 Maple Avenue, Post Office Box 338, Shrewsbury, Massachusetts 01545. 800–842–2077. www.evasub.com

Facts on File News Services, 11 Penn Plaza, 15th floor, New York, New York 10001. 800–363–7976. www.facts.com

Faxon Company, 15 Southwest Park, Westwood, Massachusetts 02090. 800–766–0039. www.faxon.com

Follett Library Book Company, 2233 Wet Street, River Grove, Illinois 60171. 800–621–4345. www.follett.com

Hispanic Book Distributors, Inc., 240 East Yvon Drive, Tucson, Arizona 85704. 800–634–2124. www.hispanicbooks.com

Ingram Library Services, One Ingram Boulevard, La Vergne, Tennessee 37086. 800–937–5300. www.ingramlibrary.com

Midwest Library Service, 11443 St. Charles Rock River, Bridgeton, Missouri 63044. 800–743–4070. www.midwestls.com

Multi-cultural Books and Videos, Inc., 28880 Southfield Road, Suite 183, Lathrup Village, Michigan 48076. 809–567–2220. www.multicultbv.com

Periodicals Service Company, 11, Main Street, Germantown, New York 12526. 518–537–4700. www.backsets.com

Perma-Bound, East Vandalia Road, Jacksonville, Illinois 62650. 800–323–4241. www.perma-bound.com

Puvill Libros, 264 Derrom Avenue, Paterson, New Jersey 07504. 973–279–9054. www.pubill.com.

Regent Book Company 25 Saddle River Road, South Hackensack, New Jersey 07606. Post Office Box 750, Lodi, New Jersey 07644. 800–999–9554. www.regentbook.com

Swets Blackwell Information Services, 440 Creamery Way, Suite A, Exton, Pennsylvania 19341–2551. 800–447–9387. www.swetsinc.com

United States Book Exchange, 2969 West 25th Street, Cleveland, Ohio 44113. 216–241–6960. www.usbe.com

W.T. Cox Subscriptions, Inc., 201 Village Road, Shallotte, North Carolina 28470. 800–571–9554. www.wtcox.com

YBP Library Services, 999 Maple Street, Contoocick, New Hampshire 03229–3374 800–258–3774. www.ybp.com

SOURCE C: LIST OF LIBRARY FURNITURE AND SUPPLY VENDORS

Agati, 1219 West Lake Street, Chicago, Illinois 60607. 312–829–1977. www.agati.com

American Seating Co., American Seating Center, Grand Rapids, Michigan 49504. 800–748–0268. www.americanseating.com

Blanton and Moore Co., Post Office Box 70, Highway 21 South, Barium Springs, North Carolina 28010. 704–528–4506. www.blantonandmoore.com

Bretford Manufacturing, Inc., 11000 Seymour Avenue, Franklin Park, Illinois 60131. 800–521–9614. www.bretford.com

Brodart, 500 Arch Street, Williamsport, Pennsylvania 17701. Supplies—888–820–4377; Furniture—888–521–1884, ext. 360. www.brodart.com

Buckstaff, Post Office Box 2506, Oshkosh, Wisconsin 54903. 800–755–5890. www.buckstaff.com

D.B. Company, 529 Pecore, Houston, Texas 77009. 877–234–1657. www.universalairlift.com

DEMCO, Inc., Post Office Box 7488, Madison, Wisconsin 53707. 800–356–1200. www.demco.com

Display Fixtures Co., 1501 Westinghouse Boulevard, Post Office Box 410073, Charlotte, North Carolina 28241. 800–737–0880. www.displayfixtures.com

ENEM Systems by Harrier Interior Products Corporation, 319 Colfax Street, Palatine, Illinois 60067. 847–934–1310. www.enembyharrier.com

Fetzers' Inc., 1436 South West Temple, Salt Lake City, Utah 84115. 801–484–6103. www.fetzersinc.com

Fleetwood Group, Inc., Post Office Box 1259, Holland, Michigan 49424. 800–257–6390. www.fleetwooodgroup.com

Gaylord Brothers, Post Office Box 4901, Syracuse, New York 13221. 800–448–6160. www.gaylord.com

Gressco, Ltd., 328 Moravian Valley Road, Post Office Box 339, Waunakee, Wisconsin 53597. 800–345–3480. www.gresscoltd.com

Highsmith Company, West 5227 Highway 106, Fort Atkinson, Wisconsin 53538. 800–558–2110. www.highsmith.com

Herman Miller, 855 East Main Avenue, Post Office Box 302, Zeeland, Michigan 49464. 888–443–4357. www.hermanmiller.com

International Library Furniture, Inc., 525 South College, Keene, Texas 76059. 888–401–0869. www.internationallibrary.com

Kapco Library Products, 1000 Cherry Street, Kent, Ohio 44240. 800–791–8965. www.kapcolibrary.com

Library Bureau, 172 Industrial Road, Post Office Box 400, Fitchburg, Massachusetts 01420. 978–345–7942. www.librarybureau.com

Library Store, Inc., 112 East South Street, Post Office Box 964, Tremont, Illinois 61568. 800–548–7204. www.thelibrarystore.com

Midlands, Company, Inc., 3640 North Dixboro Road, Ann Arbor, Michigan 48105. 734–622–0080. www.tmefurniture.com

Mohawk Library Furniture, 1609 Sherman Avenue, Suite 312, Evanston, Illinois 60201. 847–570–0448.

Montel Aetnastak, Inc., 1170 Highway A1A, Satellite, Florida 32937. 800–772–7562. www.montel.com

Palmieri Library Furniture, 1230 Reid Street, Richmond Hill, Ontario L4B 1C4, Canada. 800–413–4440. www.palmierifurniture.com

Sauder Manufacturing Company, 930 West Barre Road, Archbold, Ohio 43502. 800–537–1530. www.saudermfg.com

Spacesaver Corporation, 1450 Janesville Avenue, Fort Atkinson, Wisconsin 52358. 920–563–63162 www.spacesaver.com

Texwood Furniture Corporation, 1353 West Second Street, Taylor, Texas 76574. 888–878–0000. www.texwood.com

Thomas Moser Cabinet Makers, 72 Wright's Landing, Auburn, Maine 04211. 800–708–9710. www.thomasmoser.com

Vernon Library Supplies, Inc., 2851 Cole Court, Norcross, Georgia 30071. 800–878–0253. www.vernlib.com

Worden, Company, 199 E. 17th Street, Holland, Michigan 49423. 800–748–0561. www.wordencompany.com

SOURCE D: AUTOMATION VENDORS

Auto-Graphics, 3201 Temple Avenue, Pomona, California 91768. 800–776–6939. www.auto-graphics.com

Book Systems Inc., 721 Clinton Avenue, Suite 11, Huntsville, Alabama 35801. 800–219–6571. www.booksys.com

Companion Corporation, 1831 Fort Union Boulevard, Salt Lake City, Utah 84121. 800–347–6439. www.companioncorp.com

Cuadra Associates, 11836 West Olympic Boulevard, Suite 855, Los Angeles, California 90064. 310–478–0066. www.cuadra.com

Endeavor Information Systems, 1350 East Touhy Avenue, Suite 200, Des Plaines, Illinois 60018. 800–762–6300. www.endinfosys.com

Ex Libris, 1919 North Sheffield, Chicago, Illinois 60614. 877–527–1689. www.exlibris-usa.com

Follett Software Company, 1391 Corporate Drive, McHenry, Illinois 60050. 800–323–339. www.fsc.follett.com

Geac Library Solutions, 100 Fifth Avenue, Waltham, Massachusetts 02451. 781–672–8892. www.library.geac.com

Hunter Systems, 1800 International Park Drive, Suite 500, Birmingham, Alabama 35243. 800–326–0527. www.huntersystems.com

InfoVision Software, Inc., 3830 Valley Centre Drive, Suite 705–703, San Diego, California 92130. 858–243–1481. www.amlib.net

Inmagic, Inc., 200 Unicorn Park Drive, Fourth Floor, Woburn, Massachusetts 01801. 800–229–8398. www.inmagic.com

Innovative Interfaces, Inc., 5850 Shellmound Way, Emeryville, California 94608. 800–878–6600. www.iii.com

Keystone Systems, Inc., 8016 Glenwood Avenue, Raleigh, North Carolina 27612. 800–222–9711. www.klas.com

The Library Corporation, Research Park, Inwood, West Virginia 25428. 800–325–7759. www.tlcdelivers.com

Library Resource Management Systems, Inc., Post Office Box 922, Van Alstyne, Texas 75495. 877–700–5767. www.lrms.com

On Point, Inc., 2606 36th Street N.W., Washington, District of Columbia 20007. 202–338–8914. www.onpointinc.com

Open Text Corporation, 5080 Tuttle Crossing Boulevard, Dublin, Ohio 43016. 800–329–2648. www.opentext.com/basis

Polaris Library Systems, 103 Commerce Boulevard, Post Office Box 4903, Syracuse, New York 13221. 800–272–3414. www.polarislibrary.com

Ringgold Management Systems, Post Office Box 368, Beavertown, Oregon 97075. 503–645–3502. www.ringgold.com

SIMA, Inc., Post Office Box 248, 9312-E Old Keene Mill Road, Springfield, Virginia 22150. 703–569–0993. www.simainc.com

Sirsi/Dynix, 101 Washington Street S.E., Huntsville, Alabama 35801. 800–917–4774. www.sirsidynix.com

VTLS, Inc., 1701 Kraft Drive, Blacksburg, Virginia 24060. 800–468–8857. www.vtls.com

SOURCE E: PROFESSIONAL ORGANIZATIONS

There are many professional organizations that are able to provide assistance to librarians. These include international library organizations, state library organizations, and type of library organizations. This source will provide location information about major library professional organizations and guidance in which organization to approach for library informational needs.

Professional organizations may be divided into general national organizations such as the American Library Association, Australian Library and Information Association, Canadian Library Association, and the Chartered Institute of Library and Informational Professionals (Great Britain); types of library organizations such as the Association of College and Research Libraries, Public Library Association, and Special Library Association; and special interest library organizations such as Association for Library Trustees and Advocates and Friends of the Libraries USA. There will also be state, provincial, or other subnational unit library associations such as British Columbia Library Association, Texas Library Association, and the CILIP South East Branch. Each of these organizations will provide information and services to the smallest library.

Which organization should be approached with an information request? If it is a public library question, one of the best first stops would be the library development office of the state library. The locations of these agencies are given in Source A. Otherwise it would be good to approach the type of library organization at either a state or national level. Many state library associations will have type of library divisions. These are good sources for initial enquiries.

National library associations and types of library associations are good sources for general materials including books, audio-visual materials, fact sheets, etc., on all aspects of librarianship, and statements of professional values. They also provide guidance and assistance in questions relating to areas such as censorship issues.

The following are some professional organizations:

National

American Library Association
50 East Huron Street
Chicago, Illinois 60611
800–545–2433
www.ala.org

Australian Library and Information Association LTD
P.O. Box 6335 Kingston
2604 Australia
Street Address:
ALIA House
9–11 Napier Close
Deakin 2600
Australia
+61–2–6215–8222
www.alia.org.au

Canadian Library Association
328 Frank Street
Ottawa, Ontario
Canada K2P 0X8
613–232–9625
www.cla.ca

Chartered Institute of Library and Information Professionals (Great Britain)
7 Ridgemount Street
London, England WC1E 7AE
0 +44 20 7255 0500
www.cilip.org.uk

TYPE OF LIBRARY

Association of College and Research Libraries
50 East Huron Street
Chicago, Illinois 60611
800–545–2433, ext. 2523
www.acrl.org

Medical Library Association
65 East Wacker Place, Suite 1900
Chicago, Illinois 60601–7246

312–419–9094
www.mlanet.org

Public Library Association
50 East Huron Street
Chicago, Illinois 60611
800–545–2433, ext. 5752
www.pla.org

Special Libraries Association
331 South Patrick Street
Alexandria, Virginia 22314–3501
703–647–4900
www.sla.org

Young Adult Library Services Association
50 East Huron Street
Chicago, Illinois 60611
800–545–2433, ext. 4390
www.ala.org/ourassociation/divisions

The Canadian Library Association has the following divisions that are accessible through the Canadian Library Association at www.cla.ca/top/divisions
Canadian Association for School Libraries
Canadian Association of College and University Libraries
Canadian Association of Public Libraries
Canadian Association of Children's Librarians
Canadian Association of Special Libraries and Information Services

Canadian Library Trustees Association

SPECIAL INTEREST LIBRARY ORGANIZATIONS

Association for Library Trustees and Advocates
50 East Huron Street
Chicago, Illinois 60611
800–545–2433, ext. 2160
www.ala.org/divisions

Friends of Libraries U.S.A.
1420 Walnut Street, Suite 450
Philadelphia, Pennsylvania 19102–4017
800–937–5872
www.folusa.org

STATE LIBRARY CHAPTERS

Information on all 50 state library chapters may be found at:
www.ala.org
The Annual *American Library Directory* published by Information Today, Inc.

The American Library Association Web site: www.ala.org under the international Relations Office, the Chapters office and the Association of School Libraries Division.

The Special Library Association Web site: www.sla.org

SOURCE F: BIBLIOGRAPHY OF USEFUL MATERIALS

General Comments

Outside resources are essential for any small library. By its very nature, with limited budget and staff, the library depends upon assistance from outside in all aspects of its service to its public. This book has sought to provide guidance and reassurance for the librarian in the small library setting. This section lists resources found in the various sections of the book, a few sources not mentioned previously, and gives guidance on where to look when questions arise.

There are several good sources for assistance. The first is the library development division of the state library. The sourcebook gives contact information for all fifty state libraries. These divisions are there to provide guidance and assistance and will also have other sources of information as well. Use them, for their purpose is to help libraries with day-to-day needs as well as long-term planning.

The second is the state library association. In many cases, the state library association will have types of library divisions, which will provide workshops, conferences, and continuing education opportunities. Check the American Library Association at www.ala.org to find contact information for the state library association.

The third are the wide variety of list servs that are available. With the Internet revolution, list servs and other means of communication are widely available. All you need is a connection to the Internet. These are a good source of assistance when you have a problem for they link you with individuals with similar situations who are always ready to provide assistance. Some list servs are operated by state library agencies or kinds of library subdivisions within each state. One good example is the VPLDA list serv for public library directors in Virginia. A division of a national association or just a group of like-minded individuals banding together may also operate list servs. Each type of library will have many opportunities for such communication.

A fourth source is the telephone. Use it. It is relatively inexpensive and your peers are always willing to lend an ear to hear concerns and offer advice and comfort.

A fifth source is the wide variety of printed materials available. A good example is the "How-To-Do-It" series of books published by Neal-Schuman, of which this book is a part. Other publishers such as Libraries Unlimited and ALA and its various divisional presses have valuable resources available for the librarian in the small library. Use the Internet to access their catalogs and interlibrary loan to access the titles.

However, none of the above sources work unless they are used. Just because an individual is in a small library setting does not mean that he/she is unimportant or that concerns are not valid. For assistance to be given it must be asked for and this is often the most difficult part.

Specific Resources:

ACRL Standards. Compiled at <www.ala.org/ala/acrl/acrlstandards/standardsguidelines.htm>

ACRL. "A Guideline for the screening and appointment of academic librarians using a search committee." 2004a. www.ala.org/ala/acrl/acrlstandards/screenapguide.htm

ACRL. *Academic Library Trends and Statistics for Carnie Classification Master's Colleges and Institutions [and] Baccalaureate Colleges.* Chicago, IL: Association of College and Research Libraries, 2005.

———. "What is the Association of College and Research Libraries?" www.ala.org/ala/acrl/aboutacrl/whatisacrl/whatacrl.htm.

ACRL. A Guideline for the Screening and Appointment of Academic Librarians Using a Search Committee. 2004.

Alabaster, Carol. *Developing an Outstanding Core Collection: A Guide for Libraries.* Chicago: American Library Association, 2002.

Alibris. www.alibris.com

Amazon. www.amazon.com

American Association of Community Colleges. (Trends and Statistics) www.aacc.nche.edu

American Association of School Librarians and Association for Educational Communications and Technology. *Information Power: Building Partnerships for Learning.* Chicago: American Library Association, 1998.

American Book Company. www.americanbookcompany .com

American Library Association. "Checklist for Creating an Internet Use Policy." Chicago: American Library Association, 2003.

———. *Intellectual Freedom Manual 6th Edition.* Chicago: American Library Association, 2002.

———. *Library Fact Sheet #15—Weeding Library Collections: A Selected Annotated Bibliography for Library Collection Evaluation.* Chicago: American Library Association, 2004.

American Library Association, Library Administration and Management Association, Buildings and Equipment Section, Functional Space Requirement Committee. *Building Blocks for Planning Functional Library Space.* Lanham, Maryland: Scarecrow, 2001.

American Library Directory, 2004–2005. Medford, NJ: Information Today, 2004.

Anderson, Rick. *Buying and Contracting for Resources and Services: A How-To-Do-It Manual for Librarians.* New York: Neal-Schuman, 2004.

Anderson. Shelia. *Extreme Teens.* Westport, CT: Libraries Unlimited, 2005.

Anonymous. *Managing Small Special Libraries, 1992: An SLA Information Kit.* Washington, DC: Special Libraries Association, 1992.

Arant, Wendi, and Pixey Anne Mosley, eds. *Library Outreach, Partnerships, and Distance Education: Reference Librarians at the Gateway.* New York: Haworth Information Press, 2000.

Association of Independent Information Professionals. www.aiip.org

Austin, James F. *The Collaborative Challenge: How Nonprofits and Businesses Succeed Through Strategic Alliances.* San Francisco: Jossey-Bass, 2000.

Authority Control Definition. http://ublib.buffalo.edu/libraries/units/cts/ac/def.html

Baker and Taylor. www.btol.com

Baldwin, David A. *The Library Compensation Handbook: A Guide for Administrators, Librarians, and Staff.* Westport, CT: Libraries Unlimited, 2003.

Barclay, Donald A. *Managing Public-Access Computers: A How-To-Do-It Manual for Librarians.* New York: Neal-Schuman, 2000.

Bauer, David G. *The "How To" Grants Manual: Successful Grantseeking Techniques for Obtaining Public and Private Grants.* Westport, CT: Praeger, 2003.

Bearings on the Future: The Tidewater Community College Strategic Plan. Norfolk, Virginia: Tidewater Community College (November 2000). <www.tcc.edu.>

Berner, Andrew, and Guy St.Clair, eds. *The Best of OPL II: Selected Readings from the 'One-person Library', 1989–1994.* Washington, DC: Special Libraries Association, 1996.

Berry, John. "Library of the Year 2004: The San Jose Model." *Library Journal,* 15 (June 2004). www.libraryjournal.com/article/CA42793.html

Bielefield, Arlene, and Lawrence Cheeseman. *Trustees, Friends and the Law.* New York: Neal-Schuman, 2002.

Bilal, Dania. *Automating Media Centers and Small Libraries: A Microcomputer-Based Approach, 2nd ed.* Westport, CT: Libraries Unlimited, 2002.

Blanshard, Catherine, ed. *Children and Young People: Library Association Guidelines for Public Library Services.* New York: Neal-Schuman, 1997.

Boon, Belinda. *The CREW Method: Expanded Guidelines for Collection Evaluation and Weeding for Small and Medium-Sized Libraries, Revised and Updated by Belinda Boon, Library Development Staff.* Austin: Texas State Library, 1995.

Bowker Annual Library and Book Trade Almanac. Medford, NJ: Information Today, 2004.

Bowman, J. H. *Essential Cataloging.* New York: Neal-Schuman, 2002.

Breeding, Marshall. *Library Technology Guides. December 2005.* Available: www.librarytechnology.org

———."The Trend Toward Outsourcing the ILS: Recognizing the Benefits of Shared Systems." *Computers in Libraries* 24, 5 (May 2004): 36–39.

———. "Wireless Networks Connect Libraries to a Mobile Society." *Computers in Libraries* 24, 9 (October 2004): 29–31.

Bremer, Suzanne W. *Long Range Planning: A How-To-Do-It Manual for Public Libraries.* New York: Neal-Schuman, 1994.

Broughton, Vanda. *Essential Classification.* New York: Neal-Schuman, 2004.

Brumley, Rebecca. *The Public Library Manager's Forms, Policies, and Procedures Handbook with CD-ROM.* New York: Neal-Schuman, 2004.

———. *The Reference Librarian's Policies, Forms, Guidelines and Procedures Handbook with CD-ROM.* New York: Neal-Schuman, 2006.

Burgett, James, et al. *Collaborative Collection Development: A Practical Guide for Your Library.* Chicago: American Library Association, 2004.

Butler, Meredith A., ed. *Successful Fundraising: Case Studies of Academic Libraries.* Washington, DC: Association of Research Libraries: 2001.

Carnegie Foundation. "The Carnegie Classification of Institutions of Higher Education." www.carnegie foundation.org/classifications/index.asp

Chapman, Liz. *Managing Acquisitions in Library and Information Services, 3rd ed.* New York: Neal-Schuman, 2004.

Chases's Calendar of Events. Chicago: Contemporary Books (annual).

Chelton, Mary K. *Excellence in Library Services for Young Adults.* Chicago: Young Adult Library Services, 2000.

Chen, Chiou-Sen Dora. *Serials Management: A Practical Guide.* Chicago: American Library Association, 1995.

Cibarelli, Pamela. *Directory of Library Automation Software, Systems and Services 2004–2005 Edition.* Medford, NJ: Information Today, 2004.

Cirino, Paul John. *The Business of Running a Library: A Handbook for Public Library Directors.* Jefferson, NC: McFarland & Company, 1991.

Classification Web. http://classificationweb.net

Clayton, Peter, and G. E. Gorman. *Managing Information Resources in Libraries and Information Services: Principles and Procedures.* New York: Neal-Schuman, 2001.

———. *Planning for Integrated Systems and Technologies: A How-To-Do-It Manual for Librarians.* New York: Neal-Schuman, 2001.

———. *Writing and Updating Technology Plans.* New York: Neal-Schuman, 1999.

Cook, Michael. *The Management of Information from Archives, 2nd ed.* Brookfield, VT: Gower, 1999.

Corson-Finnerty, Adam, and Laura Blanchard. *Fundraising and Friend-Raising on the Web.* Chicago: American Library Association, 1998.

CREW Method; Expanded Guidelines for Collection Evaluation and Weeding for Small and Medium-Sized Public Libraries. Austin: Texas State Library, 1995.

Crowther, Janet, and Barry Trott. *Partnering with Purpose: A Guide to Strategic Partnership Development for Libraries and Other Organizations.* Westport, CT: Libraries Unlimited, 2004.

Curtis, Donnelyn, and Virginia M. Scheachy. *E-Journals: A How-To-Do-It Manual for Building, Managing, and Supporting Electronic Journal Collections.* New York: Neal-Schuman, 2005.

Daedalus Books and Music. www.daedalusbooks.com

Dahlgren, Anders. *Planning the Small Library Facility 2nd ed. (LAMA Small Libraries Publication Series).* Chicago: American Library Association, 1996.

De La Pena McCook, Kathleen. *Introduction to Public Librarianship.* New York: Neal-Schuman, 2004.

DEMCO. www.demco.com

Dewey Decimal System. www.oclc.org/dewey

Dewey, Barbara I., ed. *Raising Money for Academic and Research Libraries.* New York: Neal-Schuman, 1991.

Eaglen, Audrey. *Buying Books: A How-To-Do-It Manual for Librarians, 2nd ed.* New York: Neal-Schuman, 2000.

Earlham College Library. *Collection Development Policy.* Richmond, IN: Earlham College, 2005.

EBSCO. www.ebsco.com

Ellington, Elizabeth, and Jane Friemiller. *A Year of Reading: A Month-by-Month Guide to Classics and Crowd-pleasers for You and Your Book Club.* Naperville, IL: Sourcebooks, 2002.

Eng, Susanna, and Susan Gardner. "Conducting Surveys on a Shoestring Budget." *American Libraries,* 36, 2 (February 2005): 38–39.

Erickson, Rolf, and Carol Markison. *Designing a School Library Media Center for the Future.* Chicago: ALA. 2001.

Evans, G. Edward. *Developing Library Collections.* Westport, CT: Libraries Unlimited, 1979.

Evans, G. Edward, et al. *Introduction to Library Public Services, 6th ed.* Westport, CT.: Libraries Unlimited, 1999.

Feinberg, Sandra, ed. *The Family-Centered Library Handbook.* New York: Neal-Schuman, 2006.

Fiore, Carol D. *Fiore's Summer Reading Program Handbook.* New York: Neal-Schuman, 2005.

Flying Solo (Solo Librarians Division, Special Library Association)

Friends of Libraries U.S.A. http://www.folusa.org

Fritz, Deborah A., and Richard J. Fritz. *MARC21 for Everyone: A Practical Guide.* Chicago: American Library Association, 2002.

Giesecke, Joan. *Scenario Planning for Libraries.* Chicago: American Library Association, 1998.

Giesecke, Joan, and Beth McNeil. *Fundamentals of Library Supervision.* Chicago: American Library Association, 2005.

Gill, Suzanne L. *File Management and Information Retrieval Systems: A Manual for Managers and Technicians, 3rd ed.* Englewood, CO: Libraries Unlimited, 1993.

Gillespie, John T. *Best Books for Children.* New York: R.R. Bowker, 1998.

Gillespie, John T., and Catherine Barr. *Best Books for Middle School and Junior High Readers.* Libraries Unlimited, 2004.

Glockner, Brigitte. "Accountability and Accreditation for Special Libraries: It Can Be Done." *Australian Library Journal*, 53, 3 (August 2004): 275–284.

Gorman, Michael, prep. *The Concise AACRC 4th ed.* Chicago: American Library Association, 2004.

Greiner, Joy M. *Exemplary Public Libraries: Lesions in Public Library Leadership, Management, and Services.* Westport, CT.: Libraries Unlimited, 2004.

Hale, Martha, Patti Boucher, and Cindi Hickey. "New Pathways to Planning." Northeast Kansas Library System (October 2003) http://skyways.lib.ks.us/pathway/index.html

Hallam, Arlita W., and Teresa R. Dalston. *Managing Budgets and Finances. A How-To-Do-It Manual.* New York: Neal-Schuman, 2005.

Hart, Keith. *Putting Marketing Ideas into Action.* London: Library Association, 1999.

Henczel, Susan. *The Information Audit: A Practical Guide.* Munich: Saur, 2001.

Hennen, Thomas J. Jr. *Hennen's Public Library Planner: A Manual and Interactive CD-Rom.* New York: Neal-Schuman, 2004.

Herald, Diana Tixler. *Genreflecting: A Guide to Reading Interests in Genre Fiction, 5th ed.* Westport, CT: Libraries Unlimited, 2000.

Hernon, Peter, and John R. Whitman. *Delivering Satisfaction and Service Quality: A Customer Based Approach for Libraries.* Chicago: American Library Association, 2004.

Herring Mark Y. *Raising Funds with Friends Groups: A How-To-Do-It Manual for Libraries.* New York: Neal-Schuman, 2004.

Hibberd, Betty Jo, and Allison Evatt. "Mapping Information Flows: A Practical Guide." *Information Management Journal,* 38, 1 (January/February 2004): 58–64.

Himmel, Ethel, and Bill Wilson. *Planning for Results: A Public Library Transformation Process.* Chicago, American Library Association, 1988.

Hoachlander, Gary, Anna C. Sikora, and Laura Horn. " Community College Students: Goals, Academic Preparation, and Outcomes." 2003: Report in *Educational Statistics Quarterly,* 5, 2. Tidewater Community College, Portsmouth, VA http://nces.ed.gov/programs/quarterly/vol_5/5_2/q4_1.sdp#H4

Holley, Pam Spencer. *What Do Children and Young Adults Read Next?* Chicago: Thompson Gale Research, 2002.

Holt, Glen. " Public Library Partnerships: Mission-Driven Tools for 21st Century Success." www.public-libraries.net/html/x_media/pdf/holt6en.pdf

Hsieh-Yee, Ingrid. *Organizing Audiovisual and Electronic Resources for Access.* Englewood, CO: Libraries Unlimited, 2000.

H.W. Wilson Company. www.hwwilson.com

Information Bridges International: www.ibi-opl.com

Information Outlook (Special Libraries Association)

Ingersoll, Richard, and Mei Han. *School Library Media Centers in the United States 1990–1991.* Washington, DC: U.S. Department of Education, 1994.

Ingram. www.ingramlibrary.com

Intner, Sheila S., and Jean Weihs. *Special Libraries: A Cataloging Guide.* Englewood, CO: Libraries Unlimited, 1998.

JSTOR. "JSTOR Classifications for U.S. Academic or Other Research Institutions." www.jstor.org/about/us.html#classification.

James City County. *Human Resource Forms.* Williamsburg, VA: James City County, 2005.

Janes, Joseph, et al. *The Internet Public Library Handbook.* New York: Neal-Schuman, 1999.

Johnson, Peggy. *Fundamentals of Collection Development and Management.* New York: American Library Association, 2003.

Jones, Plummer Alston. *Still Struggling for Equality: American Public Library Services with Minorities.* Westport, CT: Libraries Unlimited, 2004.

Katz, William A. *Introduction to Reference Work.* Boston: McGraw-Hill, 2002.

Kovacs, Dianne K., and Kara L. Robinson. *The Kovacs Guide to Electronic Library Collection Development: Essential Core Subject Collections, Selection Criteria, and Guidelines.* New York: Neal-Schuman, 2004.

Kreizman, Karen. *Establishing An Information Center: A Practical Guide.* London: Bowker-Saur, 1999.

Kuniholm, Roland. *The Complete Book of Model Fund-Raising Letters.* Paramus, NJ: Prentice Hall, 1995.

La Guardia, Cheryl, and Barbara Mitchell. *Finding Common Ground: Creating the Library of the Future without Diminishing the Library of the Past.* New York: Neal-Schuman, 1998.

Latham, Joyce M. "Everything old is thin again: Joyce M. Latham explains how thin clients—the current cousins of dumb terminals—might be a solution for a library's tech challenges." *School Library Journal,* 47, 11 (November 2001): 20–22.

Latham, Joyce M., and Frances Boyle. *Building an Electronic Resource Collection: A Practical Guide.* London: Facet, 2004.

Leland, Eric, and Russ King. "Wireless LANs: An Introduction to Wireless Networking Hardware." California: Tech Soup (May 2003). www.techsoup.org/howto/article/articlepage.cfm?ArticleId=336&topicid=3

LibQual. "Welcome to LibQUAL+TM!" www.libqual.org

Library-Oriented Lists and Electronic Serials: www.aladin.wrlc.org/gsdl/cgi-bin/library?p=about&c=liblists

Lima, Carolyn. *A to Zoo.* New York: R.R. Bowker, 2001.

Lukenbill, W. Bernard. *Collection Management for a New Century in the School Library Media Center.* Westport, CT: Libraries Unlimited, 2002.

Maddigan, Beth. *Big Book of Reading, Rhyming and Resources.* Westport, CT: Libraries Unlimited, 2005.

Main Book Shop. www.mainbookshop.com

Martin, Ann. *Seven Steps to an Award-Winning School Library Program.* Westport, CT: Libraries Unlimited, 2005.

Martin, Murray S., and Betsy Park. *Charging and Collecting Fees and Fines: A Handbook for Libraries.* New York: Neal-Schuman, 1998.

Matarazzo, James M., and Suzanne D. Connolly, eds. *Knowledge and Special Libraries.* Boston: Butterworth-Heinemann, 1999.

Matthews, Joseph R. *The Bottom Line: Determining and Communicating the Value of the Special Library.* Westport, CT: Libraries Unlimited, 2002.

———. *Measuring for Results: The Dimensions of Public Library Effectiveness.* Westport, CT: Libraries Unlimited, 2003.

———. *Technology Planning: Preparing and Updating a Library Technology Plan.* Westport, CT: Libraries Unlimited, 2004.

MLS: Marketing Library Services (Information Outlook)

Maurer, Charles B. "Close Encounters of Diverse Kinds: A Management Panorama for the Director of the Smaller College Library" in *College Librarianship*, edited by William Miller and D. Stephen Rockwood. Metuchen, NJ and London: Scarecrow Press, 1981.

Maxwell, Robert. *Maxwell's Guide to Authority Work.* Chicago: American Library Association, 2002.

Mayo, Diane. *Technology For Results: Developing Service-Based Plans.* Chicago: American Library Association, 2005.

Mayo, Diane, and Jeanne Goodrich. *Staffing for Results: A Guide to Working Smarter.* Chicago: Public Library Association, 2002.

Mayo, Dianne, and Sandra Nelson. *Wired for the Future: Developing Your Library Technology Plan.* Chicago: Public Library Association, 1999.

McCarthy, Richard C. *Designing Better Libraries: Selecting and Working with Building Professionals, 2nd ed.* Fort Atkinson, WI: Highsmith Press, 1999.

McClure, Charles, et al. *Planning and Role Setting for Public Libraries: A Manual of Options and Procedures.* Chicago: PLA, 1987.

McClure, Charles, et al. *Statistics and Performance Measures for Public Library Networked Services.* Chicago: American Library Association, 2001.

McMains, Victoria Golden. *The Reader's Choice: 200 Book Club Favorites.* New York: Quill, 2000

Megill, Kenneth A., and Herb Schantz. *Document Management: New Technologies for the Information Services Manager.* London: Bowker-Saur, 1999.

Midwest Library Services. www.midwestls.com

Miller, Gerald J. et al. *Performance Based Budgeting.* Boulder, CO: Westview Press, 2001.

Miller, William, and D. Stephen Rockwood, eds. *College Librarianship.* Metuchen, NJ and London: Scarecrow Press, 1981.

Mitchell, Anne M., and Brian E. Surratt. *Cataloging and Organizing Digital Information: A How-To-Do-It Manual for Librarians.* New York: Neal-Schuman, 2005.

Moore, Mary Y. *The Successful Library Trustee Handbook.* Chicago: American Library Association, 2004.

Mount, Ellis. *Special Libraries and Information Centers: An Introductory Text, 2nd ed.* Washington, DC: Special Libraries Association, 1991.

National Center for Education Statistics. *Digest of Education Statistics 2004.* Washington, DC: U.S. Department of Education, 2005.

———. *Public Libraries in the United States: Fiscal Year 2003.* Washington, D.C.: Department of Education, 2005.

———. "Welcome to Compare Academic Libraries." www.nces.ed.gov/surveys/libraries/compare/Index.asp?LibraryType=Academic.

———. "What is an academic library?" www.nces.ed.gov/surveys/libraries/AcaWhatIs.asp

———. "Welcome." www.nces.ed.gov/index.asp

Nelson, Sandra et al. *Creating Policies for Results; From Chaos to Clarity.* Chicago: Public Library Association, 2003.

———. *Managing for Results; Effective Resource Allocation for Public Libraries.* Chicago: Public Library Association, 2000.

———. *The New Planning for Results: A Streamlined Approach*. Chicago: Public Library Association, 2001.

Nelson, William Neal, and Robert Feneches. *Standards and Assessment for Academic Libraries: A Workbook*. Chicago: American Library Association, 2002.

Nisonger, Thomas E. *Evaluation of Library Collections, Access and Electronic Resources*. Westport, CT: Libraries Unlimited, 2003.

———. *Management of Serials in Libraries*. Westport, CT: Libraries Unlimited, 1998.

Npower. "TechAtlas." Washington DC: Npower, 2005. www.webjunction.techatlas.org

Office of Institutional Effectiveness. Norfolk, Virginia (February 2005.) available: www.tcc.edu.

One-person Library: A Newsletter for Librarians and Management (Information Bridges International}

Osborn, Andrew D. *Serial Publication: Their Place and Treatment in Libraries, 3rd ed.* Chicago: American Library Association, 1980.

Pace, Andrew K. "The Atkins Diet for Library Computing." *Computers in Libraries*, 24, 16 (June 2004): 38–40.

———. "Helping You Buy: Integrated Library Systems." *Computers in Libraries*, 25, 8 (September 2005): 25–32.

Patel, Heutel. "Thin Client." Piscataway, NJ: Eastern New Jersey Regional Library Cooperative (December 2005). www.infolink.org/pdf_files/thinclient.ppt.

Pearl, Nancy. *Book Lust: Recommended Reading for Every Mood, Moment, and Reason*. Seattle: Sasquatch Books, 2003.

Porter, Cathy A. et al. *Special Libraries: A Guide for Management, 4th ed.* Washington, DC: Special Libraries Association, 1991.

Price, Anne, and Juliette Yaakov, eds. *Children's Catalog, 18th ed.* New York: H. W. Wilson, 2001.

Public Library Association. *Public Library Data Service Statistical Report*. Chicago, Public Library Association, (published annually).

Reed, Sally Gardner. *Making the Case for Your Library: A How-To-Do-It Manual*. New York: Neal-Schuman, 2001.

Reed, Sally Gardner, and Beth Nawalinski. *Getting Grants in Your Community*. Philadelphia: FOLUSA, 2005.

Reed, Sally et al. *101+ Great Ideas for Libraries and Friends*. New York: Neal-Schuman, 2004.

Reitz, Joan M. *Dictionary for Library and Information Science*. Westport, CT: Libraries Unlimited, 2004.

Robb, Laura. *Literacy Links*. Portsmouth, NH: Heinemann, 2003.

Ross, Catherine Sheldrick, Kirsti Nielsen, and Patricia Dewdney. *Conducting the Reference Interview: A How-To-Do-It Manual for Librarians*. New York: Neal-Schuman, 2002.

Rubel, David. *The Reading List: Contemporary Fiction/ A Critical Guide to the Complete Works of 110 Authors*. New York: Henry Holt, 1998.

Rubin, Jack, ed. *Handbook of Public Budgeting*. New York: Marcel Dekker, 1992.

Rugge, Sue, and Alfred Glossbenner. *The Information Broker's Handbook, 2nd ed.* New York: McGraw-Hill, 1995.

Sacks, Risa. *Anatomy of a Phone Search: Primary Research Using the Original 'online'.*" *Searcher*, 13, 3 (March 2005): 42–47.

Sagawa, Shirley, and Eli Segal. *Common Interest, Common Good: Creating Value Through Business and Social Sector Partnerships*. Boston: Harvard Business School Press, 2000.

St. Clair, Guy. *Customer Service in the Information Environment*. London: Bowker-Saur, 1993.

———. *Entrepreneurial Librarianship: The Key to Effective Information Services Management*. London: Bowker-Saur, 1996.

———. *Power and Influence: Enhancing Information Services within the Organization*. London: Bowker-Saur, 1994.

———. *Total Quality Management in Information Services*. London: Bowker-Saur, 1997.

St. Clair, Guy, and Joan Williamson. *Managing the New One-person Library*. London: Bowker-Saur, 1992.

"Sample Surveys," in *Serving Our Public: Standards for Illinois Public Libraries, revised edition.* pp. 74–88. Chicago: Illinois Library Association, 1997.

Sannwald, William W. *Checklist of Library Building Design Considerations, 4th ed.* Chicago: American Library Association, 2001.

Sauers, Michael P., and Louise E. Alcorn. *Directory of Management Software for Public Access Computers*. New York: Neal-Schuman, 2003.

Schaeffer, Mark. *Library Displays Handbook*. New York: H. W. Wilson, 1991.

Schlipf, Frederick A., and John A. Moorman. *From Problem Recognition to Ribbon Cutting: The Public Library Construction Process*. www.urbanafreelibrary.org.

———. *Let There Be at Least Half-Way Decent Light: How Library Illumination Systems Work and Don't Work*. www.urbanafreelibrary.org.

Schweitzer, Aileen (Director, Thomas Nelson Community College Library and Resources Center), March 10, 2005 e-mail to Mary Mayer-Hennelly.

Seiss, Judith A. *The OPL Sourcebook: A Guide for Solo and Small Libraries.* Medford, NJ: Information Today, 2001.

———. *The Solo Librarian's Sourcebook.* Medford, NJ: Information Today, 1997.

Shaw, Sondra C. and Martha A. Taylor: *Reinventing Fundraising: Realizing the Potential of Women's Philanthropy.* San Francisco: Jossey-Bass, 1995.

———. *The Visible Librarian: Asserting Your Value with Marketing and Advocacy.* Chicago: American Library Association, 2004.

Shearer, Kenneth D., and Robert Bergin, eds. *The Reader's Advisor's Companion.* Englewood, CO: Libraries Unlimited, 2001.

Slote, Stanley J. *Weeding Library Collections: Library Weeding Methods, 4th ed.* Englewood CO: Libraries Unlimited, 1997.

Simon, Carol. "How Can You Be a Manager?: You're a Solo." Information Outlook, 9, 3 (March 2005): 13–14.

Simmons-Welburn, Janice, and Beth McNeil. *Human Resource Management in Today's Academic Library.* Westport, CT.: Libraries Unlimited, 2004.

Smith, G. Stevenson. *Accounting for Libraries and Other Not-For-Profit Organizations, 2nd ed.* Chicago: American Library Association, 1999.

Snyder, Timothy. *Getting Lead-Bottomed Administrators Excited about School Library Media Centers, 2nd ed.* Westport, CT: Greenwood Publishing Group, 2000.

South Carolina State Library. *A Pocket Reference Manual for Public Library Trustees.* Columbia: South Carolina State Library, 1999.

Special Libraries Associaton. www.sla.org.

Staley Library Collection Development Policy 2002. www.millikin.edu/staley/Collection_Development_Policy.htm.

Staley Library Mission 2000. www.millikin.edu/staley/mission.html.

State Library of Ohio. *Policies of Public Libraries.* http://winslo.oh.us/publib/policies.html

Steele, Victoria, and Stephen D. Elder. *Becoming a Fundraiser: The Principles and Practice of Library Development, 2nd ed.* Chicago: American Library Association, 2000.

Stein, Barbara L., and Risa W. Brown. *Running a School Library Media Center: A How-To-Do-It Manual, 2nd ed.* New York: Neal-Schuman, 2002.

Swan, James. *Fundraising for Libraries: 25 Proven Ways to Get More Money for Your Library.* New York: Neal-Schuman, 2002.

———. *Working Together: A How-To-Do-It Manual for Trustees and Librarians.* New York: Neal-Schuman, 1992.

SWING. www.swing-lib.org.

Taft Group. *The Big Book of Library Grant Money 2006.* Chicago: American Library Association, 2005.

Taylor, Arlene G. *Wyan's Introduction to Cataloging and Classification, Revised Ninth Edition.* Westport, CT: Libraries Unlimited, 2004.

TechSoup. "Computer Networks." San Francisco, CA: TechSoup (December 2005). www.techsoup.org/howto/articles.cfm?topicid=3&topic=Networks.

Tennent, Roy. *Managing the Digital Library.* New York: Reed, 2004.

Trotta, Marcia. *Managing Library Outreach Programs.* New York: Neal-Schuman, 1993.

Turner, Anne M. *It Comes with the Territory: Handling Problem Situations in Libraries.* Jefferson, NC: McFarland & Company, 1993.

Tuscarawas County Public Library. *Materials Reconsideration Policy.* New Philadelphia, OH: Tuscarawas County Public Library, 2005.

United Way of America. *Measuring Program Outcomes: A Practical Approach.* New York: United Way of America, 1996.

Van House, Nancy. *Project Measures for Public Libraries: A Manual of Standardized Procedures.* Chicago: Public Library Association, 1987.

Van, Zant, Nancy Patton. *Personnel Policies in Libraries.* New York: Neal-Schuman, 1980.

Virginia Community College System. *Statistical Profile 2002–2003.* Richmond, VA, 2005. www.vccs.edu.

Virginia Community College System, Academic and Student Affairs Committee. *Dual Enrollment in the VCCS Report.* Richmond, VA: 2005.

Wade, Gordon S. *Working with Library Boards: A How-To-Do-It Manual for Trustees and Librarians.* New York: Neal-Schuman, 1991.

Wallace, Linda K. *Libraries: Mission and Marketing: Writing Mission Statements That Work.* Chicago: American Library Association, 2004.

Walters, Suzanne. *Library Marketing That Works.* New York: Neal-Schuman, 2004.

Warner, Alice Sizer. *Owning Your Numbers: An Introduction to Budgeting for Special Libraries.* Washington, DC: Special Libraries Association, 1992.

Wayne, Richard. "Helping You Buy: PC Management Software." *Computers in Libraries*, 25, 2 (February): 37–45.

———. "An Overview of Public Access Computer Software Management." *Computers in Libraries*, 24, 6 (June): 25–30.

Weber, Mary Beth. *Cataloging Nonprint and Internet Resources: A How-To-Do-It Manual for Librarians.* New York: Neal-Schuman, 2002.

What Do I Read Next? Available from Thompson-Gale: www.galegroup.com.

Whitlatch, Jo Bell. *Evaluating Reference Services: A Practical Guide.* Chicago: American Library Association, 2000.

Wilkinson, Frances C., and Linda K. Lewis. *The Complete Guide to Acquisitions Management.* Westport, CT.: Libraries Unlimited, 2003.

Williamsburg Regional Library. *Director's Evaluation Form.* Williamsburg, VA: Williamsburg Regional Library, 2005.

———. *Interview Questions.* Williamsburg, VA: Williamsburg Regional Library, 2005.

———. *Job Description.* Williamsburg, VA: Williamsburg Regional Library, 2005

———. *Library Policies.* Williamsburg, VA: Williamsburg Regional Library. www.wrl.org/info/policies/policies/html.

Women's Philanthropy Institute. www.women-philanthropy.org

Wood, Steve. *Information Auditing: A Guide for Information Managers.* Ashford, Middlesex, UK: Free Pint, 2004. www.freepint.com.

World Cat Collection Analysis. www.oclc.org.

Wrightson, Denelle, and John M. Wrightson. " Acoustical Considerations in Planning and Design of Library Facilities," *Library Hi Tech* 17 (1999): 349–57.

W.T. Cox. www.wtcox.com

Yesner, Bernice L., and Hilda L. Jay. *Operating and Evaluating School Media Programs: A Handbook for Administrators and Librarians.* New York: Neal-Schuman, 1998.

Zweizig, Douglas et al. *The TELL IT! Manual: The Complete Program for Evaluating Library Performance.* Madison, WT: University of Wisconsin, 1996.

SOURCE G: PROFESSIONAL STATEMENTS

At the core of librarianship, regardless of type of library, are fundamental statements outlining the principles behind the provision of library service in a democracy. The main statements are:

The Library Bill of Rights and its many interpretations
Code of Ethics
Freedom to Read Statement
Libraries: An American Value

There are many other statements dealing with access to materials, economic barriers to information access, and guidelines for the development and implementation of policies and regulations.

The best source for these documents is the Web site of the American Library Association. Documents are housed within the Office of Intellectual Freedom section of the Web site. Go to www.ala.org and locate the Office of Intellectual Freedom for current editions of all professional statements.

INDEX

ABOUT THE EDITOR

John A. Moorman is director of the Williamsburg Regional Library in Williamsburg, Virginia. A library administrator since 1975 in North Carolina, Texas, Illinois, and Virginia, he is active in state and national library associations. Professional interests include library buildings, combined school/public libraries, and organizational theory. John has consulted with libraries for many years. In this role, he has worked with libraries on building programs and space needs studies and provided workshops on a variety of topics, including fund-raising and the organization of library support groups. A graduate of Guilford College (NC), John has a master's degree in library science from the University of North Carolina at Chapel Hill and a Ph.D. in Library and Information Science from the University of Illinois at Urbana-Champaign. He is married to Ileen G. Moorman and has three children.

ABOUT THE CONTRIBUTORS

Noreen Bernstein graduated from Barnard College, and received her MLS from the University of Maryland. Worked in Educational publishing for Grolier, Inc. and Kirchoff/Wohlberg and was Children's Librarian at The Handley Library in Winchester, Virginia, for nine years. Since 1987 Noreen has been director of Youth Services at Williamsburg (VA) Regional Library. The Youth Services Department has received numerous awards including the Lee Elliott Memorial Grant from Millbrook Press and the Giant Step Award from School Library Journal and Thompson Gale during her tenure at the library. Noreen is a frequent presenter at library and educational conferences.

Karin Borei is the University Librarian at Millikin University in Decatur, Illinois. Prior to coming to Illinois, she served in a range of technical services, systems, and administrative positions at several large research libraries, all members of ARL (Association of Research Libraries), and also as College Librarian at Trinity College of Vermont (now defunct). Ms. Borei's professional involvements have been many and varied. Her vita can be found at http:/faculty.millikin.edu/~kborei.library.mu/professional.kbresume.html.

Janet Crowther is director of the Outreach Division at the Williamsburg (VA) Regional Library, and has been with the library since 1988. She received her MSLS from the Catholic University of America in 1981. Prior experience includes working as a field consultant for the Idaho State Library, working as head of readers' services for the United States Court of Claims/U.S. Court of Customs and Patent Appeals in Washington, D.C., and as a systems librarian for a law firm. She co-authored, "Partnering with Purpose: a Guide to Strategic Partnership Development for Libraries and Other Organizations" (Libraries Unlimited, 2004) and has presented programs on partnership development for libraries at the Public Library Association National Conference, the Virginia Library Association Conference, and for SOLINET.

Mary Mayer-Hennelly has been Association Vice President for Learning Resources at Tidewater Community College since 2001. Tidewater Community College is the second largest of Virginia's Community Colleges. Previously, she served as assistant director of the Norfolk (VA) Public Library System. She holds an MLS from McGill University, an MPA from Old Dominion University, and a BA from the University of Massachusetts at Boston. She has been an active member of the Virginia Library Association, the American Library Association, and the Hampton Roads Chapter for Public Administration, serving as its president and winning the ASPA's national award for continuing education.

Jean A. Major is University Librarian Emeritus of Old Dominion University. She served as University Librarian at ODU from 1992 through 2002 and came to Old Dominion from two earlier library directorships in Mississippi and Illinois. Over her long career in library administration, Major saw the growth of development from modest beginnings to today's expectation for a fully developed, well structured program of friend- and fund-raising as a central component of library leadership.

Kendra Morgan is a technology consultant for the Library of Virginia, providing assistance to public libraries in Virginia. She received her Masters in Library and Information Science from the University of Hawaii.

Richard Rubin is Director and Professor at the School of Library and Information Science at Kent State University, Kent, Ohio. He received his A.B. in Philosophy from Oberlin College, his M.L.S. from Kent State University, and his Ph.D. from the

School of Library and Information Science at the University of Illinois-Urbana/Champaign. Dr. Rubin is the author of numerous publications including: *Human Resource Management in Libraries: Theory and Practice* (Neal-Schuman, 1991), *Hiring Library Employees* (Neal-Schuman, 1994) and *Foundations of Library and Information Science, 2nd edition* (Neal-Schuman, 2004).

Barbara Rice has been Branch Manager at the Martha Washington Community Library Branch of the Fairfax County Public Library System (VA) since 1999. Prior to coming to Fairfax County, she worked for the University of Tennessee, County Technical Assistance System and as Director for the Hawkins County Library System in Rogersville, Tennessee.

Frederick A. Schlipf is Director of the Urbana Free Library in Urbana, Illinois and Adjunct Association Professor at the Graduate School of Library and Information Science at the University of Illinois, Urbana-Champaign. Fred teaches the University's course on library buildings and has done architectural consulting for over 75 libraries.

Barry Trott is director of Adult Services at the Williamsburg (VA) Regional Library. He received his MSLS from the Catholic University of America and has worked at the Williamsburg Regional Library as reference librarian and readers' services librarian prior to becoming department head. Barry is the chair of the RUSA CODES Readers' Advisory Committee for ALA, edits the readers' advisory column for RUSQ, and writes for the NoveList readers' advisory database. He has presented programs on readers' advisory and on partnership development for the American Library Association annual conference, the Public Library Association National Conference, and the Virginia Library Association Conference among others. Barry is also a professional musician.

Richard E. Wallace is currently the manager of the Technical Information Center at the Tate & Lyle Research Center in Decatur, Illinois. He is a solo librarian with responsibility for the Library and Central Research Files. During his career Richard has worked in the libraries of several agricultural and food companies. In addition to his Master's Degree from Case Western Reserve University, he has an MBA from Illinois State University. He is active in the Special Libraries Association at the division and association levels. He has held a number of offices, including two terms as the Association treasurer. He was elected a Fellow of the Special Libraries Association in 2005.

Alicia Willson-Metzger is currently Collection Management Librarian for the Captain John Smith Library of Christopher Newport University in Newport News, Virginia. She holds masters' degrees in English Literature and Library Science from the University of Missouri-Columbia, and is a doctorial candidate in higher education at Old Dominion University. She has served in adult services positions in both public and academic libraries.

Nelson Worley is currently library director of the Johnson City, Tennessee Public Library. Previously he was the Director of the Library Development and Networking Division of the Library of Virginia. He has also been the Director of the Appomattox Regional Library System in Hopewell, Virginia. Nelson received undergraduate degrees from Ferrum College in Virginia and King College in Bristol, Tennessee. His Master of Library Science degree is from George Peabody College for Teachers at Vanderbilt University. Nelson also holds a Master of Arts in History degree from the University of Louisiana at Lafayette, Louisiana.